The *Annual Review of Adult Learning and Literacy* is an important part of the Dissemination Initiative of the National Center for the Study of Adult Learning and Literacy (NCSALL). NCSALL is a collaborative effort between the Harvard Graduate School of Education and World Education, a nonprofit organization based in Boston. NCSALL's partners include The Center for Literacy Studies at the University of Tennessee, Rutgers University in New Jersey, and Portland State University in Oregon. NCSALL is funded by the Educational Research and Development Centers Program, award number R309B60002, as administered by the U.S. Department of Education's Office of Educational Research and Innovation through its National Institute for Postsecondary Education, Libraries, and Lifelong Learning.

NCSALL is pursuing a program of basic and applied research that is meant to improve programs that provide educational services for adults who have low literacy skills, who do not speak English, or who do not have a high school diploma. Ongoing studies include research in the areas of learner motivation, teaching and learning, staff development, and accountability.

The contents of the *Review* do not necessarily represent the positions or policies of the U.S. Department of Education, nor are they endorsed by the federal government.

# Annual Review of Adult Learning and Literacy

Volume 2

John Comings, Barbara Garner,
Cristine Smith, Editors

# —⌇— Annual Review
# of Adult Learning
# and Literacy

## Volume 2

*2001*

A Project of

The National Center for the Study of
Adult Learning and Literacy

 JOSSEY-BASS
A Wiley Company
San Francisco

The material in this publication is based on work sponsored wholly or in part by the
Office of Educational Research and Improvement, U.S. Department of Education, under
contract number R309B60002. Its contents do not necessarily reflect the views of the
department or any other agency of the U.S. Government.

Jossey-Bass books and products are available through most bookstores. To
contact Jossey-Bass directly, call (888) 378-2537, fax to (800) 605-2665, or
visit our website at www.josseybass.com.

Substantial discounts on bulk quantities of Jossey-Bass books are available to
corporations, professional associations, and other organizations. For details and
discount information, contact the special sales department at Jossey-Bass.

ISBN 0-7879-5062-9          ISSN 1527-3970

FIRST EDITION
*HB Printing*   10  9  8  7  6  5  4  3  2  1

The Jossey-Bass
Higher and Adult Education Series

# ━ᴍ━ Contents

# ——— Foreword

It was in B. Allan Quigley's book *Rethinking Literacy Education* that I remember first seeing the phrase, "Become literate about literacy." As simple and logical as it seems, this thought struck me as very insightful. As the director of adult education in the state of Washington, I understand how important it is to have a vision of what adult education should be if it is to meet the needs of our learners. But until reading Quigley's book, I had not given enough thought to the contribution that research can make to the creation of such a vision and, just as important, to all of the decisions that must be made to realize that vision.

It is easy enough to envision a future in which all adults who need basic skills will have access to the means of obtaining them. It is much harder to make the decisions necessary to achieve that vision now, when we have enough resources to serve only 8 percent of those who need basic skills. It is not easy to decide who will constitute the 8 percent we teach and thus who will be among the 92 percent whom we do not teach. What, then, is the most appropriate strategy of instruction for those who will be taught, and what makes us so sure it will truly work? What kinds of organizations can best implement the desired strategy and achieve the intended outcomes, and what kind of staff development is needed for the teachers in those organizations to do the work that is necessary?

With unlimited resources, a state could try two or three or even four totally different widespread strategies, as well as hybrids of each. The reality of limited resources does not allow for that. A very balanced and meager approach is usually all that is allowed.

It is tempting to make decisions based on anecdote or under the influence of political pressure, grabbing the short-term flavors of the month or year. Nonetheless, no matter what the level of resources is, the hard decisions must be made, and they must be made on some basis of need, capacity, and research.

The fact that every decision has a fiscal impact causes us to wonder regularly whether each decision was the best investment. Just as often, it is hard to tell if each decision we make will serve to support the intended goal or if some are disconnected from the whole. One thing we do seem to be sure of is best practices. We regularly talk about how important it is to promote and fund best practices. Best practices in instruction, staff development, learner involvement, and marketing are all considered very desirable. But how do we really know what a best practice is? Is it the most widely practiced? Is it the newest idea? Does it require the least amount of investment in the most learners—or the most investment in the least number of learners? Do short-term gains by our learners become the foundation for long-term success over a lifetime, or are they just symptoms of giving in to short-term solutions?

Quality research is necessary to guide our decision making. I will not claim that I can offer a definitive description of what constitutes quality research, but I can say that from my perspective, it must be both academically rigorous and user friendly—to learners, teachers, program administrators, and policymakers. It must resonate with the general population as much as it does with those of us in the field of adult learning and literacy. Our vision of the future and all of the decisions made in support of it will be acceptable to our stakeholders and all concerned citizens only if it is based on quality research.

We live in a complicated and constantly changing world that requires us all to embrace lifelong learning. For me, lifelong learning includes becoming literate about literacy using a curriculum that includes research—conducted not by K–12 researchers, not by the Department of Labor, not by any other party whose purpose is not specifically for the benefit of adult basic skills. Too often we learn something as a by-product of someone else's research. What we need is research designed with the specific intention of improving adult basics skills. And that research should be nationally based, conducted by adult literacy researchers for adult literacy learners, teachers, administrators, and policymakers.

In its infancy, the National Center for the Study of Adult Learning and Literacy declared its commitment to ensure "that research informs practice, that practice informs research, and that policy is linked to both." The *Annual Review of Adult Learning and Literacy* is a testament to this commitment. It demonstrates how research can improve practice and provide a sound framework for making the most difficult decisions. I am confident you will agree that the *Review,* in only its second year, has become an important part of the curriculum for those of us in adult basic education trying to become literate about literacy.

Israel Mendoza
Director
Washington State Board for
    Community and Technical Colleges
Office of Adult Literacy

# —∿— Preface

The National Center for the Study of Adult Learning and Literacy and Jossey-Bass are pleased to publish this second volume of the *Annual Review of Adult Learning and Literacy.* With this volume, we move closer to our goal of establishing a journal of record for the field of adult learning and literacy, with articles that review the literature and present best practices on key issues. The audience we have in mind for the *Review* includes policymakers, scholars, and practitioners who are dedicated to improving the quality of practice in adult basic education (ABE), adult English for speakers of other languages (ESOL), and adult secondary education (ASE) programs.

This second volume continues the format used in the first volume by beginning with a review of significant developments in the field during the year (in this case, 1999) and by including a chapter describing the adult literacy system of another country (here, Canada) and an annotated bibliography on a broad topic of current interest to the field (here, organizational development). We also continue a topical strand: In Volume One, we presented an article about the research on reading instruction and its applicability to adult students; in this second volume, we present an article on the applicability of research on writing instruction for adults.

In the foreword, Israel Mendoza, the adult basic education director for the state of Washington, talks about the importance of research in helping to make his vision of a quality system of adult basic education a reality. In his view, quality research is critical to making good decisions in a field where resources are scarce. Research is required, he says, if we are to become what educator B. Allan Quigley calls "literate about literacy," thereby learning the best way to serve adult students.

In Chapter One, "The Year 1999 in Review," Dave Speights outlines the federal funding initiatives for programs concerning adult literacy, key developments in policy, and major research activities during the year. Events such as the Summit on Twenty-First Century Skills for Twenty-First Century Jobs and preparations for the National Literacy Summit are covered. Speights also discusses the impact of the Workforce Investment Act, which began to be felt at the state and local level during the year.

In Chapter Two, Sophie Degener discusses critical theory and its application to the pedagogy used in adult basic education programs. She first provides a brief history and definition of critical pedagogy and then presents a theoretical framework for applying critical pedagogy to ABE programs. Degener argues that defining a program as solely critical or noncritical is not helpful, since programs more accurately fall on a continuum between the two. She suggests that programs could evolve toward adopting a more critical pedagogy, to varying degrees, in one or more of their program components: philosophy, structure, curriculum, teacher development, teacher-student relationship, and evaluation.

As a follow-up to the chapter on reading instruction for adults in Volume One of the *Review,* Marilyn Gillespie summarizes the research on writing instruction in Chapter Three. She traces the history of writing research with a variety of learners—children in the K–12 system, college students who are classified as "basic" writers, second-language learners, and adult literacy learners—focusing on issues and trends of most interest to adult literacy educators. She then discusses what these trends mean for the field of adult literacy, where educational approaches based on writing research are still relatively rare. Through examples she shows how a growing number of practitioners are beginning to integrate the teaching of writing more fully into their classes with adult students and then makes an argument for five actions that would promote improvements in writing instruction: a research agenda for studying composition in adult literacy contexts, funding for professional development of practitioners around integrating writing into the program and classroom, research on innovative tools for assessing the writing progress, policies to help students in General Educational Development (GED) classes prepare for the writing demands of postsecondary education, and better dissemination of writing by and for adult learners.

In Chapter Four, Stefan LoBuglio discusses the politics and practices of educational programs for adults in correctional facilities. LoBuglio argues that the politics of such programs, and the resulting reduction in funding for them, is related to the reaction of political leaders to public opinion about whether the primary purpose of imprisonment is to keep dangerous individuals off the street or to rehabilitate them. He also describes several innovative correctional education programs, including programs in which the quality of the education has been improved as a result of the influence of larger goals for educational reform and accountability efforts. He advocates further research on the extent to which education may reduce recidivism rates and calls for a survey of best practices in correctional education programs.

Professional development for practitioners is a key issue for state adult basic education systems. In Chapter Five, Alisa Belzer, Cassandra Drennon, and Cristine Smith provide an overview of the challenges facing state-level professional development systems. They profile the professional development systems in five states according to characteristics such as scope, cooperative leadership, coherence, and accessibility. Among the challenges common to the five states featured is the call for professional development staff to meet the needs of practitioners on the one hand and policymakers on the other, needs that are sometimes at odds with each other. The authors believe that professional development staff in different states need more opportunities to share information about their systems and about how to plan and deliver effective professional development activities that meet the needs of a mostly part-time and underpaid workforce.

In Chapter Six, Linda Shohet describes the Canadian system of adult literacy, highlighting the history of its development within a complicated cultural history of four groups: Anglo-Saxon, French, and Native cultures, and more recent immigrants from a range of countries. She describes the various organizations that have played a role in the development of services for adult learners as well as the political events that have influenced the funding of such services. Her overview of the challenges facing the Canadian adult literacy system—defining literacy, integrating new technology, professionalizing practitioners, shifting investments to workplace and family literacy programs, establishing partnerships, providing literacy for non-English or non-French speakers, and sustaining the system—reveals important differences and similarities in the challenges facing the Canadian and U.S. ABE and literacy systems.

In Chapter Seven, Marcia Drew Hohn gives us a history of organizational development theory and then provides key resources in an annotated bibliography that will be of interest to those engaged in ABE program improvement.

As the *Review* goes to press, the summit process described by Dave Speights in Chapter One is gaining momentum with the publication of *From the Margins to the Mainstream: An Action Agenda for Literacy.* Over the next year, summit organizers will make efforts to engage practitioners and policymakers at all levels to take action to make the agenda come to life. As the field progresses in its effort to secure greater resources, improvements in quality, and increases in access to services for adult learners, we hope that the *Review* will continue to be a valuable resource for those working in the field.

JOHN COMINGS
BARBARA GARNER
CRISTINE SMITH
EDITORS

# ～ The Editors

*John Comings* is the director of the National Center for the Study of Adult Learning and Literacy (NCSALL) at the Harvard Graduate School of Education. Before coming to Harvard, he spent twelve years as vice president of World Education. Comings worked on adult education programs in Nepal for six years and in Indonesia for two years and has helped design and evaluate adult education programs in several countries in Asia, Africa, and the Caribbean. In the United States, he has served as the director of the State Literacy Resource Center in Massachusetts, assisted in the design of instructor training programs, and directed projects that focused on improving the teaching of math and health in adult education programs. His research and writing have focused on the impact of adult literacy programs on reading ability and life changes such as health and family planning practices, the program factors that lead to that impact, and the issue of persistence in learning in the United States and developing countries.

*Barbara Garner,* director of publications for NCSALL and a senior program officer at World Education, currently edits the NCSALL publication *Focus on Basics.* She has held many different positions in the field of adult basic education, including teacher, staff developer, program administrator, and curriculum writer.

*Cristine Smith* is NCSALL coordinator and a senior program officer at World Education. Smith coordinates NCSALL's dissemination initiative, is directing a four-year study on adult basic education staff development under NCSALL, and is the national coordinator for NCSALL's Practitioner Dissemination and Research Network. She has worked on staff development issues in the field of adult literacy for twelve years.

# ---*--- The Contributors

*Alisa Belzer* is assistant professor of adult literacy education at Rutgers University and is currently evaluating the adult basic and literacy education professional development system for the state of Pennsylvania. Previously she was the director of the Pennsylvania Adult Literacy Practitioner Inquiry Network, an inquiry-based professional development initiative. She has done research and program evaluation in areas related to assessment, classroom practice, retention, family literacy, and professional development. She has contributed to *Focus on Basics* and to *Inside/Outside: Teacher Research and Knowledge,* edited by M. Cochran-Smith and S. Lytle, and she is the author of several other publications on adult literacy.

*Sophie C. Degener* is a researcher for NCSALL's Literacy Practices of Adult Learners Study. She also works as a data analyst for the University of Chicago's Consortium on Chicago School Research. She is working on a doctorate at the Harvard Graduate School of Education, focusing on instructional practices in family literacy programs. During her previous work as an elementary school teacher, she developed and was a teacher for a school-based family literacy program.

*Cassandra Drennon* is a private educational consultant in Athens, Georgia, providing adult literacy organizations throughout the United States with research, project management, and professional development services. Formerly she was a state-level staff development specialist and led the design and implementation of Virginia's inquiry-based professional development system. She is coauthor with H. A. Fingeret of *Literacy for Life: Adult Learners, New Practices* and has published several articles, book chapters, and resource materials on the topic of practitioner inquiry.

*Marilyn K. Gillespie* is an educational researcher in adult literacy education at SRI International in Arlington, Virginia. She has conducted research and evaluation studies in the areas of adult literacy English for speakers of other languages, curriculum development for adult basic education, native-language literacy, and the workplace and vocational training needs of adult literacy learners and has produced numerous curriculum materials for adult educators. She was founding director of the Read Write Now Adult Literacy Center in Springfield, Massachusetts, and the former director of the National Clearing House on ESL Literacy. She is also a research team member for the NCSALL staff development study.

*Marcia Drew Hohn* is director of the Northeast Regional Support of the System for Adult Basic Education Support in Massachusetts. The center is located at Northern Essex Community College, where Hohn has also held positions as director of specialized adult education and training projects, such as the Municipal Management Institute and Transitional Education for Health Careers. She is the author of research reports and articles on organizational change, systems integration, and the integration of health and literacy education, including the National Institute for Literacy Fellowship report *Empowerment Health Education in Adult Literacy*.

*Stefan LoBuglio* has worked for the past eight years for the Suffolk County Sheriff's Department in Boston, Massachusetts, on programs that prepare incarcerated adults to make the transition to community life successfully. For six years, he directed a comprehensive correctional education program at the Suffolk County House of Correction, one of the largest correctional facilities in New England. This program served more than five hundred inmates daily and offered basic literacy instruction; life skill classes in parenting, health awareness, and career readiness; and college-level courses. LoBuglio, a NCSALL fellow, has presented papers on correctional education at many local, state, and federal conferences and was the plenary session speaker for the North American Conference on Fathers Behind Bars and on the Street. Before working in the field of criminal justice, he was an engineer.

*Israel Mendoza* is the director of the Office of Adult Literacy for the state of Washington. He was previously the director of policy development, communications, and legislative activities for the state Employment Security Department, where he worked for more than twenty years. He is a founding member of the state Adult Education Advisory Council and has worked with several governor-appointed boards and councils, including the Workforce Training and Education Coordinating Board, the Governor's Economic Development Cabinet, the Family Independence Program Executive Committee, and the Governor's Timber Team.

*Linda Shohet* is the founder and director of the Center for Literacy of Quebec, an independent resource, research, and training center located at Dawson College in Montreal. Since 1984 she has worked in the field of school-based and adult literacy, editing *Literacy Across the CurriculuMedia Focus,* an international newsletter, and presenting frequently at conferences. She has recently focused on the area of health and literacy, for which the Center for Literacy won the 2000 Weiler Award, a national award recognizing commitment to social justice in Canada. She has contributed book chapters on women's ways of learning and on British models of basic skills training in the workplace and sits on several national boards and advisory bodies related to literacy, technology, and workforce education. Shohet is a faculty member in the English Department at Dawson College, where she worked for many years with underprepared students in need of basic skills support.

*Dave Speights* is the founding editor of *Report on Literacy Programs,* the only independent newsletter devoted to adult and family literacy. He is also editor of *Report on Education of the Disadvantaged,* a newsletter devoted to education programs for low-income children. He is a career journalist who has worked in Washington, D.C., Philadelphia, and Atlanta and on the Navajo Indian Reservation. His work has appeared in *Congressional Quarterly* and on National Public Radio.

# CHAPTER ONE

# The Year 1999 in Review

*Dave Speights*

F rom the perspective of the field of adult literacy, the year 1999 is best seen not as the penultimate year of the millennium but as the year bookended by the reauthorization of the National Literacy Act in late 1998 and the National Literacy Summit of early 2000. Both of those events represent a huge milestone, and 1999 may be regarded as the time when people in the field were preoccupied by reacting to the former and preparing for the latter.

The new Adult Education and Family Literacy Act, which was technically Title II of the Workforce Investment Act, mandated controversial new student performance measures for all federally funded programs and required all states to rewrite their adult education plans. The performance measures focused on job readiness rather than more holistic concerns, a fact that continues to outrage many people in the field.

Given this context, the National Literacy Summit, planned for years as a means to develop a consensus about how best to move the field forward, also came to be regarded as an opportunity for adult educators to respond to Washington and tell the politicians and bureaucrats how to get it right. It remains to be seen if the powers that be will heed the manifesto.

There were also a number of relatively routine but nevertheless significant developments in 1999, and that is where this overview begins. Federal funding for adult literacy–related programs is covered first, then developments in policy, then research activities, and, finally, events such as the National Literacy Summit and the Summit on Twenty-First Century Skills for Twenty-First Century Jobs hosted by Vice President Al Gore.

## FEDERAL FUNDING

After six years in office, the Clinton administration embraced the adult literacy cause in early 1999 with a level of public commitment not seen since Barbara Bush was first lady. In his State of the Union speech on January 19, President Clinton called for "a dramatic increase in federal support for adult literacy." Separately, he said his budget proposal for fiscal 2000 would "significantly" expand federal efforts to help immigrants learn English and learn about democracy.

### Clinton's Budget

As promised, Clinton's budget proposal for fiscal year 2000 called for massive funding increases for adult literacy programs. He wanted to increase adult education state grants by 28 percent and the overall adult education budget by 49.4 percent. "The income gap . . . is largely a skills gap," Clinton said on January 28, as he announced his new literacy and job training initiatives. "We've closed the budget deficit, now we've got to close the skills deficit. We cannot have the earnings gap in America— the income gap—get bigger because we didn't make the skills gap smaller. Now is the time to do it. We will never have a better time."

The first item on his list of specific proposals was "a national campaign to dramatically increase our efforts at adult basic education and family literacy, to help the millions and millions of adults who struggle with basic reading or math." The budget President Clinton submitted to Congress included the following programs:

• *Reading Excellence Act (America Reads).* This initiative was approved by Congress in October 1998 and had an appropriation of $260 million for fiscal year (FY) 1999. It provides states with competitive three-year grants for reading partnerships; states will then make subgrants to local partnerships that must include family literacy programs. Clinton's $286 million request for FY2000 would allow twenty-two to twenty-four additional state grants and would more than double the number of children served to almost 1.1 million.

• *Adult education state grants.* Clinton requested $468 million, an increase of $103 million over the FY1999. The administration said part of the requested increase would be used for "a strengthened emphasis on program accountability," as called for in the Adult Education and Family Literacy Act of 1998. The administration also considered this proposed increase as part of a so-called Hispanic initiative, which included several K–12 programs, such as bilingual education and emergency immigrant education. The U.S. Department of Education (DOE) said the spending increase in adult education would be "aimed primarily at expanding state efforts to help immigrant and other limited-English-proficient adults, including Hispanics, to learn English and make a successful entry into the workforce and the mainstream of society."

• *National leadership activities.* These are evaluation, technical assistance, and demonstration programs run by the DOE's Division of Adult Education and Literacy. The administration wanted to increase funding more than seven-fold, from $14 million to $101 million, to finance several new initiatives. Common Ground Partnership grants to states and localities significantly affected by immigration were to receive $70 million. The grants (another part of the Hispanic initiative) would support demonstration programs providing young adult immigrants and other participants with English literacy and life skills instruction and information about the rights and responsibilities of citizenship. An allocation of $23 million was proposed for discretionary grants to help states and private sector partners increase access to technology for adult education instruction. There would be forty pilot projects. The amount of $2 million was proposed for a High Skills Communities Campaign that would help selected states and local communities promote adult literacy and lifelong learning and measure progress in both areas. According to the DOE, these assessments would allow schools and employers "to determine if individuals have the literacy skills needed for available jobs."

• *Community-based technology centers.* President Clinton requested an increase from $10 million in FY1999 to $65 million in FY2000. This program, one of a dozen technology programs run by the DOE, makes grants to public housing facilities, community centers, libraries, and other community-based programs to make technology available to poor people in urban and rural areas. Grantees provide access to programs for preschool, family literacy, after school, adult education, and English for speakers of other languages (ESOL) as well as to on-line databases with job listings. The additional $55 million requested would increase the number of such grants from forty to three hundred.

• *Twenty-First Century Community Learning Centers.* President Clinton proposed to triple funding for this school-based program, from $200 million to $600 million, enough to provide school districts with about two thousand new grants. These centers are primarily intended to provide after-school, weekend, and summer academic and recreational services for K–12 students, but in many cases they also provide parents with educational, job training, and job placement services.

## National Coalition Lobbying Efforts

By March, all twenty-eight sustaining (voting) members of the National Coalition for Literacy (NCL) agreed to ask Congress to provide more funds than the Clinton administration requested. They agreed to lobby for the following amounts: $286 million for the Reading Excellence Act (America Reads); $568 million for state grants, "a critical first step toward a five-year goal of $1 billion"; $116 million for "national leadership" activities sponsored by the DOE's Division of Adult Education and Literacy; $7 million for the National Institute for Literacy (NIFL); and $145 million for the Even Start Family Literacy program (the same amount Clinton proposed).

## Campaign for Even Start

In May, Congressman William Goodling (R-Pennsylvania), legislative father of Even Start, said he would ask his colleagues to increase the program's annual appropriation from the FY1999 level of $135 million to $500 million for FY2000. Goodling made the announcement at an oversight hearing on Even Start before the House Committee on Education and the Workforce, which he chaired. The friendly witnesses included Sharon Darling, president of the National Center for Family Literacy (NCFL), and Andy Hartman, director of the National Institute for Literacy.

A $500 million appropriation would have been larger than the entire FY1999 appropriation for adult literacy programs ($385 million), but it would still have been dwarfed by the $4.7 billion appropriation for

Head Start, which, like Even Start, is an intergenerational program. Even Start served about 31,000 families in 1999 (up from 2,500 in 1989), whereas Head Start served 800,000.

Although Goodling's committee had a direct role in the pending reauthorization of the Elementary and Secondary Education Act, which authorizes Even Start, the committee had no direct control over appropriations. Few observers expected the House and Senate appropriations committees to grant Goodling's request, and they did not.

## Capacity-Building Grants

Volunteer and community-based organizations within the NCL lobbied Congress to include a new $15 million set-aside for themselves within the adult education budget. The money was to be earmarked for "institutional support," or capacity building. It would have allowed groups such as Literacy Volunteers of America, Laubach Literacy, and the National Alliance of Urban Literacy Coalitions to do such things as mount professional development efforts and gather data on the performance of their local affiliates. The money would not have provided grants for local affiliates, but it had the potential to help them claim a larger share of federal grant money in the future.

Since the passage of the National Literacy Act of 1991, volunteer and other community-based literacy groups have been guaranteed "direct and equitable access" to federal adult education funds, but by 1999 they were still receiving only a fraction of the federal pass-through funds doled out by state education officials. Those officials often said that local volunteer organizations did not receive funding because they could not demonstrate their professionalism or prove their effectiveness. But neither the local organizations nor their national umbrella organizations had the resources to upgrade tutor training significantly or conduct the kind of data gathering needed to demonstrate success. They argued that that was why they needed the $15 million set-aside. In the end, congressional appropriators would not be swayed by such arguments. The Republicans, who controlled Congress, had made it common practice to abolish existing set-asides and earmarks, and most of them were disinclined to create a new one.

By October, the NCL had given up on its drive for funding levels higher than Clinton's requested amounts, as well as its request for $15 million in new capacity-building funds.

By mid-November, President Clinton and Congress agreed to a
23 percent increase for adult education state grants over the FY1999
level, from $365 million to $450 million. Nevertheless, total spending on adult education would remain $105 million below the level
Clinton originally requested. He had wanted a total of $575 million,
with most of the $190 million year-to-year increase earmarked for a
Common Ground Partnership initiative: new ESOL and civics programs run by the states and the DOE. As part of the compromise with
Congress, the administration was allowed to earmark $25.5 million
of the $85 million increase for adult education state grants for the
ESOL/civics program. The final allocations were as follows:

*Reading Excellence.* Level funding of $260 million.

*Even Start.* An increase from $135 million to $150 million.

*Adult education state grants.* An increase from $365 million to
$450 million.

*National leadership activities.* Level funding of $14 million, with
nothing for capacity-building grants.

*National Institute for Literacy.* Level funding of $6 million.

*Twenty-First Century Community Learning Centers.* In another
compromise, Congress and the White House agreed on
$450 million for Twenty-First Century Community Learning
Centers in FY2000. This represents an increase of $250 million
over the FY1999 amount, but it was still $150 million less than
the president had originally requested.

*Community-based technology centers.* An increase from
$10 million to $32.5 million. The administration said the
new funding level would allow the program to reach at least
120 communities.

*Star Schools.* An increase from $45 million to $51 million.
(This program funds distance-learning projects, including the
PBS LiteracyLink project targeting adult learners.)

## POLICY DEVELOPMENTS

As usual, Congress and the administration paid little attention to adult
education and literacy in 1999. Meanwhile, state and local adult education officials continued to struggle with the mandates laid down by

the Adult Education and Family Literacy Act of 1998 and with the Education Department's National Reporting System.

## The Administration's Elementary and Secondary Education Bill

In May, the Clinton administration unveiled its proposal for reauthorizing the Elementary and Secondary Education Act (ESEA). The proposal put several literacy-related programs in line for changes, including Even Start, Reading Excellence, educational technology, and bilingual education. The ESEA dates back to 1965 and President Lyndon Johnson's war on poverty initiatives. Fully $8 billion of the ESEA's annual funding is for Title I, the federal government's effort to improve education for the disadvantaged. Even Start is part of Title I, as are various migrant education programs. The "Educational Excellence for All Children Act," as the administration called it, would have made the following changes:

*Even Start*

- Require local programs to hire teachers with relevant certifications or endorsements by July 1, 2002. Aides providing instructional support, such as follow-up educational activities in home visits, would have at least two years of college and be under the direct supervision of a teacher.

- Increase compatibility with welfare reform initiatives and list career counseling and job placement services as allowable project expenses.

- Require states to submit plans describing their efforts to develop and use quality indicators when evaluating local projects, their efforts to ensure that projects fully implement all of the Even Start program elements (early childhood education, parenting education, and adult literacy), their competition procedures for subgrants to local projects, and their procedures for coordinating resources.

- Increase the quality of services by encouraging the use of research-based instructional methods, encouraging state-level collaborations and coordinated services, and requiring state officials to review independent evaluations of local projects.

- Increase the intensity of programs by encouraging instruction through the summer months, encouraging the use of distance-learning technology, and requiring states to assess the retention efforts of local programs.
- Allow states to fund up to two model projects to serve as mentors for others.

*Reading Excellence Act*

- Limit funding to programs serving students in the third grade and below and their families.
- Require states to submit descriptions of the processes and criteria they use to evaluate applications from school districts.
- Allow states to receive new grants after their first ones run out. (The original authorizing legislation allowed only one grant during the multiyear authorization period.)
- Allow the DOE to use 1 percent of each year's funding for technical assistance and for replicating model projects.

*Educational Technology*

- Consolidate Technology Innovation Challenge Grants and Star Schools into a Next Generation Grants program for public and private consortia.
- Target grants to the neediest schools and communities, including grants for community technology centers for poor children and adults.

*Bilingual Education*

- Emphasize the importance of English proficiency by requiring schools to conduct annual assessments and report the results to parents and by providing incentive grants to successful schools.
- Require schools to provide clear program descriptions to parents and notices of their right to withdraw their children at any time.
- Authorize a "Training for All Teachers" program to provide ongoing professional development.
- Authorize a career ladder program for aides who want to become teachers.

• Authorize bilingual education teachers and personnel grants to improve the capacity and curricula of teachers' colleges.

Although much of this activity is directly relevant to children, not adult learners, the adult education community has an interest in K–12 reforms for the effect they will have on the adult learners of the future. Many adult learners still seethe about the poor education they received as children and are quite militant about K–12 reform, caring deeply about K–12 programs even though their funding streams generally do not intersect with adult education funding streams. Moreover, trends in K–12 legislation, such as accountability, usually show up later in adult education programs, and adult education is sometimes supported by K–12 programs.

## GOP Introduces "Straight A's Act"

The Republican Congress rejected the administration's ESEA bill out of hand. In June, House Republicans introduced the Academic Achievement for All Act (Straight A's), which would allow states to take most of their federal K–12 education funding in a lump sum, including funds for Even Start. The proposed legislation would have allowed states to combine all of the federal K–12 programs they administer, including Compensatory Education for the Disadvantaged (Title I of the ESEA, which includes Even Start), the Technology Literacy Challenge Fund, immigrant education, homeless education, and vocational education. The act would not have affected state adult education grants or the federally administered Even Start grants earmarked for programs serving migrant families, Native American tribes, and outlying areas.

The Clinton administration denounced the bill as an assault on categorical programs targeted to the disadvantaged. These categorical programs are federal aid targeted to specific disadvantaged groups. Democrats believe Republicans want to fold these programs into block grants so state and local officials can steer the money to affluent constituent groups that do not need it. More than half of all schools get Title I aid, including many that have below-average poverty rates. Yet some truly poor schools get none.

Congress took no final action on Straight A's during 1999. As of mid-2000, it remained bogged down in a partisan stalemate. It appeared that it would be left up to the next president and the next Congress to resolve this issue.

## House and Senate Title I Bills

By late October, the House and Senate had each taken up bills that would reauthorize Title I. (Straight A's would have changed some of the rules governing Title I, but separate legislation was required to reauthorize, or renew, the program. Typically reauthorization bills also involve rule changes.) Each reauthorization bill included several provisions that, if enacted, would have had a significant impact on literacy programs for children and families. For example, the House approved a reauthorization bill (H.R. 2) on October 21 that would have required schools receiving Title I funds to use reading curricula based on the most current, scientifically based research.

As for bilingual education, H.R. 2 would have required parental approval before students could be placed in traditional bilingual education programs, as opposed to English-immersion programs. It would also have required testing of all students who had attended school in the United States for at least three consecutive years in reading and language arts in English.

In the section dealing with Indian education, H.R. 2 would have added family literacy services as an allowable use of federal funds earmarked for Indian schools. Also, schools funded by the Federal Bureau of Indian Affairs would have been required to see to it that various providers of family literacy services coordinated their activities. The sections dealing with Native Hawaiian and Alaska Native education programs also included language adding family literacy services as an allowable use of federal funds.

The Clinton administration was muted in its response to H.R. 2. It wanted to see some changes, but it did not issue a veto threat. With regard to literacy-related provisions, the administration backed Hispanic House members who opposed the parental notification provision for bilingual education and wanted students with limited English proficiency to be tested in their native languages in all subjects other than English. Hispanic House members argued that H.R. 2 would penalize students who needed an extended time to become fluent in English. They and the administration lobbied against the House provisions, waiting to see what the Senate might do and hoping to eliminate them from the final bill.

The Senate Committee on Health, Education, Labor, and Pensions released a draft summary of its Title I reauthorization bill on October 15. At the behest of the chairman, James Jeffords (R-Vermont), and committee member Patty Murray (D-Washington), the draft included an increase in the authorization level for Even Start to $500 million— the same amount sought by fellow literacy advocate Bill Goodling in the House.

The Senate bill would have maintained the then-current authorization level for the Reading Excellence program at $260 million. It also included a new five-year early learning initiative with a total authorization of $7 billion. The initiative was targeted to children, but local projects could include education for parents and family literacy programs. The bill would also have increased the authorization level for Twenty-First Century Community Learning Centers to $800 million per year. The FY1999 appropriation was $200 million. Finally, the bill would have renewed the stand-alone authorization for the Star Schools program. That contradicted the administration's proposal to combine Star Schools with Technology Innovation Challenge Grants. The bill would have increased the Star Schools' authorization level slightly. Star Schools' funds also support the development of adult education media projects.

As with the Straight A's Act, Congress took no action on Title I reauthorization in 1999. It too would seem to be left for the next president and Congress to consider.

The House bill, H.R. 2, did not address the authorization levels for Even Start, Reading Excellence, Twenty-First Century Centers, or Star Schools. The House planned to deal with those programs in separate legislation.

## Goodling Presses for Even Start Bill

Congressman Goodling hoped to cap off his twenty-six-year career in Congress by introducing a bill to reauthorize and expand his Even Start program. Goodling hoped the bill would pass in 2000, coinciding with his retirement. As introduced, the Literacy Involves Families Together (LIFT) Act (H.R. 3222) would have increased the annual authorization for Even Start to $500 million, just as the

Senate's S. 2 would have done. Congress approved funding of $150 million, well short of the $500 million Goodling and fellow senator James Jeffords had requested. The bill has the following major provisions:

*Accountability.* States would be required to review the progress of local Even Start programs to make sure they were doing a good job. States would use these findings when making decisions about continuation grants.

*Training and technical assistance.* States would be allowed to use some of their Even Start funds to provide training and technical assistance to Even Start instructors, so long as they did not cut back on service to families. States would pay an experienced organization, such as the NCFL, to provide the training and technical assistance.

*Extended funding.* Programs that had received federal funds for eight years (the limit) would be allowed to keep receiving them at a reduced rate, with the federal government matching 35 percent of expenses.

*Research standards.* Just like other federally funded reading programs, Even Start programs would be required to base their instruction on scientific research findings.

*Adult reading research.* Because relatively little research has been done on how adults learn to read, the bill would have provided the National Institute for Literacy with $2 million per year for a new research project.

*Migrant programs.* The bill would have amended Title I and the migrant education program to allow states to use those funds to establish more family literacy projects. It would have also increased the existing Even Start set-asides for migrants and Indians from 5 percent to 6 percent whenever annual appropriations exceeded $250 million.

*Older children.* Children older than age eight would receive Even Start services, provided their schools used funds from their basic Title I grants to cover part of the cost.

*Indian programs.* The bill would have encouraged coordination among Even Start and other family literacy programs operated by the Federal Bureau of Indian Affairs, as would the corresponding Senate legislation.

Goodling was also sponsoring the Straight A's bill that would allow states to fold their Even Start funding into a block grant along with their federal funding originally earmarked for other K–12 programs. As he introduced the LIFT bill, he said he was confident that block grant states would keep funding Even Start "because it's a successful program." H.R. 3222 had the enthusiastic support of the National Even Start Association and the NCFL, although NCFL president Sharon Darling said she did not want the program block granted.

Congress decided not to wait until 2000 before extending federal funding for Even Start projects beyond the soon-to-be-expired maximum of eight years. To prevent any delay while his LIFT bill was pending, Congressman Goodling persuaded the House to include the extension in its version of the appropriations bill that would fund the DOE for FY2000. He then persuaded the Senate to accept the provision during final negotiations on the appropriations measure. The extension provision also imposed accountability measures. States were required to assess the progress made by all local projects using "indicators of program quality" approved by Washington. This requirement applies to all decisions about continuations of funding beyond the first year, not just continuations beyond eight years.

Congress took no final action on Even Start reauthorization in 1999. As with the Straight A's Act and Title I reauthorization, it seems this will be left for the next president and Congress.

## Policy Developments at the State Level

With the passage of the Workforce Investment Act of 1998 (WIA), the Adult Education Act and its 1991 update, the National Literacy Act, passed into history on June 30, 1999. The WIA included a new Adult Education and Family Literacy Act as its Title II. The new act required state directors of adult education programs and their staff to submit new state plans by April 1999, with the plans to go into effect July 1.

First, program staff and administrators had to choose one of three options: (1) join with job training, unemployment, welfare, and other state officials to submit a unified workforce plan immediately, (2) prepare a discrete five-year plan for adult education, or (3) prepare a one-year transitional plan that would serve as a placeholder while the other state-level departments hashed out a workforce plan by themselves. (The WIA did not require workforce plans to be submitted until July 1, 2000.) The act also required the states to focus on a number of

critical new issues. One key issue in the development of adult education plans was the establishment of student performance standards
based on each state's history of service in the following three areas:
educational gains; success in postsecondary programs, job attainment
and retention, and advanced training programs; and completion of
secondary education.

Ironically, although the WIA's accountability and continuous-
improvement provisions required states to undertake extensive
reforms, the act also reduced the states' ancillary and support funds.
States could spend no more than 12.5 percent of their federal grant
funds on teacher training, curriculum development, and other support services. The old set-aside had been 15 percent; in addition, states
had also been allowed to use a portion of the federal funds earmarked
for local services on such things as technical assistance.

Once the adult education plans were approved by Washington and
the funding adjustments made, state officials turned their attention to
meeting other WIA requirements, including the establishment of adult
education representation on state-level workforce boards and the integration of adult education services into the new One-Stop Career
Centers. Much of this work would continue into 2000.

## Problems with the National Reporting System

As state and local officials continued to wrestle with the new WIA
requirements, pilot testing revealed that adult education and literacy
programs faced real difficulties in their efforts to track learners who
had left local programs. This development had the potential to make
Congress reluctant to increase funding. The problems came to light
as the DOE and the National Association of State Directors of Adult
Education worked on redesigning the National Reporting System
(NRS), which measures learner outcomes. The redesign project was
launched in the mid-1990s, partly in response to the Republican
takeover of Congress following the 1994 elections. The GOP looked
askance at programs that could not show measurable results, and the
results produced by adult education programs had long been hard to
measure or simply poor. The head of the project was Mike Dean of
the Office of Vocational and Adult Education. The actual implementation was carried out by the Pelavin Research Center, part of the
American Institutes for Research in Washington.

Congress provided a new impetus for NRS improvement in 1998 when it passed the WIA with its new accountability requirements. As Barbara Garner (1999) of the National Center for the Study of Adult Learning and Literacy (NCSALL) summed it up, the act "reflects a priority toward more intensive, higher-quality services rather than rewarding [programs for the] number of students served. It also puts a much greater emphasis on learner outcomes, and therefore on accurate measurement and reporting" (p. 11). Under the old NRS, data collection and reporting had been hit-or-miss. As Dean told Garner, "There were no real consequences" if programs were unable to track students.

Programs that field-tested the NRS reported mixed results. On the one hand, the system allowed programs to report student progress (as measured by the Test of Adult Basic Education) on a new scale that gave students credit for small advances that would have been ignored under the old system. "The pilot allowed us to claim more successes," said Bill Walker of the Knox County Adult Basic Education Department in Knoxville, Tennessee. But when it came to tracking the results students achieved in life after leaving adult education programs—exactly the sort of data required by the new act—pilot testers had mixed results. "It's a tricky challenge: to show evidence of the impact of participation in adult basic education requires substantial resources, which may not be forthcoming until the evidence is produced," Garner concluded. In fact, the programs not only had difficulty tracking learners because this is hard to do but also because the NRS design required them to track *each and every* student served rather than a representative sampling of students. Sampling would have put much less of a burden on programs and probably produced better-quality information (C. Smith, personal communication, July 30, 2000).

The new performance measures required by the act were nonetheless due to go into effect July 1, 2000.

## Funding Applications Decline

Program applications for federal adult education pass-through funds were down by about half in California in 1998, and they were somewhat lower in Connecticut, according to Ronald Pugsley, director of the DOE's Division of Adult Education and Literacy. Officials speculated that the accountability and quality requirements imposed by the

WIA, and new state policies issued in response to the act, could be discouraging programs from applying.

California, for example, had adopted a "pay for performance" system for all local adult education programs receiving federal pass-through funds. Rather than fund local programs on the basis of hours attended by students, the state distributed funds on the basis of student outcomes. The state also noted on its application form for local programs the WIA requirement that all funded programs have access to computerized management information systems. Similar standards were in place in Connecticut, where local programs were also forced to work against an unusually tight deadline for the submission of funding proposals.

# RESEARCH ACTIVITIES

There were no landmark research findings on the order of the 1992 National Adult Literacy Survey reported in 1999, but many researchers continued to toil in more modest vineyards. Three of the most notable were Hal Beder of Rutgers University, Susan Imel of Ohio State University, and Tom Sticht, head of Applied Behavioral and Cognitive Sciences in El Cajon, California.

## Evidence of Program Success Is Elusive

Beder (1998) reviewed a host of research studies and found insufficient data to show that participants in adult basic education programs actually made gains in basic skills. After reviewing the twenty-nine most credible studies on the outcomes and impacts of adult education programs conducted since the late 1960s, he reported that "the evidence was insufficient" to determine whether adult learners actually learn. "In contradiction, however, learners in 10 studies were asked if they gained in reading, writing, and mathematics, and they overwhelmingly reported large gains," Beder reported. "What led to this contradiction, and what is the answer to the gain question?" he asked rhetorically. As to the former question, he suggested "that self-reported perceptions of basic skills gain [from students] are inflated by the normal human tendency to answer with socially acceptable responses and a reluctance to say unfavorable things in a program evaluation." As for the question of "real" or measurable gain, Beder said it "remains to be answered."

## Researcher Says Adult Educators Should Rethink, Redesign Programs

If adult educators want to attract more people to their programs and keep them enrolled longer, "they must change how they think about their programs," argued Ohio State University researcher Susan Imel in a report funded by the DOE (1999). Citing 1997 research by B. A. Quigley, Imel reported that only 8 percent of all people eligible to participate in government-funded adult basic education and literacy programs actually did so. Of those who did participate, 74 percent left their programs within the first year. Although there are several explanations for these statistics, including "the complicated nature of the lives of many adults," Imel said that "the way adult basic and literacy education [ABLE] programs are structured may also be a factor. . . . The fact that most ABLE programs still resemble school may mean that many adults may not choose to participate, or, once enrolled, do not find a compelling reason for persisting until their educational needs are met." Indeed, many adult learners have said they were loathe to return to a setting just like the one where they were unable to learn as children.

One way to address this problem, Imel suggested, would be to redesign programs using adult education principles rather than K–12 principles, and she devoted the bulk of her paper to describing that new model, drawing on her own research and the work of several others. Her recommendations include the following:

*Involve learners in planning and implementing learning activities.* Imel said that learners can begin with input on the intake or "needs-assessment" process and then help set program goals and help out all the way through to the evaluation phase.

*Draw on learners' experiences as a resource.* Adults' own "life tasks and problems" are often what lead them to programs, Imel said, so they provide a "reservoir for learning."

*Cultivate self-direction in learners.* Although many adults who have had difficulty following directions from teachers and other authority figures are not self-starters, Imel, quoting S. D. Brookfield, said that once adults are encouraged to become self-directed, they begin to see themselves as continuously recreating their circumstances rather than reacting to them.

*Create a climate that encourages and supports learning.* This means a climate marked by trust and mutual respect that fosters self-esteem. Imel said conflicts should be handled in a way "that challenges learners to acquire new perspectives and supports them in their efforts to do so."

*Foster a spirit of collaboration.* This often means that the teacher and student roles are interchangeable, with each learning from the other.

*Use small groups.* Small groups promote teamwork, encourage the involvement of all participants, and can "emphasize the importance of learning from peers."

Teachers "frequently give lip service" to learner involvement, according to Imel, but fail to follow through. She said they must really listen to learners and use their input in program development. She suggested letting students orient newcomers and serve on advisory boards. She also suggested that teachers use instructional materials that link academic subjects to students' real lives, often referred to as "contextualized learning." It is thought to make lessons more compelling to students, and it may be based on common work experiences, gender, race, ethnic culture, or class.

## Practitioners See Their Work as Therapy, Not Revolution

Adult educators in North America prefer to view themselves as psychotherapists rather than as revolutionaries, soldiers, or parents, according to a 1999 survey by Tom Sticht (1999). During workshops he led in the United States and Canada, Sticht asked eighty-one practitioners to consider eight sets of "dominant metaphors and analogies," each an attempt to summarize the roles of teachers and their adult students. The practitioners were asked to rate the appropriateness of each set. In descending order of popularity, they were

- Psychotherapy (education as a self-esteem booster)
- Business (teacher as purveyor of a service)
- Economics (education as an investment in human capital)

- Public schools (education as a way to produce productive citizens)
- Revolution (education as a means to liberation)
- Medicine (education as a cure)
- The military (education as a battle against illiteracy)
- Parenting (teacher as parent)

Canadian teachers said the most appropriate metaphors were psychotherapy, economics, and business. American teachers working in correctional education chose business, economics, and public schools. American teachers from community-based organizations chose psychotherapy, public schools, and business.

"Interestingly, the revolutionary metaphor, which might be associated with social justice and the critical literacy movement, especially the work of Paulo Freire, did not emerge in the top three metaphors or analogies thought appropriate for adult literacy education by the 81 participants," Sticht noted. "In contrast, the business and/or economic metaphors were always in the top three. . . . The predominance of the psychotherapy metaphor . . . while the revolutionary metaphor was ranked [lower] may indicate that adult literacy workers . . . view depression rather than oppression as a more serious problem to be overcome."

## National Assessment of Adult Literacy, 2002

By January 1999 the DOE had set up a Web site (http://nces.ed.gov/nadlits) to provide information on what it has decided to call the National Assessment of Adult Literacy (NAAL), scheduled for 2002. It will be the ten-year follow-up to the landmark National Adult Literacy Survey (NALS) conducted in 1992.

Like the NALS, the NAAL will be a household survey of people age sixteen and up. Also like the NALS, the NAAL will collect data and analyze the prose, document, and quantitative literacy skills of American adults, but this time the data are to be fully broken down by states and major subpopulations. The NAAL is also expected to provide trend data reaching back beyond the NALS to the 1985 assessment of young adult literacy conducted by the Educational Testing Service. Finally, the NAAL is expected to compare adult American literacy rates with those of other countries. A previous study found the United States about average among industrial nations.

In March, the National Center for Education Statistics (NCES), part of the DOE's Office of Educational Research and Improvement, formally invited proposals from potential contractors capable of conducting the survey. The NALS was conducted by the Educational Testing Service under an NCES contract.

## EVENTS

The year included two high-profile events that were important prerequisites to a third that would not happen until 2000, the National Literacy Summit. Organizers of this long-planned summit had repeatedly postponed it throughout 1998 and into 1999 while waiting for Vice President Al Gore and former Senator Paul Simon (D-Illinois) to hold their own separate literacy-related events. The delay tactics were a political strategy; the organizers did not want to get out in front of such influential friends. They reasoned that it would be better to follow the leads of Gore and Simon rather than try to lead them in policy directions they may or may not want to go.

### Gore Summit

One week before President Clinton's State of the Union speech, at Vice President Al Gore's January 12 Summit on Twenty-First Century Skills for Twenty-First Century Jobs, Gore proposed a new federal tax credit for employer-provided workplace literacy programs. He said the credit would apply to expenditures on literacy, ESOL, and other basic skills programs. It would cover 10 percent of such expenditures, with an annual maximum of $525 per participating employee. (Tax credits directly reduce an employer's tax owed, as opposed to tax deductions, which reduce taxable income.)

Gore also proposed several other initiatives. One of these would provide up to ten "High Skills Communities" with awards from the president and vice president each year "for achieving concrete results in improving the skills of their adult workforce," including adult literacy skills. Another was a $60 million plan to help train workers for high-skill jobs in industries facing skill shortages. This program would be run by regional workforce development boards. A third initiative was the proposed expansion of the existing tax credit for employer-paid training and education at the collegiate and postgraduate levels. Gore also called for an advisory panel that would analyze incentives for postsecondary education and training, such as low-income loans, grants, and tax incentives. Options might include individual "lifetime learning accounts" that would combine personal savings, employer contributions, and federal aid.

Congress had not given Gore's tax proposals any serious consideration by the end of 1999. The Clinton administration, not waiting for congressional authorization or an appropriation, began to designate High Skills Communities on its own authority. These were essentially symbolic declarations by local officials and business and labor leaders to cooperate on programs to upgrade workers' skills. Gore also took action by creating a thirty-one-member "leadership group" and directed it to come up with new ways to help train workers for high-skill jobs. The group included representatives of the National Institute for Literacy and the American Council on Education (ACE), the parent organization of the GED Testing Service. In a *Blueprint for Lifelong Learning* released in November 1999, members of the group made several rather platitudinous recommendations for national action and pledged themselves to various activities to further those recommendations. For example, NIFL pledged to conduct pilot testing on a training course for retail workers that is based on NIFL's Equipped for the Future curriculum standards. The ACE pledged to work with the AFL-CIO to increase the number of adults who take the General Educational Development (GED) test each year.

## Simon Forum and National Summit

Meeting in Carbondale, Illinois, in late March, the nation's leading literacy advocates called for summit meetings to be convened in every county in the nation as the first step in a new mobilization effort. The advocates had gathered at the invitation of former Senator Paul Simon for a forum to answer the question, "Literacy: Where Do We Go from Here?" Simon headed the new Public Policy Institute at Southern Illinois University. "This is the moment," said Alice Johnson, a former Simon staff member who had gone on to work at the National Institute for Literacy. She was referring to the momentum created by Vice President Gore's January Summit on Twenty-First Century Skills and President Clinton's subsequent call for new literacy initiatives and fiscal 2000 spending increases. "I want this conference to stretch our thinking," Simon said. "You know, you can get in ruts in any field, and that includes the literacy field. I want to see us start dreaming some big dreams and then fighting for those dreams."

At the end of the two-day forum, participants adopted an action plan with the following components:

- The library director in the biggest town in every county to convene a meeting of educators, religious leaders, welfare officials, businesspeople, labor leaders, and others to assess local literacy needs and mobilize new efforts to address them

- Mandatory literacy programs in every prison, with screening for learning disabilities and incentives for prisoners to improve their skills to at least the level of attainment of the GED credential

- A one-year campaign, in cooperation with broadcasters and advertisers, to encourage people with skill deficiencies to seek help

- "Significant" tax incentives for employers to offer workplace literacy programs (greater than the 10 percent proposed by the Clinton administration)

- An expanded effort to identify learning disabilities in young children

- Automatic tie-ins between literacy programs and all human service agencies, including welfare and employment offices

- Expanded family literacy efforts

- Greater cooperation among existing literacy programs and agencies

- More training for volunteers and better training for professionals

- Improved learner recruitment and retention efforts, based on interviews with dropouts, and including such services as day care and transportation

- Program assessment standards by 2005 that link learner outcomes to effective practice, followed by a National Literacy Report Card published every two or three years

"Since the enactment of the National Literacy Act in 1991, we have inched forward toward the goal of eliminating illiteracy in the United States," Simon said. "I believe these concrete, specific recommendations would help us move forward much more aggressively. . . . The question is not one of resources [but] of will. Are we really going to pay attention to this problem?"

Those attending the forum included Congressman Tom Sawyer (D-Ohio), coauthor with Simon of the National Literacy Act of 1991, former first lady Barbara Bush, and the leaders of the NIFL, the DOE's Division of Adult Education and Literacy, the National Center for Family Literacy, Laubach Literacy, the Literacy Volunteers of America, and Voice for Adult Literacy United for Education. Other organizations represented at the forum included the National Center for Adult Literacy, the Newspaper Association of America, the Lila Wallace–Reader's Digest Fund, the American Library Association, and the State Literacy Resource Centers Association. The no-shows included Senators James Jeffords and Patty Murray, Congressmen Bill Goodling and Tim Roemer (D-Indiana), the mayors of Baltimore and Philadelphia, columnist William Raspberry, and the leaders of the National Association for the Advancement of Colored People and the National Council of La Raza.

## National Literacy Summit

Once Gore and Simon had held their literacy-related events, leaders in the field began making plans for a summit in Washington to set a national literacy agenda.[1] It was conceived as a ten-year follow-up to the landmark report *Jump Start: The Federal Role in Adult Literacy.* Planners included the National Institute for Literacy, the DOE's Division of Adult Education and Literacy, and the National Center for the Study of Adult Learning and Literacy. In the *Jump Start* report, Forrest Chisman of the Southport Institute for Policy Analysis had laid out an agenda including the call for a national center for adult literacy (which would become the National Institute), a federal mandate requiring comprehensive state plans for adult education and literacy, state literacy resource centers, and access to federal funds for nonprofit and volunteer organizations. Most of these proposals were realized with the passage of the National Literacy Act of 1991. The new summit was intended to produce a new manifesto. Regional literacy summits would follow the national event, and a final manifesto would emerge later.

After many delays and postponements, the summit was slated for February 2000, when 150 to 175 invited attendees would hammer out a tentative new agenda for the adult literacy field. In addition to the organizers, other participants would include the National Coalition for Literacy, the National Council of State Directors of Adult

Education, other federal agencies with an interest in literacy, and representatives of labor, business, community colleges, and other key constituencies. The Lila Wallace–Reader's Digest Foundation agreed to provide $72,500 to sponsor the summit and the follow-up meetings.

## Voice for Adult Literacy United for Education

Archie Willard, chairman of the new adult learners' group Voice for Adult Literacy United for Education (VALUE), attended the February 10 meeting of the National Coalition for Literacy (NCL) with a request for funding. (The NCL includes virtually all of the nation's leading literacy organizations, including VALUE, which was created in 1998 by a group of about fifty adult learners and adult education professionals.) In a short and moving appeal, he said VALUE deserved support because adult learners were the best possible advocates for increased government support. "Congress needs to see the finished product," Willard said, referring to the NCL's underwhelming Capitol Hill lobbying effort of the previous day. Only fifteen people had shown up, and only a handful of those had confirmed appointments with members of Congress or their staff. Willard said VALUE needed funding for lobbying efforts and other activities. One objective was to get Congress to earmark federal funds for student leadership activities. Willard came away from the meeting with a commitment of $1,000 from the NCL treasury and an even greater amount in checks and pledges from individual representatives of NCL member organizations.

## CONCLUSION

The year 1999 may best be regarded as the beginning of a new reality for the adult education and literacy field. It was the year when state officials and local program personnel began to rethink and redefine their jobs under terms dictated by the Workforce Investment Act of 1998. It was also the year when members of the field finalized plans for their National Literacy Summit, which would give them a solid, visible platform from which to voice their opinion of the WIA. It would be facile to describe 1999 as a year of fundamental change leading to some bright new future. The real fundamentals did not change. Too many adults continued to struggle with inadequate skills. Too many adult education and literacy practitioners continued to struggle with inadequate resources. Too many children continued to be neglected by schools that lacked the resources and perhaps the will to make them literate.

Things may change for the better in the new millennium. As 1999 drew to a close, the need for change remained glaringly clear.

## Note

1. The literacy summit had first been proposed in 1996 by Jean Lowe, then director of the GED Testing Service. She said the field lacked an infrastructure for sharing proven instructional ideas, and she hoped a summit would help create one. She also hoped the summit could define the nature and extent of the nation's literacy problems, produce standards for measuring progress toward solutions, and calculate the amounts of government funding needed to make such progress. Officials at the NIFL and NCSALL had been talking about a summit almost since Lowe first suggested it, but their tentative plans were repeatedly postponed—first by plans for Gore's conference and then by those for Simon's forum in Illinois.

## References

Beder, H. (1998). Lessons from NCSALL's outcomes and impacts study. *Focus on Basics, 2*(D).

Garner, B. (1999). Nationwide accountability: The National Reporting System. *Focus on Basics, 3*(B).

Imel, S. (1999, Feb.). *Using adult learning principles in adult basic and literacy education.* Practice Application Brief published by the ERIC Clearinghouse on Adult, Career, and Vocational Education, housed at Ohio State University. Available at: http://www.ericacve.org.

Sticht, T. (1999, Oct. 2). National Literacy Advocacy listserv. Research Note 10/2/99, Metaphors and analogies in adult literacy education. Available at: http://literacy.nifl.gov/cgi-bin/list.

Vice President's Leadership Group on Twenty-First Century Skills for Twenty-First Century Jobs. (1999, Nov. 4). *Blueprint for lifelong learning.*

# CHAPTER TWO

# Making Sense of Critical Pedagogy in Adult Literacy Education

*Sophie C. Degener*

I n the field of adult education, there is much debate about how programs can best serve students. Some educators and researchers believe that adult education programs should reflect a critical pedagogy, providing services that are culturally relevant, participant driven, and socially empowering (Auerbach, 1989; Freire, 1993; Lankshear & McLaren, 1993; Quigley, 1997; Shor, 1992). Critical theorists (Bartolomé, 1996; Freire & Macedo, 1987; Lankshear & McLaren, 1993; Shor, 1992) have criticized many adult education programs for applying a "one model fits all" approach—with a preset structure and curriculum that rarely take into account the specific background and needs of the individuals involved. These noncritical programs place a primacy on skills acquisition, reflecting some educators' belief that literacy and other academic skills alone will help to rectify the marginalized positions of the students who are enrolled. Noncritical programs are criticized for ignoring the political, social, and economic factors that have conspired to marginalize people in the first place (Macedo, 1994). Students in these programs are seen as passive recipients of the teacher's knowledge, with little sense of their own agency in transforming their lives (Shor, 1992).

Critical theorists believe that adult literacy programs should not be confined to teaching specific literacy skills but rather should contextualize instruction within a framework of social activism and societal transformation. Critical adult literacy programs should be designed around the backgrounds, needs, and interests of students and should encourage a "dialogic" (as defined by Freire, 1993) relationship between teachers and students.[1] More important, programs should establish a democratic setting where students are able to use their developing literacy skills to analyze critically their place in society, understand how certain cultural assumptions and biases have put them and their families at risk, and ultimately learn how to challenge the status quo. Critical adult education programs do not simply teach literacy and other basic skills; rather, they show students how they can use those skills to transform their lives and the society in which they live.

Critical pedagogy in literacy programs around the world, including Cuba's "Great Campaign" of the early 1960s, the Nicaraguan Literacy Crusade of the early 1980s, and the work of the Highlander school in the southern United States during the civil rights movement, has been shown to have an important impact on adult students' literacy attainment and their social empowerment (Horton & Freire, 1990; Kozol, 1978; Miller, 1985). Students in these programs learned how to read and write and how to use reading and writing to challenge political structures and improve their lives. Some may argue (Facundo, 1984) that critical pedagogy worked well in these programs because they existed within the context of a repressive government and a larger revolutionary movement. Standing up to the government was a matter of crucial importance for students in these programs; they needed to transform their situation because their lives were literally at risk. Literacy attainment in the United States today, however, is not perceived as a matter of life and death, and personal and societal transformation are not seen as necessary goals of an adult education program. I would argue, however, that literacy attainment *is* a matter of life and death for many students in this country. Too many people are prevented from reaching their full potential because they do not have access to the adequate nutrition, housing, health care, and education that so many of us take for granted. Learning to read and write will not change this imbalance. Adult literacy programs that make an effort to reflect a critical pedagogy try to help students understand what forces have contributed to their positions in society and to see how literacy can help them influence these forces and transform their lives. These programs hold great promise for adult learners in this country; it behooves educators to learn more about them.

Critical theorists are eloquent and prolific in their criticisms of traditional, noncritical adult education programs. Unfortunately, their criticisms have resulted in an "us versus them" mentality that often puts noncritical programs on the defensive rather than open to the idea of change. Practitioners within adult education often view the ideas of critical theorists as too theoretical and impractical (Kanpol, 1998). Teachers often feel that implementation of critical pedagogy is impeded by too many barriers, such as the required use of specific curricula or assessments by government agencies that provide funding for programs, students who are resistant to critical pedagogy, and administrators who expect students to show improvement on standardized assessments.[2]

Dividing adult education programs into two categories is too simplistic and does not adequately represent the field. In reality, there may be programs that reflect some critical and some noncritical elements. In addition, some programs may be noncritical but may also have the potential to evolve—that is, they may be making program changes that reflect a shift toward critical pedagogy. Rather than labeling programs as either critical or noncritical, it may be more useful and beneficial to the field to think about adult education programs as falling somewhere on a continuum between noncritical and critical. Dependence on government-sponsored funding may force some programs, for example, to use a specific curriculum or assessment tool. Teachers in the program may have to use that curriculum but may also attempt to make their instruction more reflective of critical pedagogy. Such teachers could be seen as attempting to shift their pedagogy from noncritical to critical. Such changes do not occur immediately, nor would we expect them to. As Freire (1998) himself argues, critical educational practice is not a specific methodology to be applied blindly but rather one that emerges when teachers can practice teaching from a critical perspective and have the time to reflect on their pedagogy. I believe this is a more constructive way of mending the division between critical and noncritical pedagogy in adult education; programs may have little incentive to change if they believe they must change everything at once. This chapter challenges the assumption that adult education programs must be defined as solely critical or noncritical and shows how a bridge between the two camps might be built.

The principal frame for this chapter is critical theory.[3] Critical theory in literacy (also called critical literacy) looks at how one's identity is inscribed by literacy practices. A person's level of literacy, the nature of the printed material that this person reads and writes, and the role that literacy plays in his or her community all contribute to how that person is perceived by him- or herself and by society. Critical theorists believe that becoming literate involves not just learning how to read and write but also learning how to use literacy to examine critically one's position in life in terms of socioeconomic status, gender, educational background, and race (Auerbach, 1989; Freire, 1993; Freire & Macedo, 1987; Giroux & McLaren, 1992; Street, 1995). Within a critical literacy framework, there is not just one literacy but many (Street, 1993), and an individual may need to practice many kinds of literacy to fulfill his or her roles in society. The literacy needs of the home or the community may be entirely different from the kinds of literacy practices required at work or at school. According to Lankshear and McLaren (1993), these literacies "are socially constructed within political contexts: that is, within contexts where access to economic, cultural, political, and institutional power is structured unequally. Moreover, these same literacies evolve and are employed in daily life settings that are riven with conflicting and otherwise competing interests" (p. xviii).

The content of this chapter is also informed by Vygotsky's (1978) theory of social constructivism, which takes the view that an individual's intellectual development results from social interactions within specific cultural contexts. More specifically, Vygotsky sees the community as playing an integral role in intellectual development, arguing that it is the people most central in our lives who influence the way we perceive the world, and therefore how and what we learn. From a social constructivist viewpoint, education should occur in meaningful contexts, and every effort should be made to connect school experiences with students' out-of-school experiences.

## CRITICAL PEDAGOGY: EDUCATION IS POLITICAL

To understand how critical pedagogy can be applied to adult education, it is first important to have a general understanding of it. Of all the educators and theorists espousing a critical pedagogy, Paulo Freire is probably the best known among adult educators. His work in adult education, though carried out largely in developing countries, including his native Brazil, has been extremely influential among adult educators in the United States. Many others as well have contributed to our understanding of critical pedagogy.

European social and political theorists of the nineteenth and twentieth centuries have influenced Freire and other modern critical pedagogues. One such influence is Marx, who theorized that economics in large part dictates social and cultural relations (Klages, 1997; Wink, 1997). Marx also theorized that dominant ideologies work to justify a society's social and economic hierarchies. In a capitalist society, for example, Marx would say that all major institutions—educational, religious, government, business—promote ideologies that allow certain people to prosper while others remain marginalized. Another major influence in critical pedagogy is Gramsci, who used the term *hegemony*—the domination of one group over another—to describe how societal institutions maintain their power (Wink, 1997). The term *critical theory* and the ideas behind it can be traced to the Frankfurt school, a German institute of social research where Max Horkheimer, Jürgen Habermas, Erich Fromm, Hannah Arendt, Herbert Marcuse, and other social thinkers developed influential sociological, political, and cultural theories based in part on Marx's theories (Greene, 1996).

In the United States, Dewey and Horton have had major influences on critical pedagogy. Dewey (1963) theorized that only students who were actively involved in their learning could become informed participants in a democracy. He believed that rote learning contributed to the passive acceptance of one's place in society, whereas learning through problem solving and practical application would lead students to take a more active role in determining their experiences and positions within society. Horton, who opened the Highlander Folk School in Tennessee in 1932, believed that education must be tied to larger social movements. His work with adults reflected his belief that education must be grounded in the real-life problems and struggles of students and must help them understand how to master their fate (Heaney, 1996).[4]

This chapter, while acknowledging the important role that critical theorists and educators from the nineteenth and first half of the twentieth centuries played in the formation of critical pedagogy, focuses on critical theorists and educators of the latter part of the twentieth century, particularly those who have influenced education in the United States. It is important to note that critical pedagogy is not tied exclusively to adult education. Freire, Horton, Shor, and Auerbach focus almost exclusively on adult students, but many of the writings on critical pedagogy concern education in general (Macedo, Giroux, McLaren, Lankshear, Street) or K–12 education (Bartolomé, Shannon). I have synthesized these different approaches in order to present a more cohesive portrait of critical pedagogy.

Perhaps the most important theme running through the literature is the belief that educational systems the world over are political (Freire, 1993; Freire & Macedo, 1987; Giroux, 1997; Shannon, 1992; Shor, 1992).[5] Decisions about whom to hire, what curricula to follow, which books to buy, and what language to use are all political. Teachers who claim to be neutral are also, de facto, political. Horton contends that the idea of a neutral educational system and neutral educators is a false one (Horton & Freire, 1990). He believes that calling education "neutral" is actually a code for supporting the status quo. Neutrality means following the crowd, doing what is expected, and refraining from questioning the political decisions that are made daily in schools all over the world. According to Shannon (1992), all of the decisions that educators make regarding program and lesson goals, the materials to be used, and the nature of teacher interaction with students "are actually negotiations over whose values, interests, and beliefs will be validated at school" (p. 2). These decisions are indisputably political.

Critical theorists claim not only that education is political but that critical educators *must* be political if they are to see through curricula that promote mainstream beliefs, culture, politics, and goals (Anderson & Irvine, 1993; Edelsky, 1996; Giroux, 1997; Lankshear & McLaren, 1993). Critical theorists challenge the popularly held belief that becoming literate will by itself effect dramatic change in the lives of marginalized people. They believe that educators should not only teach content but should also educate students about the political and social inequities that have prevented them from becoming academically successful thus far.

Educators cannot help students understand these social and political inequities unless they understand them themselves. Some critical theorists (Bartolomé, 1996; Freire & Macedo, 1987) write about the need for teachers to develop political clarity, which Bartolomé (1996) defines as the "process by which individuals achieve a deepening awareness of the sociopolitical and economic realities that shape their lives and their capacity to recreate them" (p. 235). To achieve political clarity, teachers need to understand that what happens in the larger society has significant impact on what happens in school. Schools are not isolated from larger sociocultural realities, and the academic achievement of subordinated students can be seen as a by-product of what is occurring at the societal level. Teachers with political clarity understand that the sociocultural reality within their classrooms and schools must be transformed so that class and school cultures do not mirror society's inequities.

The idea that education is political is certainly the central theme of critical pedagogy. Within that theme are several additional assumptions about education put forth by critical educators:

- Dominant ideologies and culture dictate educational practices.
- Students must be actively involved in their education.
- Language is ideological and serves to construct norms within classrooms.

Each of these ideas overlaps with the others, but I will discuss them separately to delineate the most important ideas of critical pedagogy.

## Dominant Ideologies and Culture Dictate Educational Practices

Closely tied to the idea that education is political is the idea that the structure of schools, the way in which teachers are educated in teacher preparation programs, the official curricula, and the methodologies that teachers implement are all influenced by those who currently hold power, including government, religious, and private sector leaders. Critical theorists maintain that dominant ideologies have dictated what is taught and that the culture represented by these dominant ideologies is the most highly privileged (Giroux, 1997; Lankshear & McLaren, 1993; Macedo, 1994). This privileged culture has more of what critical theorists refer to as *cultural capital,* which means that its mainstream cultural practices are more highly valued than those of marginalized groups. The "English-only" movement (Tatalovich, 1995) and Hirsch's (1987) "cultural literacy" are both examples of how cultural capital can influence political and educational policies and thought, imposing mainstream language and culture on political and educational structures.[6]

Macedo (1994) believes that those who defend a "Western cultural heritage" fail to recognize that marginalized groups do not possess the same cultural capital as those in dominant groups; this failure contributes to unequal power relations in schools. Teachers tend to value students more highly who more closely represent the mainstream in their language, ethnicity, socioeconomic background, language, and life experiences than those of nonmainstream groups (Bartolomé, 1996). Taylor (1997) writes, "Race, gender, and socioeconomic status are all factors that critically affect whose 'literacy' counts. There seems to be a limit to how much success there is to go around, and not all types of knowledge or ways of knowing are recognized" (p. 2).

Delgado-Gaitan (1996) believes that schools' failure to involve families in school activities and to engage parents in helping their children become academically successful is due to the fact that schools are influenced by competitive, capitalistic principles that do not attempt to comprehend the cultures and values of the communities they serve. Freire (1998) sees the problem as one of intolerance, which he defines as the tendency to believe that whatever is different from "us" is inferior. People tend to believe that the way they do things is correct and therefore superior to the ways others might do things. This kind of belief system has the most impact on marginalized groups because they lack the power to impose their ways on others. Freire (1998) goes so far as to say that the dominant class does not intend for there to be equality between the classes; rather, it wants to maintain the differences and distance between groups and to use political systems such as schools to identify and emphasize the inferiority of the dominated classes while at the same time confirming its own superiority. One major way in which school systems support this "mainstream is superior" attitude is through curriculum. The decisions about what to teach and how to teach it lie largely with white, mainstream administrators and educators who place the highest value on their own ways of knowing while ignoring other ways of knowing that are part of different social classes, values, and languages.

If it is as Freire says, then we are up against a school system that places subordinate students in the position of having to reject their own cultural knowledge and ways of knowing in order to fit in and be successful in school. Bartolomé (1996) goes further when she writes that schools dehumanize students by "robbing [them] of their culture, language, history, and values" (p. 233). She believes that attempting to address the academic failure of subordinated students is futile if schools do not address their own discriminatory practices.

Critical theorists believe that one of the most important things educators, curriculum designers, and policymakers can do is to learn about the culture, everyday experiences, language, and community that make up the reality of subordinated students (Freire, 1993; 1998; Giroux, 1997; Shor, 1992). Giroux (1997) believes it is necessary to develop pedagogy that is "attentive to the histories, dreams, and experiences that such students bring to school" (p. 140). Only through being attentive to students' realities will critical educators develop teaching practices that accept and validate the different kinds of cultural capital that influence the way students make meaning of their learning.

If the knowledge that we gain about marginalized students does not significantly affect our curriculum or the way we teach, then that understanding is, from a critical perspective, useless. Similarly, multicultural education that amounts only to add-ons (such as Black History Month or the celebration of the Chinese New Year) and that is not evident in meaningful ways within the day-to-day curriculum will not affect the educational achievement of subordinated groups in any substantial way (Lankshear & McLaren, 1993). According to Giroux (1997), a critical multiculturalism should not be exclusively focused on subordinate groups, because this tends to single them out and often highlights their deficits. Critical multiculturalism should instead examine racism from a historical and institutional perspective so that students are able to understand the factors that have helped to create an unequal society—one that has a political, socioeconomic, and educational impact on their lives every day.

## Students Must Be Actively Involved in Their Education

Critical pedagogy does not end with the idea of using student experiences to frame curricula. Rather, it proposes that education should always go beyond that point by encouraging students to become active participants in their education (Anderson & Irvine, 1993; Macedo, 1994; Shor, 1992). Students who are active participants are engaged with the teacher and the curriculum. They contribute their own ideas and learn to wrestle with ambiguities and challenge assumptions. Active participation also means that they cocreate curricula with the teacher to ensure that their needs and interests are given primary importance. Finally, it means taking action and transforming the world in order to eliminate disadvantage. Social transformation is the ultimate goal of critical education.

Students who are presented with a curriculum rooted in mainstream culture and ideology but cannot relate to that culture and ideology tend to become passive learners. Shor (1992) notes that all people begin life as motivated learners, but when students sit year after year in classrooms that are not tuned into their backgrounds and experiences and where their own ideas are not valued, they lose their natural curiosity and become passive or even nonparticipants.

Freire (1998) refers to the importance of dialogic communication between teachers and learners as one means of actively involving students in their own education. In his opinion, dialogism is the cornerstone of critical education. To teach students in a meaningful, personal way, educators must open their minds to what learners have to say. Freire (1993) writes, "Only dialogue, which requires critical thinking, is also capable of generating critical thinking. Without dialogue there is no communication, and without communication, there can be no true education" (p. 73). In traditional classrooms, the teacher is the holder of the knowledge, and the students, who are perceived as ignorant, are the receptacles for this knowledge. Freire refers to this as a "banking model" of education and criticizes it for its view of learners as objects of learning. Dialogic communication, on the other hand, views both teachers and learners as important contributors to the learning process.

Although marginalized students are often viewed—and view themselves—as knowing nothing of value, these learners come to realize through dialogic communication that they *have* learned many things in their relations with the world and with others. Freire (1993) believes in a more fluid relationship between teachers and students, so that learning goes both ways: teachers are learners and learners are teachers.

To prevent their classrooms from reflecting a "banking" sensibility, critical educators should consciously help their students to become active learners. A critical literacy, for example, is about much more than learning how to read words on a page. Freire and Macedo (1987) believe that marginalized learners must learn to "read the world" before they "read the word." In other words, students must come to an understanding of the cultural, political, and social practices that constitute their world and their reality before they can begin to make sense of the written words that describe that reality.

In his work with adult literacy students in Brazil, Freire (1993) developed what he called *generative themes,* which were used to help adults learn to "read the word" while simultaneously learning to "read the world." Based on his observations and discussions with community members and students, the generative themes were designed to bring up issues important to the particular students in his classes, perhaps representing conflict or social problems in their lives. Freire believes it is important to engage students in discussions of such issues to help them understand that even without the ability to read the word, they are capable of reading their world and therefore are active subjects in their learning.

Generative themes are instrumental in giving students a means to critically examine their lives and the society in which they live. Macedo (1994) explains that when marginalized people begin to realize that they are capable of reading and naming their world, they start to question the culture that has been imposed on them and start seeing themselves as the makers of their own culture. They become politically literate and begin to see how reading and writing will benefit them as they begin to challenge the status quo.

In discussing issues that they find important, students realize that they already possess much knowledge and awareness about important matters. Freire makes clear, however, that students need to move beyond their initial naive consciousness of the world. He believes that students have "the right to know better what they already know" (Horton & Freire, 1990, p. 157). One of the most important roles of a critical educator is to help students get beyond common sense, to understand the reasons behind the facts. For example, it is not enough to know that the school in one's neighborhood is old and falling apart and that the students who attend that school generally do not achieve academically what students in the newer suburban schools achieve. As Freire (1993) writes, marginalized learners need to reflect on their concrete situations. They must discover why things are the way they are. What political, socioeconomic, racial, and cultural factors contribute to the deterioration of city schools, while suburban schools are more technologically advanced, more structurally sound, and much more amply provided with teachers and support staff? When students begin to understand the reasons behind their problems, they begin to understand their world and what they need to do to change it. When disadvantaged learners are able to reflect on their common-sense knowledge and get beyond it, they begin to understand that they can take action to transform their lives. Freire describes this shift as one from naive consciousness to critical consciousness.

Shor (1992) describes critical consciousness as the process of coming to understand the relationship between our own individual experiences and the social system. Shor writes that critical consciousness allows students to understand that "society and history are made by contending forces and interests, that human action makes society, and that society is unfinished and can be transformed" (p. 129).

Another important part of critical consciousness, according to Giroux (1997), is for students to understand the dominant forms of knowledge in order to be able to critique them. This is distinctly different from the banking model of education, in that students are acquiring this knowledge in order to understand it, critique it, and incorporate it into their ways of knowing so that they can challenge and transform it. Freire agrees that teachers are doing their students no favors if they never move them beyond their own lived experiences. He writes, "To acquire the selected knowledge contained in the dominant curriculum should be a goal attained by subordinate students in the process of self and group empowerment. They can use the dominant knowledge effectively in their struggle to change the material and historical conditions that have enslaved them" (in Macedo, 1994, p. 121).

Critical theorists (Edelsky, 1996; Giroux, 1997; Lankshear & McLaren, 1993; Macedo, 1994; Quigley, 1997) believe that critical education should guide students toward becoming political. Different theorists have different names for this process—*emancipatory education, liberatory education, democratic education, transformative education*—but it all boils down to the importance of moving students beyond learning content and toward taking political action. To achieve this, educators should teach in opposition to the inequalities that exist in their students' lives—racial inequalities, gender inequalities, and socioeconomic inequalities (Edelsky, 1996). Marginalized students need to understand the role that systemic factors play in placing them at a disadvantage. Their economic or educational limitations may have less to do with their lack of ability than with the damaging effects of the structure of the mainstream culture (Lankshear & McLaren, 1993). Educators should help their students understand that trying to work within the institutions that keep them marginalized will not be enough; they may need to change the wider conditions that conspire to prevent their academic and socioeconomic success.

As students develop a critical consciousness, they begin to understand that society as they know it and the history that informs it are not set in stone but have been formed by different interests and powers, that human action has created society as they know it, and that their own human action can transform it (Shor, 1992). Once marginalized people recognize that society is changeable and that they have the power to transform the structures that put them at a disadvantage,[7] they develop what is often called agency. *Agency,* according to Shor (1992), means learning about the social, political, and economic structures in society that maintain the status quo and then using that knowledge to transform lives, individually and collectively.

## Language Is Ideological

The issue of language is of crucial importance in critical pedagogy. According to Macedo (1994), language should never be seen as merely a tool for communication. Indeed, language can be seen as ideological in that it is able to impose specific norms within classrooms (Anderson & Irvine, 1993; Giroux, 1997). The ability of marginalized people to reflect on their lives, discover the root causes of their disadvantaged situation, and take action to transform that situation depends on their ability to discover their own voices in the process. Too often teachers who place great importance on learning to speak, read, and write in the standard language representing the mainstream delegitimize the language experiences that students bring with them to the classroom (Freire & Macedo, 1987; Macedo, 1994). When the dominant language is most highly valued in the learning process, minority language speakers (including those who speak nonstandard English) are automatically devalued, and their words and ideas are seen as less important—if they are heard at all. These students are often forced to become passive objects of the educational process. Unless and until they are able to learn the language of the mainstream, they have no voice with which they can read and write their worlds.

Language plays an important part in critical pedagogy in two distinct ways: (1) if students are to become active participants in their learning, teachers must legitimize their language needs and the curriculum should be grounded in their language; (2) students need to develop a voice or form of discourse that helps them to read their world as well as participate in its transformation.

First, students must be able to speak their own language in their classrooms because it is through that language that they make sense of their reality and their own experiences in the world (Giroux & McLaren, 1992; Macedo, 1994). A critical pedagogy that provides students with the tools for transforming their own reality needs to recognize the plurality of students' voices and engage them in learning that democratically accepts all languages. Through their own language, students can begin to develop the means to name their world (Freire & Macedo, 1987). Schools have the power to privilege certain languages over others, thus granting higher status to those groups able to speak the dominant language. When language-minority learners are forced to read their world using a language in which they lack proficiency, they are unable to develop a voice that goes beyond the surface level of understanding. They may learn the appropriate labels for things, such as "food," "money," or "job," but they will not be able to go beyond that level of understanding to reflect on and interpret their reality. The transformation of their reality, which depends on their ability to read and reflect on their world with much greater depth of understanding, will be impossible.

Critical educators should use students' own languages as a starting point for educational development (Freire, 1998). Educators should become familiar with the communicative practices associated with the written and oral forms of their students' languages. Every effort should be made to learn about the grammar and syntax of students' languages and to understand how different cultural practices may influence language usage—for example, with regard to how students address or interact with others or how students may tell a story. Even when all students in a class speak the same language, there may be differences in the ways they use that language. Teachers should understand this and must be careful not to favor one kind of interaction over another. Gee (1993) discusses how students from different backgrounds tell stories differently. Mainstream students tend to have storytelling styles that mimic the structure of storybooks, beginning with "Once upon a time" and incorporating a problem and solution into the story. African American students may have a storytelling style that is more like a performance, with rhythmic language and repetition. Gee explains that the first kind of storytelling is valued more highly in schools because it more closely mirrors the kind of bookish language associated with school learning. Critical educators must be careful not to discount certain kinds of communication by students solely because it does not match their expectations for school language use. Teachers must acknowledge that student self-expression is about more than the student's language; it is reflective of cultural, class, and racial backgrounds as well as gender.

When students perceive that the teacher accepts and values their language, they begin to see that their ideas are important and do matter to the teacher and their classmates. At the same time, teachers should not restrict students to their own language. Shor believes that nonstandard student speech must be recognized as the legitimate and rule-governed dialect that it is and that it should be used and studied *in tandem* with standard English, which students need to learn. Educators might consider engaging in critical discussions about language so that students can confront the power structures that make certain languages and forms of language dominant (Shor, 1992). Students need to understand that to work toward changing their worlds, they may often need to appropriate certain aspects of the dominant language (Freire & Macedo, 1987).

Another way that language can serve to empower or oppress marginalized students is in the type of discourse that takes place in the classroom. Educators are in a position of power and so can decide whose voices will be heard in the classroom and whose will be submerged (Giroux, 1997; Lankshear & McLaren, 1993). In traditional classrooms, the teacher is an authoritarian figure whose voice dominates the class, controlling what is taught, how it is taught, and how students interact with texts and other learning materials. By providing students with knowledge and the means for self-understanding, teachers can guide students toward critical consciousness. However, even the best-intentioned teachers can use their voices to impose their own points of view or to silence their students' voices.

Freire's vision of dialogical education has much to do with the concept of voice. In a dialogical classroom, the teacher can be seen as a problem poser—encouraging students to question existing knowledge rather than presenting subject matter as immutable and universal (Freire, 1993; Lankshear & McLaren, 1993). It is this process of mutual inquiry that leads students to discover their own voices. Macedo (1994) notes that it is not possible for teachers to give students their voices. Finding one's voice requires struggling with preconceived notions about whose knowledge counts and learning to analyze and critique that knowledge that has heretofore been considered fact. Nonetheless, critical educators have the responsibility to create a classroom environment that allows for these silenced voices to emerge. Macedo calls voice "a human right" and a "democratic right" (p. 4).

Dialogue is a democratic and critical form of discourse that does not occur in traditional classrooms. Shor (1992) sees dialogue as a means for changing the nature of communication between students and teachers, which has typically been characterized by the authoritarian position of the teacher. He believes dialogue is a discourse created jointly by students and teachers, one that questions existing knowledge and also calls into question the traditional power relations in schools and society that have kept certain groups marginalized.

A dialogic classroom is *not* simply about having discussions in class where everyone is allowed to share their opinion (Macedo, 1994). Rather, dialogical education expects teachers to listen to their students to learn about the issues and problems that are important within their communities and ask questions that will enable students to understand those problems from a societal perspective and then figure out ways to take political action to solve them (Shor, 1992). Teachers must not be afraid to share their own expertise in these situations. Although the nature of dialogical education requires a fluid relationship between teacher and student, teachers have knowledge that will enable students to broaden their understanding of issues of importance. Allowing students to share what they know does not mean that teachers should submerge their own competency (Shor & Freire, 1987). A teacher is obliged to be an authority on his or her subject matter but should also be open to relearning what he or she knows through interaction with students (Horton & Freire, 1990). According to Bartolomé (1996), creating a dialogic learning environment for ethnic minority and low-socioeconomic-status students "requires that teachers . . . genuinely value and utilize students' existing knowledge bases in their teaching. In order to do so, teachers should confront and challenge their own social biases so as to begin to perceive their students as capable learners. Furthermore, they should remain open to the fact that they will also learn from their students. Learning is not a one-way undertaking" (pp. 239–240).

Dialogue should not be characterized by teacher-dominated exchanges. Dialogue, from a critical perspective, must balance teacher authority with student input (Shor, 1992). There is no room for authoritarianism in such a setting. Student participation in decision making is an important part of the dialogical classroom. Students should be able to contribute to curricular decisions. They should be asked to propose areas of study and to choose the associated reading materials.

At the same time, teachers need to recognize that not all students may be able to or want to speak up. Students have the right to be silent

(Shor & Freire, 1987). Because they have traditionally been encouraged, through authoritarian classrooms, to devalue their own voices, they may be resistant to sharing the power within a classroom or school setting (Shor, 1992). It may be hard for them to let go of the long-perpetuated notion that certain kinds of knowledge or ways of knowing are more highly valued. In fact, they may firmly believe that their own ways of knowing do not count. It takes time and patience on the part of critical educators to help students understand that their voices do count and that the canons of knowledge are merely social constructs that can be questioned and held up for examination.

When students begin to recognize their ability to use their own voices to name their world, and to critique and analyze their own situations, they will begin to understand that they possess the power to change their world. This ultimate goal of critical pedagogy is achieved when educators recognize the political nature of education.

## A CRITICAL PEDAGOGY FRAMEWORK FOR ADULT EDUCATION PROGRAMS

This section looks at how the central ideas of critical pedagogy could be applied in an adult education program.

### Philosophy, Presuppositions, and Goals

The idea that education is political is central to the basic philosophy behind a critical adult education program. All other features of the program likely stem from this basic belief. A critical program would acknowledge that literacy learning alone is not the answer to the problems of marginalized adults (Street, 1993). Rather, the mastery of literacy and other basic skills would be seen as one means for students to negotiate society's realities, as one of the tools they need to analyze critically and transform their position in society (Lankshear & McLaren, 1993). The mission of such a program would be to help students "read their world" in order to understand better their own power to change it and use literacy to help them to do so (Freire & Macedo, 1987). A critical program would never impose dominant literacy practices and discourse styles on the students in the program. Rather, it would show how the use of academic skills can help students negotiate the world that has traditionally put them at a disadvantage, and it would do so without asking them to give up forms of discourse and literacy that are important to their own cultures (Freire & Macedo, 1987; Giroux & McLaren, 1992; Shor, 1992).

## Program Structure

A critical adult education program would be built from the bottom up, not the top down. A program would never just "open up" in a community without consulting members of that community (Freire, 1993). Planning the program would be a grassroots affair (Macedo, 1994). If starting the program were not the community members' idea in the first place, then certainly the planning process would include the opinions and ideas of potential students, staff members, community members, and teachers (Giroux, 1997). Such decisions as where the program would be housed, what kinds of classes would be offered, when those classes would meet, who would teach them, and who would oversee the day-to-day running of the program would be made jointly. All final decisions would be up for approval by the community, so that the program would embody the democratic principles so crucial to critical education (Shor, 1992).

## Curriculum and Materials

First and foremost, the curriculum for a critical adult education program would be based on the premise that no one methodology works for all populations. A set curriculum would never be imposed on a program (Bartolomé, 1996). All curricular decisions would be based on the needs and interests of the students involved, and choices as to what would be studied, and how, would be made jointly by teachers and students (Giroux, 1997; Shor, 1992). Furthermore, the curriculum would always be linked as closely as possible to the immediate realities of the learners (Freire & Macedo, 1987). Teachers would understand, respect, and legitimize the cultures and languages of their students, and every effort would be made to root the program in these different cultures and languages (Giroux & McLaren, 1992). Teachers and administrators would spend time meeting with students and other community members, both formally and informally, to learn about the most important issues in learners' lives. Class activities and materials would initially be centered on those issues, perhaps, but not necessarily, in the form of generative themes (Freire, 1993; Shor, 1992). Gradually, as students became confident readers of their own world, curricular activities and materials would become more conceptual and academic.

The reading that students engage in, no matter what their literacy level, would have relevance to their own lives. Discrete skill work, including work with phonics, spelling, and vocabulary, would be done only when a context had been created for it (Street, 1995). Materials would never be simplistic or patronizing because the program would trust in the ability of its students to read their own world and to examine critically their own social situations (Freire & Macedo, 1987). Whether students were able to read the word, they would be assumed able to read the world, and the materials used in class would acknowledge this.

Possible learning activities to support the critical adult education program might include, but would not be limited to, self-reflective journal keeping, cooperative group work, the reading of texts for class discussion (not just reading practice), extended peer discussion of problems posed in class, and long-term, active research projects (Shor, 1992). Texts would be developed from students' own writing, based on their reading of the world.

In reading texts, emphasis would be placed not only on the comprehension of those texts but also on students' critique of those texts (Giroux, 1997). Students would be encouraged to reflect on and be critical of what they read. They would learn to look below surface-level meaning to understand the ideas that inform that meaning. Finally, they would be encouraged to read to transform, using reading materials as a springboard for discussion that would help them consider actions they might take to improve their lives.

The curriculum would be transformative in that it would promote students' acquisition of the necessary strategies and skills to help them become social critics capable of making decisions that would affect their social, political, and economic realities (Giroux & McLaren, 1992). This would ultimately involve learning skills reflecting the dominant culture, but in learning these skills, students would understand *why* they should learn them (Freire & Macedo, 1987). For example, in learning to write a business letter, students would never be taught that this is simply another practical skill. Instead, letter writing would be seen as a mainstream writing skill that is important to master in order to negotiate with people or institutions using a discourse that they understand. Teachers would encourage students to write letters to people or agencies to try to address problems in their personal lives or their community.

## Teacher Development

Teachers are an integral part of any critical adult literacy program. Because they are the ones who spend the most time with learners, they have the greatest potential influence on the program itself, on the adults who participate in it, and on how learning takes place in the classroom.

In a critical adult literacy program, teachers would be immersed in the community in which they are to teach before they begin teaching (Giroux, 1997; Macedo, 1994; Shor, 1992). They would learn about the community—its hopes, its dreams, and its most pressing issues. They would visit the institutions that play important roles in the community, and they would talk to community leaders such as clergy, doctors, social workers, businesspeople, educators, and local politicians. Beyond that, teachers would develop an understanding of the role that literacy plays in the community. How do community members use literacy in their day-to-day lives? What purpose do reading and writing serve?

Even more ideal would be for teachers to live in and have a firsthand understanding of the community. Learners would not perceive their teachers as outsiders but as community members who understand its social structure, its advantages and disadvantages. Learners graduating from the program would be highly valued as tutors and, ideally, with additional training, would be employed as teachers. New learners would see these former learner-teachers as role models and could be confident of their unique understanding of learners' backgrounds, needs, and interests.

To ensure that teachers are knowledgeable about the factors that contribute to social inequalities, their preservice education would include the study of critical theory, educational theory, linguistic theory, literacy theory, and social theory (Street, 1995). Teachers would try to make explicit their assumptions about cultural relations and cultural identity to understand better the prejudices they may bring to teaching certain groups of people (Bartolomé, 1996; Macedo, 1994). Moreover, teachers would receive training that would help them to understand how to set up a class that reflects critical pedagogy: how best to elicit student opinions about program structure and curriculum, how to set up a classroom that is most conducive to dialogic interaction, how to trouble-shoot when class discussions get bogged down. This aspect of training is crucial. It is not enough to believe in critical pedagogy; without the tools and the knowledge to understand how to put critical pedagogy into practice, teachers could very easily get frustrated.

Once teachers begin teaching, they would be carefully tuned in to their students' specific needs for literacy and would not paternalistically impose their own narrow view of literacy on students (Freire & Macedo, 1987). They would keep their doors open to student and community input, so that when students or community members feel uncomfortable with the class agenda, or when they believe the class should offer more or be doing things differently, they would have open access to the teacher and a means for addressing the perceived need for change. Teachers would engage in "praxis"—understanding how educational theory translates into their own everyday practice and being ever mindful of the specific population they are serving (Bartolomé, 1996; Freire, 1998).[8] Teachers would constantly seek political clarity and always consider the ways their instruction is linked to wider social movements, making those connections explicitly clear to their students (Bartolomé, 1996; Freire & Macedo, 1987). To that end, it is important that teachers be given autonomy within their classrooms. Methodologies or curricula cannot be imposed on teachers if they are to connect instruction to the lives of their students (Bartolomé, 1996; Giroux, 1997).

## Teacher-Student Relationship

If social transformation is the ultimate goal of critical pedagogy, then the relationship between students and teachers is central to creating an environment in which such social change becomes possible (Freire & Macedo, 1987; Lankshear & McLaren, 1993). A dialogical relationship between students and teachers would be essential (Freire & Macedo, 1987; Shor, 1992). Teachers and students would together negotiate the structure and curriculum of the class. Understanding that students need to see themselves as sharing power with the teacher, teachers would create a safe environment where students would feel free to express themselves. Teachers would not be authoritarian but rather willing to learn from their students, respecting their dreams and expectations (Freire, 1998). At the same time, teachers would not be permissive. Dialogue between teacher and students is not a "feel good" sort of thing but requires political analysis. The sharing of experiences would be framed within a social praxis that includes reflection and action (Macedo, 1994).

Teachers might see their role as problem poser, asking questions that would help students think more analytically about aspects of their lives that they may assume cannot be changed (Freire, 1993; Shor, 1992). The teacher would never impose his or her own notions about how to deal with such problems but would listen to what different students have to say, acknowledge what students perceive to be the main issues, and pose questions designed to help students think critically about the situation and make decisions about what action to take.

In a class on English for speakers of other languages (ESOL), for example, concerns about inadequate or poor service at health clinics might emerge. If the issue was that students were unable to use health clinic forms to explain their symptoms or illnesses effectively because the forms were written in English, the teacher might ask students to consider what it means on a societal level that no attempt has been made to translate the forms into Spanish (or any other minority language) or to have interpreters available. The teacher might ask: "Whose language is being used? What group of people is more likely to have its medical needs met adequately and efficiently? Why is English more highly valued? What reasons might there be for not creating Spanish translations of medical forms?" Once students reflect on these questions, they may begin to realize that they should not feel ashamed or inadequate because they are unable to obtain sufficient medical care simply because they do not yet have sufficient proficiency in English. Rather, they may begin to see that government agencies and society are often structured in ways that contribute to the marginalization of certain groups. This may lead students to discuss the ways in which they could overcome this problem—perhaps by approaching clinic administrators to suggest translating important medical forms into languages that patients understand. Students might even volunteer to help with the translations or find a willing member of their community. Through dialogue, problem posing, and reflection (a form of praxis), students can come to a deeper understanding of the factors that contribute to their marginalization and the steps they might take to eliminate them.

## Evaluation

An ongoing evaluation of both student and program progress is an essential part of a critical adult education program (Freire, 1998). Students would be asked to set goals for themselves that might include work on their literacy skills, their ability to help their children with their schoolwork, or their ability to communicate effectively with schools and other institutions and advocate on behalf of their children or themselves. Goals would reflect actual literacy needs rather than the development of decontextualized skills. While teachers may suggest long-term goals for students, they would never impose their own notions on students' goals. On a regular basis, teacher and students would discuss these goals and the progress made toward attaining them (Shor, 1992). Evaluation would likely be narrative and not based on standardized test scores (unless students' goals have to do with acquiring a certificate of general educational development or other such academic goals). Students would evaluate their own progress and, together with the teacher, would decide when and if their goals have been achieved.

As with student evaluation, program evaluation would take place on a regular basis, not only at the end of the semester. Teachers and administrators would get feedback from adult learners at the individual and group levels. This feedback would be used to refine the program structure and the class instruction continually (Freire, 1998). As students' needs change, so would the program. Students would be able to see how their input affects the program and would thus see themselves as active participants. Programs might also develop formal structures, such as a student board, so that students would have an organization in which to work hand-in-hand with administrators to create a program that accurately reflects student and community needs.

## DEFINING A MIDDLE GROUND BETWEEN NONCRITICAL AND CRITICAL PEDAGOGY

This framework for critical pedagogy in adult education is an ideal one. In reality, very few programs have the freedom or resources to be critical in every area of endeavor. Many programs must use noncritical, standardized assessments to remain eligible for funding from government agencies and private foundations. Some programs may lack the necessary resources to update curricula or materials to better match learners' needs, interests, and experiences. Others may have a structure that cannot be changed to meet students' needs because of access to community centers or associations with community colleges that regulate class times and meeting places. Although it may be possible for programs to reflect critical pedagogy in all areas, many programs have some areas that are critical and others that are not.

Rather than labeling programs as either critical or noncritical, it may be more useful to look at programs in terms of the degree to which they reflect critical pedagogy. For example, a program's curriculum may not be entirely critical or noncritical. It may instead be somewhat noncritical, meaning it tends to reflect noncritical pedagogy for the most part but may also have some critical elements that differentiate it from highly noncritical programs. Whereas a highly noncritical curriculum would be fixed and unchanging, a somewhat noncritical program might be preestablished but subject to modification based on student interests and experiences. Table 2.1 shows how the six program areas might look given varying degrees of critical pedagogy, from highly and somewhat critical to highly and somewhat noncritical.

It seems entirely possible for a program to have critical features and still be considered a noncritical program. Consider, for example, a program that provides teachers with in-depth training on multiple literacies and multicultural awareness and involves its students in collaborations on assessment and program structure. Despite having these critical elements, the program espouses the philosophy that learning basic literacy skills is the only key needed to changing the lives of learners. It employs a curriculum that is not at all related to the lives of students but, rather, covers skills sequentially and uses decontextualized workbooks and texts. This kind of program could not be characterized as critical. Its philosophy, curriculum, and materials anchor it at the noncritical end of the continuum.

The key to differentiating noncritical programs from those with the potential to become critical may lie in program philosophy. A large part of critical pedagogy involves the belief that education is political and that structures in the educational system privilege the dominant culture while placing minority cultures at a disadvantage. A program with a highly noncritical philosophy is not likely to evolve from noncritical to critical even if it has some features that are somewhat or highly critical. Programs with philosophies that implicitly blame

| | Presuppositions, Philosophy, and Goals | Structure | Curriculum and Materials | Teacher Development | Teacher-Student Relationship | Evaluation |
|---|---|---|---|---|---|---|
| Highly critical | • Education should be used for personal growth and empowerment.<br>• Learning is a meaning-making process that takes place within specific contexts.<br>• Education is political in nature and important for enhancing students' abilities to advocate for change in their lives. | • Student input is sought continually.<br>• Students are involved in deciding when classes meet.<br>• Community members have a partnership role in programming planning. | • Emphasis is placed on reading, writing, and other activities that help students deal with personal needs and concerns, at home and within the community.<br>• Writing, reading, and other skills are seen as tools to help students deal with life issues and political action. | • Teachers are tuned into the types of literacy materials and practices that students use outside school.<br>• Teachers learn about issues of importance to individual students as well as community issues. | • Students are seen as teachers, teachers as learners. Teachers actively demonstrate their willingness to learn from students.<br>• Dialogue between students and teachers helps students to discover their voices.<br>• Teachers and students share control of and responsibility for the program.<br>• Teachers guide students toward taking action to solve problems. | • Greatest emphasis is placed on whether students meet goals they have set for themselves.<br>• Students are active partners in evaluation; conferences with students take place throughout the term.<br>• Standardized tests are not used. Program success is measured by how well students use the skills they have acquired to negotiate change in their world. |

| Somewhat critical | • Education should be used for personal growth and empowerment.<br>• Learning is a meaning-making process that takes place within a specific context. | • Student input is sought before the program begins; class agendas are organized around student needs and interests.<br>• Students are involved in deciding when and where classes will meet. | • There is no pre-set curriculum.<br>• Literacy and other basic skills are taught in the context of socially or culturally relevant activities.<br>• Students are given choices as to which materials and activities will be used in class. | • Teachers' belief systems are considered integral to program success, as are the curriculum or materials being used.<br>• Training focuses on multicultural learning styles and different literacy environments. | • Students are seen as teachers, teachers as learners.<br>• Dialogue between students and teachers helps students to discover their voices. | • Portfolios may be used as part of the evaluation process; students decide on its content.<br>• Students play a large role in their assessment, including setting and evaluating goals.<br>• Students' ability to negotiate with social institutions outside the program is seen as an indicator of success.<br>• Standardized tests may be used. |
| --- | --- | --- | --- | --- | --- | --- |

**Table 2.1. Four Degrees of Critical Pedagogy Across Six Elements of Adult Education Programs.**

| | Presuppositions, Philosophy, and Goals | Structure | Curriculum and Materials | Teacher Development | Teacher-Student Relationship | Evaluation |
|---|---|---|---|---|---|---|
| Somewhat noncritical | • Literacy and other basic skill development is the answer to the social and economic problems of marginalized groups. <br> • Students bring with them to the classroom some basic knowledge and experiences that programs build from. | • Students are included in program initiation and are asked for input. <br> • Students are involved in supplementary decision making. | • The curriculum is generally planned, but attempts are made to link the curriculum to students' everyday experiences. <br> • The curriculum is modified to match students' interests or needs. <br> • Students participate in discussions that help them relate the reading material to their own lives. | • Teachers modify materials and curricula to meet student needs. <br> • Training emphasizes the importance of understanding the community in which one teaches. <br> • Training exposes teachers to theories on learning so that they have a theoretical framework on which to base their instruction. | • Classes are teacher directed, but teachers make an effort to tune into the life needs of students. <br> • Open communication between students and teachers is seen as very important. <br> • Teachers ask students for input on the topics covered in class. | • Heavy emphasis is placed on academic progress, measured by standardized tests. <br> • Program success is partially measured by the extent to which students meet their own goals. <br> • Students provide feedback throughout the term. <br> • Evaluation may be based on interviews with students and their self-reported success. |

| Highly noncritical | • Literacy and other basic skill development is the answer to the social and economic problems of marginalized groups.<br>• So many students fail because they or their families (or both) do not value education. | • Students are not included in any part of the program planning process. | • Curricula are preset and unchanging, no matter what students' cultural or language needs.<br>• The curriculum does not reflect students' interests or crucial life issues; it may reflect student skill levels. | • Emphasis is placed on learning to plan class time and using time wisely.<br>• Teachers learn specific methodologies and must have a good understanding of basic skills. | • Classes are teacher directed.<br>• Teachers make no effort to learn about students or to modify instruction to meet student needs or interests. | • Heavy emphasis is placed on academic progress, measured by standardized tests.<br>• Evaluation is based on program goals and expectations, not students' goals.<br>• Evaluation takes place only at the end of the term. |

Table 2.1. Four Degrees of Critical Pedagogy Across Six Elements of Adult Education Programs (*continued*).

students for their academic failures or view literacy acquisition as a panacea cannot be considered critical even if some of their endeavors can be considered critical. Programs that focus singularly on teaching mainstream literacy skills, with no consideration of learners' backgrounds, needs, and interests, and that neglect to engage students in efforts to understand the societal structures that marginalize certain groups cannot be considered critical.

On the other hand, programs that have one or more noncritical features but also a somewhat or highly critical philosophy may be seen as having the potential to become critical. Consider a hypothetical program that espouses the beliefs that meaning making is the main goal of basic literacy and skills instruction and that learning takes place in a variety of social contexts. One of the program's goals is to promote students' personal growth, apart from their educational growth. This program also has a somewhat critical curriculum, designed around the students' backgrounds and experiences and allowing for student input. Evaluation methods are somewhat critical, based largely on whether students meet the goals they have set for themselves. The structure of this program, however, is highly uncritical, with students involved in neither its inception nor ongoing planning for class meetings and locations. Although the structure reflects noncritical pedagogy, the program has more critical than noncritical features, and because of its critical philosophy, it may at the very least represent a program that has the potential to become more highly critical.

The journey from noncritical to critical pedagogy should be seen as just that: a journey. It is not a quick fix, and it is not a pedagogy that can be learned during a two-hour in-service workshop or even over the course of a year. A pedagogical shift from noncritical to critical may take many years, if not a lifetime. In truth, all programs have the potential to change, but it is unlikely that any program could change all of its features at once. Certain programs are probably more likely to change than others. For example, a teacher who purports to have a critical philosophy will be more likely to develop a more highly critical pedagogy than a teacher who does not. A teacher who is aware of the belief system inherent in a critical pedagogy will be more likely to identify program features that are not informed by that philosophy than one who is not.

Cowper (1998) gives an example of her own evolution as an ESOL practitioner. Her classroom philosophy had included the somewhat critical idea that her class should be learner centered, in that she felt it was important to collaborate with students in creating curriculum and learning objectives that focused on their real-life needs. However, when given the chance to meet with other practitioners during a series of retreats and reflect on what such a philosophy really meant, she realized that her classroom practice did not reflect her philosophy. Although she had given her students choices in completing teacher-assigned activities, she had never taken the time to learn about how and what they wanted to learn. She did not know about their interests, needs, or learning styles, and she had never included them in decisions regarding which materials and activities to use. She came to understand that it was not enough to say she held a certain philosophy; that philosophy needed to be demonstrated in all aspects of her practice. If she had not had the philosophy in the first place, it is less likely that she would have seen any problems with her classroom practice.

## IMPLICATIONS FOR RESEARCH, PRACTICE, AND POLICY

The most important concept in critical pedagogy concerns the belief that education is political. Every idea that critical educators and theorists espouse about schooling, teachers, language, curriculum, marginalized students, and so on derives from the political nature of education. Education is not seen as neutral, and it is thought that those educators who want to make a difference in the lives of their nonmainstream students must resist the status quo that privileges mainstream students' cultural practices, language, and experiences in every aspect of the educational system. For adult educators, this would mean refusing to place primary importance on reading and writing activities that reflect mainstream literacy practices. It would also mean acknowledging that the acquisition of literacy and other basic academic and language skills is not a panacea. No matter what the driving philosophy is, education is not a quick fix, and even if every undereducated person in the country were to become literate, there would likely still be poverty, violence, and academic underachievement. Literacy and language using this pedagogy would be viewed as tools, and only two of many that provide adult education students with the means for questioning the status quo and for effecting change. Learning activities would be taught in the context of issues that really matter to students.

Given the several complex components of adult education programs—philosophy, structure, curriculum, teacher development, teacher-student relationship, and evaluation—it would be very hard for any program to reflect critical pedagogy to the highest degree in all of them. For the most part, adult education programs must work within a system that does not support or even understand critical pedagogy. It is unrealistic to expect programs to become entirely critical. Instead, if a program were interested in becoming more critical, it would be more helpful for program staff to begin to think of critical pedagogy as something they can work toward over time, in different aspects of their program. Some programs that have both critical and noncritical features may in fact be in the process of evolving from noncritical to critical. Certainly those programs with philosophies that reflect an understanding of the political nature of education, even when some program features do not manifest that philosophy, may be seen as having the potential to evolve.

The likelihood that many adult education programs are neither entirely critical nor entirely noncritical but somewhere in between suggests the need for more research on classroom practice and pedagogy within adult education programs. The field would benefit greatly from a better understanding of what exactly is taking place in classrooms. In-depth surveys designed to capture the degree to which different aspects of classroom and program practice reflect critical pedagogy, sent to a wide variety of programs across the country, could help broaden our understanding of the prevalence of critical practice. In addition, it would be quite valuable to conduct in-depth research on programs that are attempting to modify their services to reflect critical pedagogy as well as those that already reflect critical pedagogy in many respects. Observing classes, interviewing students and teachers, and seeing the different materials that are used in class and for evaluation would provide a deeper understanding of the everyday practices of programs that purport to be influenced by critical pedagogy.

It is also important to initiate research that compares the impact of critical versus noncritical programs on learners—that is, it is necessary to understand what differentiates critical from noncritical programs in terms of outcomes and to answer questions such as these: Do learners in critical programs have a more positive attitude toward their experiences? Do they perceive greater gains being made in both their literacy achievement and their dealings with different institutions, such as schools, employers, and government agencies? In which type of class do learners feel more empowered? How do teachers perceive the progress of their students? Is student progress borne out by assessments? Are learners in one type of program more likely to have better attendance or retention than those in another? Until we can answer these questions, educators and administrators may lack the information they need to decide whether critical pedagogy in adult education is a worthwhile undertaking.

The ideas of critical educators and theorists can be off-putting to literacy practitioners because they seem abstract and difficult to put into practice in the real world of the classroom. A thorough investigation of and report on critical and potentially critical programs would be of practical use to adult education providers if it could reveal how teachers have been able to embody critical pedagogy principles in their daily work with adult students. Such an investigation could also address the difficulties and benefits teachers experience as a result of having embarked on this course. By describing programs that are in different stages of evolution from noncritical to critical, such research would also reveal possible modifications that programs have made over time so that practitioners deciding to take a more critical approach would not feel overwhelmed by the idea that they must change everything at once. If critical adult education programs hold as much promise for marginalized students as critical educators believe they do, then research that can clarify how and why they work is essential.

A better understanding of critical pedagogy in adult education also has the potential to influence educational policy. Current policy concerning adult education—which reflects the trend toward national standards-based education and standardized assessments (Stites, 1999)—is often perceived as conflicting with the philosophy of a highly critical pedagogy because it does not take into account the specific backgrounds, needs, and interests of individual students. Imposing the same standards and the same measures of success on all students, no matter where they live or what their current social or economic situation, is extremely problematic to critical educators. However, programs that want to be more critical in their classroom practices may be discouraged by their need to be accountable for the test scores of their students. Research that looks at the individual successes of students in highly critical and somewhat or "evolving toward" critical programs—not on the basis of standardized tests but in terms of how they use literacy and other skills to negotiate successfully with institutions such as welfare offices, employers, schools, and housing authorities—may provide policymakers with examples of the utility of nonstandardized measures of success. Such a shift in sentiment may ultimately give programs greater freedom to initiate changes that will bring to bear a more critical pedagogy.[9]

## Notes

1. Dialogue, according to Freire (1993), "is the encounter between men, mediated by the world, in order to name the world" (p. 69). A dialogic relationship between teacher and students is believed to create students who actively participate in their own learning rather than just passively accepting what the teacher says. This concept is discussed in more detail later in the chapter.

2. This observation is based on feedback I received from adult educators during my work on an ongoing study at Harvard University about the literacy practices of adult learners. The study, headed by Victoria Purcell-Gates at Michigan State University, looked at two particular features of critical pedagogy: (1) the degree to which class materials and activities were culturally and experientially relevant to the lives of the learners and (2) the degree to which relationships between learners and teachers were considered dialogic, or collaborative. Our research involved determining how those two features of the classroom experience can bring about changes in out-of-school literacy practices. After explaining the critical framework to study participants, I heard from many teachers that while they may have read Freire and other critical theorists, and may even believe in and value the *concept* of critical pedagogy, they simply did not have the time, the curricular freedom, or the theoretical understanding to bring those ideas into their classrooms. Critical pedagogy, quite simply, was seen as theory—not as something that could easily be translated into their own adult education practice. In addition, some teachers noted that they had tried initiating a more dialogic relationship with their students but met with resistance because students were more comfortable taking a passive role in the classroom.

3. The terms *critical theory, critical literacy,* and *critical pedagogy* are used in this chapter. They are similar in meaning but not interchangeable. *Critical theory* refers to a school of thought that came out of the

Frankfurt school in Germany and has its roots in Marxist theory. Critical theory, in brief, considers how different societal institutions serve to promote the interests of some individuals and groups while placing others in a marginalized position that prevents their needs and interests from being met. *Critical literacy* acknowledges that reading and writing are not isolated activities; rather, they take place within a historical, cultural, social, and political context. Critical literacy encourages people to use reading and writing to understand their positions in society better and subsequently to change societal inequalities. *Critical pedagogy,* the main focus of this chapter, refers to educational practices based on the ideas of critical theory and critical literacy.

4. These are some of the major historical influences on critical pedagogy, but they are not the only ones. Wink (1997) well summarizes the history of critical pedagogy in lay terms. For a more thorough discussion of the history of critical pedagogy within adult education in the United States, refer to Heaney (1996).

5. Being "political" in this case does not mean the educator supports a Democratic or Republican platform or identifies with the left or the right. Rather, it means that the educator comprehends all of the different forces—racism, classism, sexism, ethnocentrism—that contribute to the disadvantaged position many adult students find themselves in and can thereby help students to understand those forces.

6. English Only has been an attempt on the part of U.S. politicians as well as two organizations called English First and U.S. English to put forth legislation that would proclaim English as the official language of the United States. In brief, this kind of legislation would either eliminate bilingual instruction altogether or put a cap on the amount of time that students with limited proficiency in English could spend in bilingual classrooms. It would also require that all government business be conducted in English and that public documents be printed in English. Although some states have passed this legislation, there is, as of now, no federal legislation mandating English Only. Cultural literacy is the brainchild of Hirsch (1987), who has published a set of books—the Core Knowledge Series—that specifies what children at each grade level need to know to be considered literate. The series has been criticized for plainly stating which kinds of knowledge are important and which kinds are unimportant. It has also been criticized for valuing knowledge from the dominant culture while ignoring the knowledge of marginalized groups. (See Macedo, 1994, for an in-depth critique of Hirsch's cultural literacy.)

7. Most critical literacy histories use the term *oppressed* rather than *disadvantaged*. This substitution was made for clarity given that the intended audience of this book may be unfamiliar with the vocabulary of critical theory.

8. Praxis is a process of critical reflection that requires an individual or group to plan an action based on their understanding of a situation and then reflect on that action to change their understanding. They then plan and act again, but reflect again and change their understanding. This is a continuous process that deepens their understanding of the situation they are dealing with, improves their plans, and makes their actions more effective.

9. The Equipped for the Future initiative (EFF) is a program, developed by the National Institute for Literacy in partnership with the National Education Goals Panel, that has created performance-based standards for adult learners, based on feedback from teachers, policymakers, and adult learners (Stein, 1999). To the extent that performance-based assessments can be designed to correspond with EFF standards, there is hope that adult educators can get away from the "teach to the test" mentality that pervades classes where student performance is judged solely on their CASAS (Comprehensive Adult Student Assessment System) or TABE (Test of Adult Basic Education) scores. See Stites (1999) for a thorough discussion of the pros and cons of standards-based assessments in adult education.

## References

Anderson, G. L., & Irvine, P. (1993). Informing critical literacy with ethnography. In C. Lankshear & P. McLaren (Eds.), *Critical literacy: Politics, praxis, and the postmodern* (pp. 81–104). Albany: State University of New York Press.

Auerbach, E. R. (1989). Toward a social-contextual approach to family literacy. *Harvard Educational Review, 59*(2), 165–181.

Bartolomé, L. (1996). Beyond the methods fetish: Toward a humanizing pedagogy. In P. Leistyna, A. Woodrum, & S. Sherblom (Eds.), *Breaking free: The transformative power of critical pedagogy* (pp. 229–252). *Harvard Educational Review,* Reprint Series No. 27.

Cowper, E. (1998). An unexpected outcome. *Focus on Basics, 2*(C), 22–24.

Delgado-Gaitan, C. (1996). *Protean literacy: Extending the discourse on empowerment.* Bristol, PA: Falmer Press.

Dewey, J. (1963). *Experience and education.* New York: Collier Books. (Originally published in 1938.)

Edelsky, C. (1996). *With literacy and justice for all: Rethinking the social in language and education.* Bristol, PA: Taylor & Francis.

Facundo, B. (1984). *Issues for an evaluation of Freire-inspired programs in the United States and Puerto Rico.* Washington, DC: Fund for the Improvement of Postsecondary Education. (ERIC Document Reproduction Service No. ED 243 998)

Freire, P. (1993). *Pedagogy of the oppressed.* New York: Continuum.

Freire, P. (1998). *Teachers as cultural workers: Letters to those who dare to teach.* Boulder, CO: Westview Press.

Freire, P., & Macedo, D. (1987). *Literacy: Reading the word and the world.* Westport, CT: Bergin & Garvey.

Gee, J. P. (1993). Postmodernism and literacies. In C. Lankshear & P. McLaren (Eds.), *Critical literacy: Politics, praxis, and the postmodern* (pp. 271–296). Albany, NY: State University of New York Press.

Giroux, H. A. (1997). *Pedagogy and the politics of hope: Theory, culture, and schooling. A critical reader.* Boulder, CO: Westview Press.

Giroux, H. A., & McLaren, P. (1992). Writing from the margins: Geographies of identity, pedagogy, and power. *Journal of Education, 174*(1), 7–30.

Greene, M. (1996). In search of a critical pedagogy. In P. Leistyna, A. Woodrum, & S. Sherblom (Eds.), *Breaking free: The transformative power of critical pedagogy* (pp. 13–30). *Harvard Educational Review,* Reprint Series No. 27.

Heaney, T. (1996). *Adult education for social change: From center stage to the wings and back again.* Washington, DC: Office of Educational Research and Improvement. (ERIC Document Reproduction Service No. ED 396 190)

Hirsch, E. D. (1987). *Cultural literacy: What every American needs to know.* Boston: Houghton Mifflin.

Horton, M., & Freire, P. (1990). *We make the road by walking: Conversations on education and social change.* Philadelphia: Temple University Press.

Kanpol, B. (1998). Critical pedagogy for beginning teachers: The movement from despair to hope. *Journal of Critical Pedagogy* [on-line], *2*(1). Available at: http://www.lib.wmc.edu/pub/jcp/jcp.html.

Klages, M. (1997). *Marxism and ideology* [on-line]. Available at http://www.colorado.edu/English/ENGL2012Klages/marxism.html.

Kozol, J. (1978). *Children of the revolution: A Yankee teacher in the Cuban schools.* New York: Delacorte Press.

Lankshear, C., & McLaren, P. (Eds.). (1993). *Critical literacy: Politics, praxis, and the postmodern.* Albany, NY: State University of New York Press.

Macedo, D. P. (1994). *Literacies of power: What Americans are not allowed to know.* Boulder, CO: Westview Press.

Miller, V. L. (1985). *Between struggle and hope: The Nicaraguan literacy crusade.* Boulder, CO: Westview Press.

Quigley, B. A. (1997). *Rethinking literacy education: The critical need for practice-based change.* San Francisco: Jossey-Bass.

Shannon, P. (Ed.). (1992). *Becoming political: Readings and writings in the politics of literacy education.* Portsmouth, NH: Heinemann.

Shor, I. (1992). *Empowering education: Critical teaching for social change.* Chicago: University of Chicago Press.

Shor, I., & Freire, P. (1987). What is the "dialogical method" of teaching? *Journal of Education, 169*(3), 11–31.

Stein, S. (1999). Equipped for the Future: The evolution of a standards-based approach to system reform. *Focus on Basics, 3*(C), 11–14.

Stites, R. (1999). A user's guide to standards-based educational reform: From theory to practice. *Focus on Basics, 3*(C), 1–7.

Street, B. (1993). Cross-cultural perspectives on literacy. In J. Maybin (Ed.), *Language and literacy in social practice: A reader* (pp. 139–150). Clevedon, England: Multilingual Matters.

Street, B. (1995). *Social literacies: Critical approaches to literacy in development, ethnography, and education.* New York: Longman.

Tatalovich, R. (1995). *Nativism reborn? The official English language movement and the American states.* Lexington: University Press of Kentucky.

Taylor, D. (1997). *Many families, many literacies: An international declaration of principles.* Portsmouth, NH: Heinemann.

Vygotsky, L. (1978). *Mind in society: The development of the higher psychological processes.* Cambridge, MA: Harvard University Press.

Wink, J. (1997). *Critical pedagogy: Notes from the real world.* New York: Longman.

# CHAPTER THREE

# Research in Writing

## Implications for Adult
## Literacy Education

*Marilyn K. Gillespie*

W ithin the field of literacy, writing has some-
times been described as "the forgotten of the three R's" (Freedman,
Flower, Hull, & Hayes, 1995, p. 1). Until as late as the 1970s, surprisingly little was known about how writing skills develop. Most people
assumed that there was essentially one process of writing that served
all writers for all their various purposes; writers decided on what to
write in advance and primarily worked alone. The attention of most
educators was directed toward how to evaluate the final product. Over
the past three decades, our knowledge of what writers do when they
write has changed considerably. Much progress has been made in
understanding writing as a cognitive process, understanding its sociocultural dimensions, and understanding how best to teach it in the
classroom. Although new research on the teaching of writing has had
an impact on some adult literacy classrooms, most adult literacy educators remain unfamiliar with this body of knowledge and its potential value for adult learners.

This chapter brings the teaching of writing more sharply into
focus as an integral and essential part of our work as adult literacy
educators.

# UNDERSTANDING WHAT WRITERS DO

The shift from looking solely at the products of writing to the study of what writers do when they write is often cited as beginning in the United States with the work of Janet Emig. In *The Composing Practices of Twelfth Graders* (1971), she pioneered a think-aloud protocol and the use of case study methodology to observe her students as they composed. By asking students to describe how they planned what to write, what they were thinking when they paused, and how and when they reread, revised, and edited, she determined that the writing process was considerably more complex than had been realized.

In the years that followed, the number of studies related to the composing process grew. Within the K–12 arena, the mid- to late 1970s brought several important, detailed observations of young children as they wrote. Graves (1975), for example, studied the processes that children used to write, revise, and share their work. Read (1975) discovered that children who analyzed the sounds they could hear in their own pronunciation of sentences could invent a writing system for themselves. Calkins (1975) broke ground by closely observing how just one child learned to write. In England, Britton, Burgess, Martin, and Rosen (1975) completed a seminal work on secondary school students' writing practices, their purposes for writing, and their awareness of their reading audience. In the years that followed, a plethora of studies on the writing of K–12 learners emerged. (A good summary of these can be found in Dyson & Freedman, 1991.)

Of particular interest to adult literacy educators was a body of research that began to focus on remedial writing at the postsecondary level. By the early 1970s, many colleges had begun a new policy of open admissions. For the first time, college instructors were faced with large numbers of nontraditional students, many of whom had limited experiences with writing. Many students who were not prepared for the writing required of them in college were placed in noncredit remedial writing courses. With her book *Errors and Expectations* (1977), Shaughnessy christened an area of study that came to be known as basic writing. By looking closely at hundreds of essays written by students considered to be remedial writers, she offered a counterpoint to the view that these learners were cognitively deficient and incapable of the rigors of college-level study. The errors in their writing, she observed, made sense if looked at from the perspective of someone who is unpracticed in expressing complex ideas in writing, and she could detect predictable patterns in the kinds of errors they made.

Underprepared students write the way they do, she explained, "not because they are slow or non-verbal, indifferent to or incapable of academic excellence, but because they are beginners and must, like all beginners, learn by making mistakes" (p. 3).

Soon other researchers, pointing out the limitations of an interpretation of writers' errors as no more than marks on the page, began to use case study methodologies to follow basic writers as they composed. At the City University of New York, a sense of urgency developed when nontraditional students flooded the campuses and teachers struggled for ways to address their needs. Sondra Perl (1979) asked five of her basic writing students to think aloud as they composed essays. She found that many began to follow a train of thought as they wrote but then lost it when they had to interrupt their thoughts to attend to more mechanical concerns, such as letter formation, punctuation, and spelling. Rose (1980) investigated more closely the experiences of basic writers with writer's block. He found that these writers became blocked because they followed a set of rigid rules, trying to apply them to situations where they did not apply. Sommers (1980) found that basic writers typically solved problems simply by rewriting, without analyzing the problems with their text. By listening to basic writers read their essays aloud and asking them to stop to correct errors as they read, Bartholomae (1980) was able to show that his students demonstrated the use of an intermediate grammar somewhere between speech and writing. In comparing expert with more novice college writers, Flower (1979) found that while writing, expert writers thought about their reader more than did novice writers, which helped them to plan their essays and generate text. Beginning writers, on the other hand, wrote what she called "writer-based prose." They did not think about their reader while writing but were concerned primarily with the text. Taken together, the studies of this period showed that to move from the status of a basic to a more expert writer, students had to learn to revise what they write, consider the reader in their planning, and attend to more global problems, such as resequencing and rewriting units of text.

## Toward a Model of the Cognitive Writing Process

By 1980, Flower and Hayes were able to gather the findings from the many studies of composing practices with varied populations then emerging and to propose a working model of the writing process

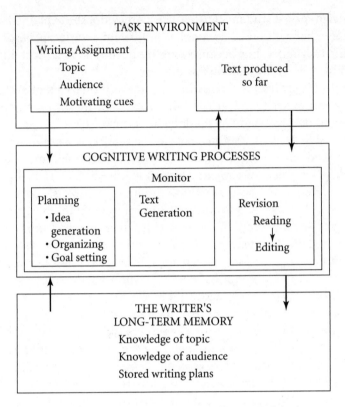

**Figure 3.1. The 1980 Hayes-Flower Model.**

*Source:* Reprinted with permission from Figure 1.2,
"The Hayes-Flower Model (1980) Redrawn for Clarification," in Hayes, 1996, p. 3.

(see Figure 3.1). Flower and Hayes (1980) suggested that there are essentially three cognitive writing processes: planning (deciding what to say and how to say it), text generation (turning plans into written text), and revision (improving existing text). These processes do not occur in any fixed order but proceed in an organized way that is largely determined by the individual writer's goals (Dyson & Freedman, 1991). At one moment writers might be writing, moving their ideas and their discourse forward; at the next they were backtracking, rereading, and digesting what had been written. The finding that these processes are recursive, with subprocesses such as planning and editing often interrupting each other, represented an important shift in the understanding of the writing process. An adaptation of this model of composing has often made its way into the classroom as the "writing process approach."

A key premise of the model is that writing is hierarchically organized and that it is, above all, a goal-directed, problem-solving process (Flower & Hayes, 1980). Whenever a person writes, he or she poses a problem to be solved on multiple levels. To solve the problem, the writer must set up subgoals and solve subproblems. For example, a woman writing a letter to her child's school must determine her goal for writing the letter and her subgoals for making sure she has covered all the issues she wants to address. She also has to solve subproblems related to how to form the letters on the page and how to spell unfamiliar words. She may do a little planning, begin to write, stop and plan a bit more, interrupt her planning to consult a dictionary, spend some time worrying about her handwriting, pause to talk to a friend about her child's problem, reread and revise what she has written, and so forth. As writers gain experience, many of the lower-level processes (such as forming letters and spelling) become automatic and unconscious. Other processes require planning and skill, no matter how experienced the writer is.

## Alternatives to the Hayes and Flower Model

From the beginning, this writing process model was criticized, and later even the notion that such a model could exist was questioned (Kent, 1999). Some researchers posited alternative models. One of the best known, proposed by Bereiter and Scardamalia in 1987, challenged the implication of the Hayes and Flower model that experts do the same things that less skilled writers do, only much better. Less skilled writers, they claimed, use a "retrieve-and-tell" approach to writing tasks, or a *knowledge-telling model*. These writers produce much less elaborate and abstract sets of prewriting notes. They concern themselves with generating content during composing and spend much less time considering goals, plans, and problems posed by the writing. This is because less experienced writers, when beginning to compose texts, need to keep the task relatively uncomplicated in order to direct their working memory to the basic task of converting oral language experiences into written form. Until these lower-level processes of putting text on the page become automatic, writers are less able to focus on the kinds of higher-level processes needed for making global revisions. For beginners, the primary goal is to tell someone what they have retrieved and to translate these thoughts into letters, words, and sentences. These strategies work especially well when recounting a personal story, where coherence can easily be created by following a basic chronology.

Taking this into account, the knowledge-telling model is an efficient means of writing for less skilled writers. In contrast, in the knowledge-transforming model, the writing task leads directly to problem analysis and goal setting. The resulting goals, and the problems anticipated, lead to plans for how to resolve them, whether they are problems of content or problems concerning the best way to organize the narrative in the light of previously presented information and the audience to be addressed (rhetorical problems). As one problem is solved, others are created, and in this way new content is generated or new ideas about how to organize the ideas are developed. As solutions to problems are formed, they feed into the knowledge-telling component of the process and are written down. Bereiter and Scardamalia (1987) argued that the writer's effort to resolve content and rhetorical problems by moving between these "problem spaces" invokes a dialectical process that allows for more reflection. This process, they believe, may be excluded from simpler writing tasks. (In later work [1993], these researchers developed and tested strategies for teaching some of the higher-level writing processes associated with planning and revision.)

## A Sociocontextual View of the Writing Process

The work of these pioneers in the writing process represented a significant shift away from a focus solely on written products toward seeing the student as the primary object of study. During the early 1980s another shift began that focused research on understanding the complex sociocultural dimensions of writing, seeing this dimension not as peripheral but as central to our understanding of composition.

One of the first substantial critiques of the cognitive approach to the study of writing came from Bartholomae (1985). After teaching nontraditional students for several years, he had come to see that the essays he read were not simply egocentric reader-based prose. They did not represent only "the interior monologue of a writer thinking and talking to himself" (Rose, 1989, citing Flower, 1981, p. 64). Another key issue, Bartholomae observed, was that his students were being asked to write in a world different from their own, an academic world of which they had never before been a part. "Students are not so much trapped in a private language," he said, "as they are shut out from one of the privileged languages of public life, a language they are aware of but cannot yet control" (1985, p. 276).

"Every time a student sits down to write for us," Bartholomae concluded, "he has to invent the university for the occasion. . . . He has to learn to speak our language, to speak as we do, to try on the peculiar ways of knowing, selecting, evaluating, reporting, concluding, and arguing that define the discourse of our community" (1985, p. 273). His students, he came to realize, had to appropriate (or be appropriated by) a specialized discourse, and they had to do this "as though they were easily or comfortably one with their audience" (p. 276). Looked at this way, the problem of audience awareness becomes much more complicated. To enter the world of academia, a writer has to build a bridge between his point of view and that of his readers. He must find a way both to imagine and write from a position of privilege. Basic writers must imagine for themselves the privilege of being insiders—"that is, of being both inside of an established and powerful discourse, and of being granted a special right to speak" (p. 277).

Research began to show how notions that learners have a fixed number of linguistic defects that can be pinpointed and corrected through drill and practice obscured the social and historical factors that allow some people into academia and keep others out. In *Lives on the Boundaries: The Struggles and Achievements of America's Underprepared* (1989), Rose recounts the stories of adults who are trying to "cross the boundaries" and enter into the academic world. Rose's stories poignantly describe the events leading up to the decision to drop out made by many students who are underprepared for college and disoriented in the culture of higher education. They drop back into a world "in the margins" where they can expect only low-paying jobs. "Through all my experiences with people struggling to learn," Rose reflects, "the one thing that strikes me most is the ease with which we misperceive failed performance and the degree to which this misperception both reflects and reinforces the social order. Class and culture erect boundaries that hinder our vision—blind us to the logic of error and the ever-present stirring of language—and encourage the designation of otherness, difference, deficiency" (1989, p. 205). This research led to a new understanding of the role of the basic writing classroom as a site where students could begin to recognize these competing positions and interests. Researchers began to consider how the classroom could be a place where students could give voice to different and suppressed stories and where their struggles to accept (as well as resist) the dominant discourse could be made explicit and examined.

In recent composition studies, researchers have tried to integrate cognition and context and to involve learners in the interpretation of research. In *The Construction of Negotiated Meaning: A Social Cognitive Theory of Writing,* Flower (1994) provides a framework for the design of studies in collaboration with learners that focus on students' interpretation of tasks, feedback, and situations, as well as sites of conflict, acts of negotiation, and the insights from students' reflections.

## The Influence of New Literacy Studies

Research on the social dimensions of basic writing is just one example of a broader social turn in a number of fields concerned with literacy theory, among them developmental psychology, cultural psychology, anthropology, branches of cognitive science, and interdisciplinary social science research on learning. One researcher who was instrumental in defining the emerging field that has come to be known as new literacy studies was social anthropologist Brian Street (1984, 1995). Looking at literacy across a wide range of contexts around the world, Street rejected the notion that literacy is a set of discrete skills that exist regardless of context. The meaning of literacy, he contended, depends on the social and cultural institutions in which it is embedded. It is the processes whereby reading and writing are learned that construct the meaning of literacy for particular individuals. Literacy cannot be separated from its cultural and political significance and treated as if it is autonomous. In fact, he asserted, it is more appropriate to refer to multiple literacies rather than a single literacy.

Rather than looking at literacy in isolation from its social context, researchers within this tradition began to study literacy events (particular activities in which literacy has a role) and literacy practices (ways of using literacy that are carried from one situation to another, similar situation) (Scribner & Cole, 1981; Graff, 1987; Szwed, 1981; Street, 1984; Gee, 1989; Willinsky, 1990). Ethnographic researchers in this tradition began to study literacy practices in various communities. Heath (1983) looked closely at the functions and uses of reading and writing in three working-class communities in North and South Carolina, observing the differences and incongruities between home and mainstream school literacy. Using a similar framework, Taylor and

Dorsey-Gaines (1988) studied the literacy practices of African American mothers living in an urban housing project and their efforts to involve their children in literacy activities (such as making grocery lists, playing word games, and keeping journals). The authors' detailed observations challenged the common conception that low-income mothers seldom engage in literacy practices with their children. Reder (1987) asked members of Hmong, Eskimo, and Hispanic communities to describe the social organization, roles, and status of given literacy practices. He found that in these communities, reading and writing events were often shared activities. A young person, for example, might be engaged in a literacy event by taking down a letter dictated by his mother, who is functionally engaged in the same task even though her literacy skills are limited. Another family member might contribute to this same literacy event through her knowledge of the implications of the letter for the life of the community. At the Mexican-Origin Language and Literacy Project at the University of Illinois, Farr and Guerra (1995) conducted a longitudinal study of one social network of Mexican immigrant families over several years. They found that although many adult members of families had relatively limited literacy skills owing to restricted access to formal education, they nevertheless managed a variety of literacy tasks to a greater extent than most people were aware.

In a collection of articles edited by Barton and Ivanič, *Writing in the Community* (1991), researchers took a second look at writing in a variety of community contexts. For example, Klassen (1991) studied how nine Latino men living in Toronto used written language in their everyday lives. He found that they managed to get along very effectively in some literacy domains, such as at home, in the streets, and in local shops. In fact, it was in the domain of English for speakers of other languages (ESOL) literacy classes where they felt most estranged and unable to manage literacy tasks.

Barton and Padmore (1991) reported on a multiyear study that examined the role literacy plays in the everyday lives of adults living in Lancaster, a small city in northwest England. All of the adults in the study had left school at the minimum age, fifteen or sixteen years, although many had gone back as adults. Everything the participants wrote as they went about their lives was catalogued, including writing to maintain their households, maintain communication with friends and family, and express personal feelings in forms such as poetry and journal writing.

The book *Local Literacies: Reading and Writing in the Community* (Barton & Hamilton, 1998) describes the results of this same study. After years of observation, researchers noted that when people talked about writing, they imbued it with power. Some adults felt frustration at the inadequacy of their written work; they knew what they wanted to say but could not find the words to express their thoughts. But others preferred writing to reading or felt they could express themselves better by writing than by speaking. They took great pleasure and comfort in writing and felt empowered by it. Although many doubted that they could effect change through writing, for a few, writing letters to newspapers or school officials was part of a process of learning to exercise their power in the community.

Researchers have also studied literacy in the social context of the workplace. In *Changing Work, Changing Workers: Critical Perspectives on Language, Literacy, and Skills* (Hull, 1997), chapter authors provide a critical analysis of what goes on in vocational and literacy classrooms that aim to prepare people for work as well as an analysis of the literacy demands and social practices of actual workplaces. The authors reveal a counterpoint to the common notion that workers' lack of basic skills are responsible for problems in the workplace. The chapter authors report on a wide variety of cultural, political, and economic barriers to employment, such as the way in which tests serve as gatekeepers to skilled trades, the limitations of vocational and occupational literacy programs that assume an overly simplistic understanding of the skills requirements of the workplace, and the way in which gender, class, and race influence employability. They point out that literacy educators need to pay closer attention to the complex social dimensions of literacy in the workplace, including how the writing demands of the workplace are socially constructed.

These findings about literacy in the workplace are especially important as research indicates that the amount and types of writing performed in the workplace are growing. In nearly all job categories that Mikulecky (1998) studied, significant percentages of workers, including employees without a college education, were found to write regularly as part of their job. They most frequently write memos and reports and fill in forms. Only 24 percent of workers reported that they never write memos and 36 percent that they never write reports. Tasks that once belonged to middle-level managers are now often assigned to work teams as companies downsize. The implication that Mikulecky points out is a greater need to adjust school writing curricula to prepare individuals for workplace writing, and not just for individual writing but for work on writing tasks in teams. Hart-Landsberg and Reder (1997) found that much of the writing (and reading) that took place in one workplace they studied was done in collaboration with others. Workers often learned new workplace literacy skills by working in teams on hands-on projects and through mentoring and apprenticeship relationships.

## Composing in a Second Language

Another area where research has seen a shift from product to process and then to social context is second-language composition. This body of research is important because half of all learners in adult literacy programs are enrolled in ESOL classes (Tracy-Mumford, 2000). A growing number of ESOL students also make the transition from higher-level ESOL classes to General Educational Development (GED) classes. More and more students who require training in ESOL are also enrolling in community colleges, vocational schools, and universities. In classes where all the learners are nonnative speakers, there is considerable diversity in terms of first language and cultural background, prior schooling and literacy levels, and English-language proficiency. However, college classes are also increasingly linguistically diverse, containing a mixture of native speakers, speakers of vernacular dialects of English, nonnative-speaking young people who have gone through elementary and high school in the United States, and new immigrants (see Wolfram, 1994).

Research in the teaching of second-language composition has often been separated from general composition research. Matsuda (1999), for example, reviewed the historical conditions that have led to what he calls a "disciplinary division of labor" between composition studies and ESOL at the university level. He found that "few composition theorists include second-language perspectives in their discussions and only a handful of empirical studies written and read by composition specialists consider second-language writers in their research" (1999, p. 699).

As in any other context where writing is learned, second-language writing is influenced by the social and educational context in which it is taught. This requires attention to what teachers and students do, think, and accomplish with writing in particular settings rather than conceiving of second-language writing in the abstract (Silva,

Leki, & Carson, 1997). But writing in a second language also occurs within situations of biliteracy (Cumming, 1998; Hornberger & Hardman, 1994). Biliterate situations vary according to individuals' personal histories and proficiencies in the first and second languages, as well as according to issues such as the differing status of the languages within a society and the degrees of difference between the first and second language (Cumming, 1998). In addition, the language difficulties ESOL writers face often continue long after students move out of ESOL classes. For example, in a study of students in public schools, Ramirez (1992) found that the ability to use English in abstract and decontextualized situations (such as writing) may lag considerably behind the ability to communicate effectively in face-to-face, contextualized situations. The students he studied often took many years to become proficient in the use of English in abstract contexts such as academic writing and the taking of standardized tests.

Second-language writing researchers now criticize scholars who conduct studies that describe what they believe to be first-language rhetorical practices and then contrast these practices with those of the second language, as well as studies that compare students of differing linguistic groups (Raimes, 1998). These contrastive studies, Raimes points out, "tend to lead to a normative, essentializing stance; observations of different students in different settings are generalized to all students of the same linguistic background regardless of the contexts and purpose of their learning to write, or their age, race, class, gender, education and prior experience" (p. 143). One example she cites is a survey by Hedgcock and Atkinson (1993). This study of 272 university students revealed a correlation between first-language writing proficiency and school reading experiences in the first language but found no correlation between writing proficiency in the second language and reading skills in either the first or second language. Raimes (1998) points out that this contradicts findings with younger ESOL students (Elley, 1994) and reinforces the need to distinguish research populations before making teaching recommendations.

Current studies (Zamel, 1997) reflect an increasing trend to replace a transmission mode of second-language education (which involves showing second-language students how the language should be used and how the first language causes "problems" in the second language) to a "transculturation" mode (in which students select, absorb, and adapt features of another language and culture). Case studies have illuminated the circumstances of former ESOL students writing in the specific milieu of university courses and the kinds of socialization into literate practices they require (Raimes, 1998). One study of special interest to adult literacy educators is Spack's detailed observation (1997) of one Japanese student's three-year process of acquiring academic literacy across various courses and disciplines, from ESOL to major courses. This study used multiple sources of data to show how this student became not so much a product of academic culture but a creator of her own multiculturalism. In another case study, Guerra (1996) looked at the autobiographical narratives of the lives of three young women in the Mexican-origin community of Pilsen in Chicago to understand the barriers they faced in trying to continue their education and the ways they negotiated life in dual cultures.

Reviews of trends in the teaching of writing as a second language can be found in Cumming (1998) and Raimes (1998), as well as in texts that prepare educators to teach ESOL writing, including Reid (1993), Leki (1992), Ferris and Hedgcock (1998), and Campbell (1998).

## Recent Research in Handwriting and Spelling

Work in the cognitive dimensions of writing has continued to evolve. In particular, adult literacy educators should not overlook recent research in handwriting and spelling. In the current understanding of the writing process, handwriting and spelling are considered lower-level processes. Processes for planning, generating language at the sentence and text levels, and reviewing and revising written text are considered higher-level processes (Berninger & Swanson, 1994). For beginners, "the goal is to automatize the lower-level processes so that working memory resources are freed for the higher-level constructive aspects of composing" (Berninger et al., 1998, p. 652). Increasingly, researchers are seeking to understand better how these lower-level processes can best be acquired within the context of composing.

In a study of handwriting with beginning elementary school writers, Berninger and her colleagues (1997) compared the effects of different teaching approaches. They found that brief (ten-minute) but frequent handwriting instruction within a process approach to writing was more effective than traditional strategies of isolating handwriting instruction. Visual cues (numbered arrow cues indicating the nature, order, and direction of the component strokes required to produce the letter correctly) combined with memory retrieval intervention (in which children look at each letter, then cover it up, and write it from memory) seemed to be more effective than other treatments, such as either of the above treatments alone, teacher modeling without visual cues, or simple copying.

Researchers who have attempted to trace the development of spelling ability suggest that students who experience difficulty with spelling follow the same developmental course as other students, but at a slower pace (Marcel, 1980; Bear, Truex, & Barone, 1989; Worthy & Viise, 1996; Liberman, Rubin, Duques, & Carlisle, 1985; and Viise, 1996). Learning to spell begins with learning to sound out individual letters and sounds. Students begin by developing an awareness of spoken words and creating or inventing their spelling as they write (Templeton & Morris, 1999). The students' theories of how spelling works at this stage are driven by an alphabetic expectation (Berninger et al., 1998). After they understand the alphabetic layer, they must begin to tackle the more conceptually advanced pattern layer, in which groups or patterns of letters work together to represent sound. Over time, students move from learning that spelling represents sound to learning that it represents meaning. As in the acquisition of other language behavior, they learn that much of what is learned about spelling is gained by noticing recurring patterns and trying out and revising hypotheses about these patterns in other writing situations. Spelling, then, is not just a memorization process but an intellectual activity—a process of understanding the patterns that can be detected in the sound, structure, and meaning of words (Templeton & Morris, 1999).

A few studies compare the learning of adult beginning writers in literacy classes with that of young children (Marcel, 1980; Worthy & Viise, 1996; Viise, 1996). They have found that the adult literacy learners, not unlike beginners who were children, possessed a limited knowledge of the multilevel nature of English orthography and a limited comprehension of word structure. Many had not yet mastered basic phonological awareness.

Researchers recommend that students receive short study sessions in which they use word patterns, followed closely in time by an opportunity to use new and old spelling words in compositions. Students should also be helped to see that the processes of writing words and reading words draw on the same underlying base of word knowledge (Templeton & Morris, 1999).

## Recent Studies of the Social Context of Adult Literacy Education

Research focused specifically on how adult literacy learners develop as writers is quite limited. Nevertheless, a number of more general studies of the social context of adult literacy education contain examples that allude to the development of adult literacy learners as writers. Many of these studies point to contributions that the field of adult literacy can make to a more general understanding of the role that beliefs, social identity, and personal transformation play in learning to read and write. These studies reflect the extent to which prior experiences with literacy in school construct the meaning of literacy for many adult learners (Lytle, 1990; Gillespie, 1991; Fingeret & Drennon, 1997; Merrifield, Bingman, Hemphill, & deMarrais, 1997; Purcell-Gates, 1995; Belzer, 1998; Russell, 1999).

In *Other People's Words: The Cycle of Low Literacy* (1995), for example, Purcell-Gates chronicles the literacy development of Jenny, a white urban Appalachian mother who first came to a university literacy lab asking for help with her seven-year-old son, who was failing to learn to read in school. Jenny herself had struggled with reading and writing throughout her school years, dropping out in the seventh grade. At age thirty-one, she and her husband had created a full life for themselves, but one in which reading and writing played a small part. When Purcell-Gates met her, Jenny had been attending adult education classes off and on for four years. She showed Purcell-Gates her books, which contained short reading passages, comprehension questions, and fill-in-the-blank language arts exercises. Although she was able to read workbooks written at the fourth-grade level, she had transferred none of this reading and writing knowledge to her everyday life. "She had never written anything on her own, for her own purposes besides her name, a few notations on the calendar and her address on the few occasions when she had been required to do so" (Purcell-Gates, 1993, p. 213).

When Purcell-Gates suggested to Jenny that she write in a journal and then read her own writing, "She looked at me with an expression of stunned awareness. 'Why I ain't never read my *own* words before!' she exclaimed softly. . . . 'That's all I ever really did was copy stuff, you know, from a book.'" It is hard to believe, Purcell-Gates remarks, "that

Jenny had *never*—in 7 years of school, 4 years of adult school, and 31 years of life—*never* written or read her own words at the text level" (1993, p. 218).

> That is because her words were never acknowledged and affirmed, never allowed. Since people think, conceptualize, and learn with their language—with their words—Jenny was effectively shut out from the literate world. The fact that she was allowed to fail year after year until she finally dropped out of the system in frustration is part of the immorality of the story. . . . Jenny's world and Jenny's language did not fit with the language of the schools. Moreover, the texts given to her to read were not real to her. Not only could she not relate to them on the content level, she was so stuck at the word level that she was effectively paralyzed. She continued year after year, trying to memorize rules, trying to memorize terms like *adverb* and *pronoun*. None of these words, these rules, these linguistic terms were hers . . . and thus she could not succeed. [1993, p. 218]

Many adults never have the opportunity to "make words their own" within the context of typical adult education programs. Alisa Belzer (1998), in a case study of students preparing for their GED tests, studied young African American women who "consistently maintained a line of self-blame that left little room for any other explanations for failure to achieve. . . . Not only did they have little or no opportunity in school to construct knowledge, the information that was conveyed to them was of the most simplistic and shallow nature. . . . School neither engaged their intellects, nor, with 20/20 hindsight, did it have much or any connection to the lives they would lead once they left it" (p. 274).

Forester (1988) came to similar conclusions in her study of Laura, an adult literacy student who seemed unable to make progress. Forester made a breakthrough when she was able to help Laura make the connection between how she had learned to ice skate (her favorite hobby) and how she could learn to write: by allowing herself to fall down and make mistakes. "There can be no question that Laura's sudden move forward, after years of limited progress," Forester observed, "is due to the personal involvement and active thinking-trying she now brings to her writing" (p. 605).

In their in-depth study of the lives of five adult literacy learners, Fingeret and Drennon (1997) connect literacy beliefs and social identity with the notion of personal change. They seek to create a framework for thinking about literacy learning and personal change "as inextricably bound up together" (p. 67) with adults' transformation of their identity as they move into literate culture. The authors elaborate on the way in which adults move at varying rates through several stages of change. Many less literate adults, they believe, experience prolonged tension, feeling a discrepancy between the way life is and the way they think it could be. Shame often holds them back from resolving the tension. Often this sense of shame is learned early on, as they are left behind in elementary school and internalize a belief that their literacy problems are their "fault." As adults, this sense of shame, embarrassment, and self-consciousness related to literacy is pervasive. Although it does not define their lives and identities, the authors say that "it remains a force to be dealt with" (p. 69). At the same time, these learners often experience themselves as competent workers, parents, citizens, and friends. The dissonance between these two views of their own identity creates an internal tension.

Many adults remain in this stressful condition. For others, however, something happens to disrupt their coping patterns, and new possibilities open up. These turning points can take many forms, but each leads to a time of reflection and problem solving. At this time, many adults turn to educational programs for help in relieving the tension they are experiencing. Adults often are ambivalent about these programs. They may want to change in order to relieve tension in their lives but also fear the change in social relationships that the new situation may bring about. As adults explore educational opportunities, Fingeret and Drennon (1997) note, supportive relationships assume greater importance. Positive, accepting relationships with others inside the literacy program can mediate the sense of shame and isolation and support the development of enhanced self-esteem. The authors' data also show that the adults who experienced the deepest and most profound life changes engaged in new literacy practices in both public and private situations:

> As adults experience success with learning and listen to the similarities between their stories and those of their fellow students, they may begin to develop a more critical perspective on literacy and literacy development. Placing their experience in a broader framework and seeing the extent to which social and political conditions share responsibility for their problems with literacy can begin to mediate self-blame. [Fingeret & Drennon, 1997, pp. 83–84]

Fingeret and Drennon draw links between their work and the notion of perspective transformation that Mezirow (1991) and Taylor (1998) elaborated. They suggest that adult educators need to learn more about the sources of tension in students' lives (personal, cultural, economic, and social) and how programs can help students deal with these tensions. Armed with this understanding, adult literacy programs can become more deliberate about helping students move through the process of changing their lives. Although the role that writing plays in this transformation process was not a focus of the Fingeret and Drennon study, all of these learners attended classes at Literacy Volunteers of New York City (LVNYC), a program in which collaborative writing workshops are an integral, if not central, part of literacy instruction. (See Fingeret & Danin, 1991, for a description of the writing program at LVNYC.) A close reading of the five case studies reveals the extent to which these adults used writing as part of the process of examining their previous beliefs with respect to literacy and developing alternate images and possibilities for themselves.

In a related study (Gillespie, 1991), I conducted in-depth interviews with eighteen adult literacy students in three literacy programs in New England. All of these adults had engaged in writing over a period of time and had "published" their work in student anthologies or individual books. I asked these adults to describe their life histories with respect to literacy, trace the history of their writing as adults, and describe the purposes that writing fulfilled in their lives. The study revealed that these adults used writing to fulfill a variety of purposes related to reconceptualizing their identities as literate adults. In many cases, the first piece of writing they undertook was a description of their previous experience with school and their reasons for going back to school as an adult. This kind of writing appeared to play a role in the goal-setting process of these beginning writers as they made a commitment to become more literate. Writing was a public way to affirm to teachers, fellow students, and themselves that "I believe I can do it."

Subsequent writing by the adults I studied was often a way to relieve the tension of previous negative experiences. For example, one student wrote about being locked in a closet as a child by a teacher as punishment for being left-handed. Another used writing to acknowledge publicly for the first time that she had been abused as a child. Still another recounted his early experiences with stuttering. As many of these adults gained experience with publishing, the topics of their writing moved from telling their stories to giving advice to others in areas where they felt that perspectives like theirs had not been heard. They wrote to advise teenagers who were thinking of dropping out of school, mothers of children who abused drugs, and people living in poverty. Several of the adults I interviewed observed that developing an image of themselves as capable of producing knowledge was even more important than developing the actual tools for independent writing. As one learner put it, seeing herself as "someone who matters . . . my words matter" was the most important lesson she derived from her writing experiences.

Fingeret and Drennon (1997) suggest that many adult learners "never develop a critical analysis of their social world in which poor schooling, poverty, discrimination, crime, family situations or other social and structural conditions share the responsibility for slow progress in learning" (p. 66). Indeed, as the story of Jenny showed, the development of a more critical understanding of the world is often a slow process. Jenny required repeated experience with literacy to free herself of the notion that her failure in school was due to her Appalachian language patterns. "That's why it was a little hard for me startin' to . . . sound my words out . . . 'cause I talk different . . . 'cause I'm, you know . . . countrified. And my words don't come out the way they're supposed to" (Purcell-Gates, 1993, p. 212). Jenny had a long road ahead of her to acknowledge the integrity and value of her culture and language, distinguishing it from the powerful negative images of Appalachian adults found in the dominant culture. Writing, and talking about her writing, was a key tool in this process.

Taken together, these studies point to the strong connections between changing beliefs and personal identity and adult literacy learning. Further studies along these lines may help us to understand the potential role that writing can play in the personal transformation process of adult learners in varied contexts. Such studies may also illuminate instructional strategies that help teachers to bridge the gap better between students' previous conceptions of literacy and their emerging literacy practices.

## WRITING RESEARCH IN PRACTICE

The way writing was taught in the K–12 arena began to change during the late 1970s and the 1980s (Freedman et al., 1995). In elementary schools, teachers began setting aside time during the class day for writing. Based on research on emergent literacy, even very young children began to be encouraged to use "invented" spelling and drawing to convey meaning through words and pictures. As they progressed through the elementary grades, students were taught how to rehearse, or "prewrite," using idea webs, brainstorming, peer discussion, and other techniques. Students were given more time to work on their drafts in the classroom and urged to write multiple drafts. Teachers discovered ways to encourage students to collaborate to reflect on and revise their work. "Author's corners," a process through which students read their writing to their peers, became popular. In some classrooms, the teaching of the mechanical skills of writing, such as spelling, writing conventions, and handwriting, was integrated as mini-lessons within the context of writing. Many teachers began to encourage journal writing, even among the neophyte writers, as a way for students to learn the process of "talking on paper" without the pressure of writing "correctly" for an outside audience.

In the higher grades, writing took on new prominence as a problem-solving tool. Teachers from various disciplines were encouraged to see that

> writing possesses many qualities that make it a particularly good tool for learning. The permanence of written text allows writers to step back and read their ideas, to rethink them, and to revise over time. The act of writing can often help the writer to discover ideas that would not have been discovered without the experience of the writing process. Writing also demands that the writer be explicit, so that it can be understood by a reader outside the context in which it was written. It draws on both intellect and imagination. [Langer & Applebee, 1987, p. 3]

Teachers, especially at the middle and high school levels, began to learn how to work in teams across subject areas to foster writing across the curriculum (Healy & Barr, 1991). Content standards began to be written with an eye to using writing as a tool in science, social studies, history, and other subjects.

One key to the dissemination of information about the process-writing approach was the National Writing Project, a broad national staff development effort. The idea for the project grew along with the work of the National Center for the Study of Writing at the University of California at Berkeley, a U.S. Department of Education Research and Development Center that for years had spearheaded the effort to conduct and disseminate research on writing. To convey the information about how to implement the writing process and spread the information to as many teachers as possible, the project undertook an innovative "training of trainers" model. One or two teachers in each school or region were elected to attend intensive writing institutes, often held for as long as four to six weeks during the summer. At these institutes, teachers engaged in writing workshops, thus learning firsthand how to use writing as part of a learning process. They developed plans and practiced techniques for implementing similar processes in their classrooms. These teachers were then expected to carry this information back to their schools and to train fellow teachers in what they had learned. The program also included follow-up sessions with summer institute participants and the involvement of school administrators. During the 1980s and 1990s, thousands of teachers in nearly every state participated in this program (Dyson & Freedman, 1991).

By 1992, the National Assessment of Educational Progress (NAEP) had begun to implement new approaches to assess writing. In 1992, a writing assessment was administered to a representative national sample of approximately 7,000 fourth-grade students, 11,000 eighth-grade students, and 11,500 twelfth-grade students from about 1,500 public and private schools across the country. The NAEP assessed student ability to write to inform others about a topic (interactive writing), to write an essay to convince others of their point of view (persuasive writing), and to write about personal experiences (narrative writing). Students were asked to respond to two writing tasks and provided with blank paper to plan their writing. Students, teachers, and administrators in all three grades were also asked about instructional content and practices. Students were asked how frequently teachers encouraged them to plan their writing (use prewriting), define their purposes for writing, and write more than one draft and revise.

The study found that several process-writing techniques were associated with higher writing proficiency. Students of teachers who always encouraged planning and defining purpose and audience were found to be generally better writers than students of teachers who reportedly never encouraged these activities. Average writing ability was higher among students whose teachers emphasized more than one process-writing strategy. In particular, the use of prewriting was found to be associated with the highest average proficiency scores (National Assessment of Educational Progress, 1998). Recently questions have emerged about the reliability of the NAEP data and about using NAEP writing assessments to report trends (Kennedy Manzo, 2000). Subsequent studies have shown more limited improvement in writing among the students tested. Nevertheless, at the time of the 1992 report, the NAEP findings played a prominent role in promoting the adoption of process-oriented writing instruction.

Although considerable adoption of research findings has taken place, such implementation has not been universally accepted or understood. Researchers, for example, lament that too often the writing process has been translated in the classroom into a fairly rigid set of activities in the lesson plan for the week: "Monday we plan; Tuesday we draft; Wednesday we respond to drafts; Thursday we revise" (Dyson & Freedman, 1991, p. 761). Langer and Applebee (1987) suggest a conflict between the forces shaping traditional instruction and the values in process-oriented instruction for writing. Curriculum theory in the United States, they point out, is often "guided by a building block or assembly line metaphor: the final product is a body of knowledge made up of discrete component parts and these parts must be assembled in a coherent, specified order if they are to function properly" (p. 553). This way of understanding learning is deeply engrained in the American education system—and has been internalized by many teachers. Process-oriented approaches to instruction, Langer and Applebee point out, are based on the assumption that learning is not linear and sequential but recursive, involving the cycling and recycling of learning processes, and so is often at odds with traditional classroom approaches.

Within higher education too, process-oriented writing approaches were extended into first-year English courses and other university departments as well. Professors began to experiment with ways to involve college students in collaborative writing activities. Within ESOL departments at the higher education level, courses in ESOL writing became more prevalent. A wide number of articles disseminating information about effective instructional strategies for teaching ESOL writing began to emerge in the *Journal of ESL Writing, TESOL Quarterly,* and other publications. College faculty became more aware that the process of learning to write in a second language may take many years and that there was a need to help nonnative speakers with their writing beyond first-year writing courses. The cultural dimensions of learning to write in a new language also became more widely understood.

The availability of remedial education programs in community colleges and universities continued to grow during the 1980s and early 1990s as the enrollment of nontraditional students grew and the curriculum area known as basic writing became more established. Such courses were usually offered as noncredit-bearing "preuniversity" courses and taught by nontenured and part-time faculty. Teachers at this level explored ways to give students more frequent opportunities to write for varied purposes, including narrative writing. They also implemented strategies for helping students to revise their writing, consider the reader in their planning, and address not only mechanical but content-related problems.

Addressing the sociocultural implications of academic writing for nontraditional students also became more explicit in many classrooms. Increasingly, basic writing teachers saw their role as one of helping students to cross the boundary between their own world and that of higher education. The writing classroom became a place to examine social class, ethnicity, language, gender, and other forms of difference (Bizzell & Herzberg, 1996). Yet basic writing teachers struggled to address the competing needs of minority and nontraditional students. The dilemma was perhaps best described by educator Lisa Delpit (1986):

> Let there be no doubt: a "skilled" minority person who is not also capable of critical analysis becomes the trainable low level functionary of dominant society, simply the grease that keeps the institutions which orchestrate his or her oppression running smoothly. On the other hand, a critical thinker who lacks the "skills" demanded by employers and institutions of higher learning can aspire to financial and social status only within the disenfranchised underworld. Yet if minority people are to effect the change which will allow them to truly progress, we must insist on "skills" *within the context of* critical and creative thinking.

During the late 1990s, controversies regarding budgets for remedial programs for nontraditional students became more heated, even as the numbers of students who might be considered nontraditional grew (Reder, 2000). Many higher educators and policymakers have argued for literacy selection, which advises against admitting to higher education students whose literacy skills are deemed insufficient. Critics of literacy selection have, in turn, argued for literacy development, which supports equity of opportunity and allows less prepared students additional opportunities and support. In many states, financial support for programs for students with poor basic skills has been scaled back and admissions requirements tightened. For example, the City University of New York, the site of much of the original work on remedial writing at the college level, has now ended its open admissions policy and drastically reduced its remedial programs. The state university system in California has also adopted a policy of scaling back remedial courses on its twenty-two campuses (Cooper, 1998; Reder, 2000). This trend may have important implications for the adult literacy field. As the availability of basic writing courses within higher education diminishes, the responsibility for preparing nontraditional adult students for the demands of college writing may well shift to adult education programs.

## THE IMPACT OF WRITING RESEARCH ON THE ADULT LITERACY FIELD

Scant data exist about whether, how, and under what conditions writing is taking place in adult literacy classrooms. In most large-scale studies of adult education, writing has been subsumed under the more general category of literacy education rather than separated out for study (Development Associates, 1994). What little we know can be gleaned only indirectly from practitioner-written articles appearing over the years in professional journals, from learner-written publications, and from a very few research studies, all of them limited in scope and size.

### Advances

One example of the way that process writing has spread to the adult literacy field can be found in the case of literacy volunteer programs in New York City. One of the first that appears to have adopted process-oriented writing is LVNYC. The first issue of the *Big Apple Journal*, a semiannual anthology of student writing, was published by the program in 1975. Since that time, LVNYC has continued to expand its practice of involving learners in writing workshops as part of small group instruction in adult literacy, to offer Saturday writing workshops, and to hold special events where students read their writing (Fingeret & Danin, 1991; Gillespie, 1991). Early on, New York City adult literacy teachers began attending workshops offered by the National Writing Project, and in 1986 a summer writing institute designed for adult literacy educators was held at Lehman College. Since then, shorter workshops have periodically been offered by the Literacy Assistance Center, a clearinghouse for adult literacy and other organizations. In other large cities, notably Boston, Philadelphia, and Chicago, workshops for teachers on how to adapt writing-process work designed for children to adult education settings became available. In Boston, for example, student writers from various community-based programs began to contribute their work to a citywide anthology, *Need I Say More.* A student editorial board was initiated, and during the late 1980s and early 1990s, two overnight writers' weekends were held. New writers began visiting other classrooms to talk about their work through the Writer in the Classroom initiative (Gillespie, 1991).

Over the years, a number of journal articles have chronicled adult literacy practitioners' efforts to experiment with new ways to teach writing. Among the most popular have been articles about the effectiveness of journal writing in various adult education settings (see Kerka, 1996, and Anderson, 1995, for a summary). Dialogue journals, in which students maintain a dialogue on paper with their peers or with teachers, also became popular (see Peyton & Staton, 1991; Fallon, 1995). The language experience approach, in which students dictate their ideas to teachers, who then use the stories as a basis for teaching reading, also became more widespread, in particular with beginning ESOL students (Taylor, 1993).

Teachers have written about unique ways in which they have adapted writing instruction to meet the varied purposes of adult learners. For example, in "Writing: The Golden Thread in Family Learning," Goethel (1995) describes her efforts to weave writing into the fabric of family literacy. Parents and children write and illustrate stories together, and parents reflect on time spent with their children in journals and use these writings in conferences with the parenting instructor. Parents also contribute to class anthologies and participate in "writing celebrations" together with their families. Blinn (1995) describes a program piloted at a minimum-security correctional center, designed as part of an effort to reduce recidivism among high-risk inmates. Instructors used personal writing as a tool to help offenders examine the goals they had for life after prison and to teach concrete problem-solving and consequential-thinking skills. Glasgow (1994) showed how learners in prison writing classes improved when their learning styles were taken into account. Other work has chronicled the use of writing as a tool in workplace literacy programs (Rhoder & French, 1995), ESOL programs (Peyton, 1993; McGrail, 1995; Wales, 1994; Weinstein, 1992), community-based centers (Himley, Madden, Hoffman, & Penrod, 1996; Kazemek, 1984), and computer-based contexts (Scheffer, 1995). Of particular note is a text for teachers entitled *Making Meaning, Making Change: Participatory Curriculum Development for Adult ESL Literacy* (Auerbach, 1992). The author at once describes the work of an English family literacy project in Boston and offers a compendium of participatory education strategies, many of which are writing based. In a companion book, *Talking Shop* (Nash, Carson, Rhum, McGrail, & Gomez-Sanford, 1992), teachers associated with this same family literacy project document their struggle to introduce writing to beginning-level ESOL students, to use students' native language for writing in the classroom, and to employ varied forms of photo stories, oral histories, and language experience in their teaching.

Another major influence on the field was the introduction of a direct assessment of writing ability into the 1988 edition of the GED test. Up to 1987, language arts were measured indirectly through multiple-choice questions related to the conventions of written English. The new test did include a multiple-choice component that measured students' ability to edit and revise sentences for structure, usage, and mechanics, but it also required students to complete an essay within a forty-five-minute time frame. Students were asked to present an opinion or explanation regarding a situation familiar to adults. The introduction of the essay test was considered quite innovative at the time and marked a dramatic revision of the GED test. The test developers, basing their work on NAEP results related to the writing abilities of young adults, encouraged adult educators to teach the writing process explicitly, provide students with broad-based experiences in reading to develop their understanding of good writing, and provide writing experiences in different rhetorical modes, such as description, persuasion, and exposition, each of which, they pointed out, requires different skills (Dauzat & Dauzat, 1987). A number of articles suggesting approaches to teaching students to prepare for the GED essay test appeared during this period (Taylor, 1987; Fadale & Hammond, 1987). Since that time, however, there have been surprisingly few reports in adult education journals regarding successful preparation of students for the GED essay test. (One exception is a 1996 issue of *Connections: A Journal of Adult Literacy,* which devoted an entire issue to teachers' reflections on this topic.) No empirical studies of how GED teachers prepare adults for the GED test appear to have been undertaken.

One more key influence on the spread of writing in adult basic education is community writing, or what has come to be known as learner-generated writing. This movement has its roots in Britain, where various kinds of community-based writing and local publishing groups sprang up in working-class British neighborhoods in the 1970s. The groups promoted the local publication and distribution of individual biographies, poetry, fiction, oral histories, and community action materials that allowed working-class people to give voice to their individual and collective experiences. Eventually these organizations united to form the Federation of Worker Writers and Community Publishers. (The history of this movement is described in Morley & Worpole, 1982.)

Soon the notion of involving adult literacy students in the worker writing movement gained momentum. By 1974, plans were under way to produce a national newsletter by and for adult literacy learners. For more than a decade, the *Write First Time* newspaper was published three times a year. At its height, more than sixty local programs contributed articles to this publication. Production was moved from one region to another to give larger numbers of adults experience with the publication and production process. In 1985, however, the government-based funding for the newspaper was withdrawn. A growing centralization of control of adult literacy education during the 1990s led to a considerable reduction in the number of projects engaged in community writing (see Gardener, 1985; Gillespie, 1991; Mace, 1995; Hamilton & Merrifield, 2000).

Some of the British publications made their way into the hands of adult literacy practitioners in the United States and Canada and provided inspiration for a growing number of learner-generated publications during the 1980s. (See Gillespie, 1991, and Peyton, 1993, for summaries of this movement.) One project of note was *Voices,* a quarterly magazine consisting of writing by adult beginning readers and ESOL students, primarily from the United States and Canada. Accompanying each article was a biography and photograph of the student writer. The magazine, edited and published by the Lower Mainland Society for Literacy and Employment in British Columbia, was distributed to subscribers in Canada and the United States and did much to promote the idea that beginning readers can write sophisticated and meaningful text. Lack of sufficient financial support led to the demise of the project in the late 1990s.

In a few innovative cases, adult literacy learners have been involved in developing curriculum materials to teach other adults how to write. One good example is *Opening Time* (Frost & Hoy, 1987). This text presents a fresh look at learning to write through the eyes of adult beginning writers. The titles of the learning modules these adults created reflect the level of analysis that can be attained when adults are given the time and power to create their own curriculum materials— for example: "A Beginning Reader Is Not a Beginning Thinker," "It Helps to Discover Myself," "A Sense of Relief," "School: A Wasted Childhood," "The Student Is the Expert," and "It Doesn't Have to Be Perfect." *Conversations with Strangers* (Gardener, 1985) provides another example of students' and teachers' documenting their work together as writers.

Community writing projects for working-class adults have also taken place outside the arena of adult basic education classrooms. One powerful example is a community writing project that took place in an inner-city neighborhood in San Francisco. This work is documented in the book *Until We Are Strong Together* (Heller, 1997). Two other examples are the Amherst Writers and Artists Institute in Massachusetts (Schneider, 1989) and the Neighborhood Writing Alliance in Chicago, which publishes the *Journal of Ordinary Thought*.

### Stasis

Although some programs have made efforts to apply new research on writing in their adult literacy classrooms, many others continue to focus on lower-order writing process skills (such as grammar, punctuation, and spelling) and to give less attention to higher-order processes (such as planning what to write and making revisions). In one of the few studies to look at how writing is taught in adult literacy classrooms, Padak and Padak (1988) studied five adult education sites in Michigan. They found that some form of writing activity occurred at all the sites. At three of the five sites, students sometimes wrote in response to a teacher-assigned topic. However, Padak and Padak noted that the vast majority of interactions about writing involved the teacher and a single student and was focused on mechanics. Discussion of ideas or the content of writing did not occur at any of the three sites and accounted for only 7 percent and 22 percent of interactions about writing at the other two sites. Teachers rarely assigned or even suggested writing outside the classroom. "Throughout all forty-one hours of instruction," the researchers noted, " we observed only four interactions about writing that students had completed independently. In all four cases, students had written poems and stories outside of class" (p. 5).

Interviews with teachers revealed that their definition of "good" writing supported a mechanics-oriented view. Only three of eleven teachers mentioned purpose or content as characteristics of good writing. Teachers' primary goal was to help students learn the skills required to pass the GED test. "I may be in a rut," one teacher said, "but I know how to get them through. I know what books to use so they can pass the test" (p. 6).

A more recent survey, also of teachers in Michigan, was conducted by Young (1997). Her study, which looked at the use of computers in the classroom, revealed that participants primarily used drill and practice software for language arts. Students working at the computer were typically ignored by teachers until their scores appeared on the screen. Teachers and students engaged in only superficial exchanges with little educational substance. Students engaged in word processing solely to type in their own previously written texts as corrected by teachers. Young found a remarkable disparity between the research literature on the sociocontextual nature of literacy and the reality she observed in the classroom. Drawing on the work of Schön, Young noted that some teachers possessed "espoused theories" that reflected an understanding of recent process-centered instruction. When they got into the classroom, however, their "theory-in-use" reverted back to a more traditional approach. Another study on computer use (Hopey, Harvey-Morgan, & Rethemeyer, 1996) also found drill and practice to be the predominant use for computers in adult literacy classrooms.

To date, we know relatively little about how the development of writing ability in adult literacy learners compares with that of young children or of basic writers at the college level. However, we can speculate that adult literacy learners have many characteristics in common with basic, or remedial, adult writers. They may, for example, come to the classroom with a limited understanding of the higher-order processes involved in writing and thus require strategic instruction in these areas. One recent study in this regard was conducted by Russell (1999), who found that the adult learners she observed came to the task of learning to write with a mental model of writing that was different from that of their teachers. While teachers encouraged students not to worry about form, to ignore their mistakes, and to focus on the content of their writing, the students were mostly concerned with avoiding mistakes and writing the "right" way. Interviews with students revealed that they believed a "good" writer was someone who knew how to use punctuation and could write perfectly the first time. They did not fully recognize the possibility of learning from reading and then applying this new understanding to writing. Nor could they conceive of strategies that put themselves in the role of revising or correcting their own work. In effect, she observed, "teachers and learners appear to be speaking two different languages, perhaps different dialects of the language of writing instruction" (p. 20). Her work suggests the need to develop a different model of teaching writing to adult literacy learners, "one that allows learners and teachers to co-construct representations of their assumptions about the writing process, and that makes explicit the connections that may be unclear" (p. 23).

Art Halbrook, a writing specialist at the GED Testing Service, has observed that students in many adult literacy and GED classrooms are not developing higher-order skills in the processing of writing. After reading hundreds of GED essays, Halbrook (1999) described most as a "blueprint for mediocrity." Too often, he observes, students appear to be taught simply the minimum requirements of a five-paragraph formula—introductory paragraph, three supporting paragraphs, and a conclusion—and drilled in how to adapt it to nearly any assigned topic: the minimal requirement to pass the test. Learning to write a five-paragraph essay is valuable, but it appears, based on Halbrook's observations, that "writing for the test" may be the only kind of writing students learn. He saw limited evidence of the mastery of higher-order writing processes, such as planning and revising, in the content of the essays.

This conclusion is especially troubling, since, as Reder (2000) points out, moving up into well-paying jobs increasingly requires postsecondary education and credentials. Students who in the past might not have participated in postsecondary education now need to seek further education training. Without academic writing skills, students may either be screened out of or be unable to succeed in postsecondary education. The ability to pass the GED essay test, although important, may not adequately prepare adults for the demands of postsecondary writing. Moreover, as we have seen, adults increasingly may be required to do more writing on the job than in the past. Since writing skills in one rhetorical mode may not fully transfer to another mode, learning to write a short essay alone may not prepare adult GED learners for the kinds of writing they may be required to do at work, such as writing memos, short reports, and e-mail messages.

Below the GED level, the most commonly used standardized tests, such as the Test of Adult Basic Education (TABE) and the Adult Basic Learning Examination (ABLE), do not include direct measures of writing. Among the tests offered through the Comprehensive Adult Student Assessment System (CASAS), a direct test of writing does exist, but few programs appear to take advantage of it. Many of the most popular commercial workbooks available for adult literacy learners continue to offer drill and practice language arts exercises that are correlated to the kinds of questions covered by these tests.

For English-language learners, the Basic English Skills Test (BEST), designed for lower-level learners, includes a very short writing assessment that asks learners to write a note to a teacher and a thank you note. The Adult Language Assessment Scales (A-LAS) also contain a direct measure of writing, with scores reported holistically on a scale of 0 to 5. (See Van Duzer & Berdan, 2000, for a discussion of assessment in adult ESOL instruction.)

## Promising Trends

Unlike teachers in the K–12 system, many, and perhaps the majority, of adult literacy teachers appear to have had few opportunities to receive training in innovative approaches to the teaching of writing and thus may rely on more traditional approaches. A number of promising trends, however, emerged during the 1990s.

PROJECT-BASED INSTRUCTION. One such trend is project-based instruction. "In its simplest form, project-based learning involves a group of learners taking on an issue close to their hearts, developing a response, and presenting the results to a wider audience" (Wrigley, 1998, p. 13). Through project-based instruction, adult learners develop their language, literacy, and problem-solving skills as they research an issue of concern or interest. Writing often plays a central role in project-based instruction. For example, learners in one ESOL project discussed, researched, and wrote down traditional recipes (Gaer, 1998). Another decided on themes and then wrote and enacted short plays and skits. Yet another group of students decided to write an orientation handbook for future students of their literacy program. Still other projects have involved research and writing to create educational materials on health (Norton & Campbell, 1998). Projects may last from only a few days to several months. In some cases, projects turn into businesses, as did a student-run café at ELISAIR, an ESOL program in New York City. Others have come about spontaneously, such as when a group of ESOL learners decided to organize a fundraiser to help flood victims in Honduras (Wrigley, 1998). In some projects, students serve as apprentices, as, for example, when they learn from their teacher how to put together their own newspaper. Tasks, time lines, and responsibilities are often posted to track the status of a project and sometimes students to keep budgets. Often such projects have real audiences and a goal of effecting change in a community.

Although no research studies have yet been conducted that study this approach to instruction in adult contexts, proponents claim it helps adults to develop skills that are more closely matched to the literacy requirements of work and everyday life. Project-based instruction encourages collaborative learning and writing for authentic purposes. This form of instruction also helps to make visible the processes that are usually hidden from learners in typical programs, such as the publishing process (Wrigley, 1998).

EQUIPPED FOR THE FUTURE. Equipped for the Future (EFF), the standards-based system reform initiative of the National Institute for Literacy (NIFL), is another project that is encouraging the involvement of students in writing (and reading) in authentic contexts. One of EFF's most significant accomplishments has been to shift the conception of the purpose of literacy away from the acquisition of a set of skills isolated from practice and toward a conception of literacy as purposeful action rooted in the contexts of people's lives. In this respect, EFF draws on many of the same conceptual and theoretical ideas that have informed the writing-related research described in this chapter. In addition, it acknowledges the transformative qualities of adult literacy acquisition suggested by Fingeret and Drennon (1997).

The EFF standards reform initiative began in 1993, when the NIFL was asked by the National Education Goals Panel (an intergovernmental body of state and federal officials designed to assess and report on state and national progress in education) to measure and track the progress of the nation toward the following goal: "Every adult American will be literate and possess the knowledge and skills necessary to compete in a global economy, and exercise the rights and responsibilities of citizenship." This goal presented not just a technical challenge in terms of measurement but a conceptual problem: what does one have to know and be able to do to be literate? The NIFL team found that no widely held agreement on the meaning of "literate functioning" existed (Merrifield, 2000).

To try to answer this question, the NIFL team turned to adult learners, issuing a widely distributed invitation for them to respond to the following question: "What do adults need to know and be able to do in order to be literate, compete in the global economy, and exercise the rights and responsibilities of citizenship?" Fifteen hundred students in a variety of adult education programs from around the United States submitted written responses, which the NIFL team used to identify four key purposes for learning: to gain access to information, give voice to ideas, act independently, and build a bridge to the future by learning how to learn (Stein, 1995).

Using these four purposes as a base, EFF has developed a framework for standards-based system reform, at each stage seeking input from as wide a range of people as possible (Merrifield, 2000, p. 8). Content standards were derived from optimal portraits (referred to as role maps) of what adults know and do when they are effective in their three key life roles of worker, parent and family member, and citizen. The process also included an analysis of the skills and knowledge required across the three life roles, referred to as generative skills. Writing represented a key generative skill in the model. Over a two-year iterative and field-based process in many states, content standards were developed. The focus of EFF is now on the development of an assessment framework and performance standards. Writing will be one of the generative skills assessed. To date, a large number of states are involved with EFF in one way or another, including in some cases statewide adoption of the standards (Merrifield, 2000; Stein, 2000).

The EFF reform system has the potential to guide significant reform in the teaching of writing in adult literacy contexts. Its focus on "purposeful" learning "rooted in the context of people's lives" (Merrifield, 2000, p. 9) can direct teachers away from teacher-assigned writing activities with little relationship to everyday life and toward authentic writing tasks derived from needs at work, within the family, and in community life. In developing an assessment framework and performance standards, EFF designers have the potential to apply many of the writing research findings outlined in this chapter in exciting and innovative ways.

TECHNOLOGY-BASED COMMUNICATION. Innovative uses of technology may represent one of the most significant of the promising trends. In growing numbers, adult literacy learners are surfing the Web to research areas that interest them, communicating through e-mail, creating Web pages, and forming on-line groups of various kinds. (See Rosen, 2000, for a summary of technology-based activities in which students and teachers are engaged.) In ways never before available, adult students can find audiences to read and respond to their texts. They can combine visual and print literacy to communicate their ideas, and they can form long-distance collaborations with others. Each of the National Institute for Literacy's regional LINCS (Literacy Information and Communications System) sites now have links to resources by and for learners. For example, SouthernLINCS (http://hub2.coe.utk.edu.html) has links to learner-developed projects on topics such as stress, home remedies, the influence of television commercials on viewers, and ways in which inmates can keep in touch with the outside world. Brown University's literacy center maintains a site at which adult beginning readers can post their poetry, short stories, and essays (http://www.brown.edu/Departments/ Swearer Center/Literacy Resources/learner.html). Dave's ESL Café (http://www.eslcafe.com) contains more than twenty discussion forums for ESOL students and has provided the means for thousands of ESOL students to become pen pals with other ESOL students from around the world. Some programs also publish their curriculum materials and teaching tips on-line. Write on Nashville (http://cls.coe.utk.edu/lpm/writeon.html), for example, gives teachers tips on how to prepare for a public event in which students read their stories. (The Literacy List, a comprehensive, hyperlinked list of adult literacy, basic education, and ESOL Web sites, is maintained by David Rosen and can be found at http://www2.wgbh.org/mbcweis/ltc/ alri/LiteracyList.html.)

# IMPLICATIONS FOR RESEARCH, PRACTICE, AND POLICY

While research-based approaches to the teaching of writing have made their way into some adult literacy classrooms, progress overall has been quite limited. Adult literacy programs need guidance if writing is to move from an occasional activity to one that is at the heart of the educational process. Given the limited funding for research and program improvement in the field, attention should be given to activities of immediate value and strategic importance. The following list suggests some priorities.

- *Develop a research agenda for the study of composition in adult literacy education contexts.* Given funding constraints, the field needs to consider carefully what kinds of research studies are of greatest priority. Specialists in the teaching of writing should come together to establish a research agenda. This process should include experts from a number of fields, such as researchers in basic education at the postsecondary level; specialists in emergent writing; teachers and teacher trainers from adult basic education, ESOL, and vocational education; postsecondary school teachers with day-to-day experience teaching adults to write; and policymakers concerned with how best to assess progress in writing. Working together, they should make recommendations for how to select and design studies that build on existing research and are of most value to the field. In designing the studies that address this agenda, this panel of experts should employ both micro- and macrolevel analyses. If learning to write is largely a process of "personal growth in the social context" (Dyson & Freedman, 1991), then scholars will have to study varied cultural, linguistic, contextual, and individual differences that come to play in this multifaceted process. Within those social contexts, microlevel analysis of how adults develop and change as writers may help explain how adult literacy learners are both similar to and different from other populations that have been studied. Other possible topics for research include longitudinal studies of the writing development of adults who successfully make the transition into postsecondary education and work that requires writing and of the role that writing plays in the transformational process that occurs as an adult becomes literate.
- *Support policies that create a bridge between GED study and preparation for the writing demands of postsecondary education.* In today's world, moving beyond an entry-level job often requires further education. Adults who decide to enroll in a vocational school, community college, or university face many writing-related challenges. An essay test may serve as a gatekeeper to entry into the program. Once enrolled, many students will be expected to pass entry-level composition classes and to engage in writing in other academic classes. Special policies and programs need to be developed to help students make the transition to writing at the postsecondary level.

Recent research has revealed that few GED holders enter or complete postsecondary education (Reder, 2000). Since data seem to indicate that adult education students who do enter college and participate in remedial programs fare relatively well compared with their peers, transitional programs have considerable potential. With diminishing financial support for remedial writing classes at the precollege level, adult basic educators may be required to fill the gap. Rance-Roney (1995) summarizes some of the factors adult educators will have to consider in designing transitional programs. Adult educators must find ways to motivate students to believe they have the ability to face the academic demands of college; help them to understand the culture, norms, and expectations of the academic community; and help them to develop their conceptual and critical thinking skills such as synthesis, analysis, and evaluation. Second-language students need to expand their vocabulary and learn to integrate and transfer first-language skills and learning strategies to English. To aid in the development of effective programs, writing teachers at the adult, vocational, and postsecondary levels need to be encouraged to sponsor professional development activities and publications jointly.

• *Fund staff development models that better equip adult educators to develop and implement literacy programs that support writing.* The training that most adult literacy teachers receive in the teaching of writing is minimal. Few teachers have specialized, university-level training in adult literacy education or special degrees in the teaching of writing. If teachers are to adopt the kind of process-based approach to writing that writing experts now advocate, they will require additional, specialized preservice training. In considering training options, adult literacy educators should examine the experiences of the National Writing Project to ascertain which aspects of this highly regarded training model might be adapted. Mentoring and apprenticeship programs for new teachers of writing may be useful, and Web-based networks might foster and share innovative practices. At the GED level, in particular, educators require training and support if they are to shift their focus beyond preparing students to pass the GED test and toward preparing adults for the demands of further education.

Many programs are experimenting with approaches to teaching that support learning in the social context. Programs are using project-based instruction and other approaches that involve multitasked, collaborative practices in real-life contexts. Teachers in these programs need support to document how writing develops and is taught in these contexts. In particular, researchers should observe how curricula based on EFF content standards promote writing and how writing is woven into the content standards.

• *Investigate innovative tools to assess progress in writing.* Researchers and test developers are looking for ways to overcome the current mismatch between what is measured by existing standardized tests and what should be taught in the classroom. The most popular standardized tests in use today, except for the GED, only indirectly measure writing. Adult educators need to examine alternative models. The K–12 and postsecondary systems have developed models for both the large-scale testing of writing for accountability purposes and for smaller-scale, classroom-based assessment useful to teachers.

Since the 1960s, the College Entrance Examination Board has used holistic scoring of writing and has developed techniques to train readers to score writing samples, thus solving reliability problems (Freedman, 1991). By 1998, more than thirty-five states had begun to use some direct measures of writing in their K–12 assessment. In addition, for more than twenty years, the NAEP has been conducting large-scale, direct assessments of writing. The NAEP has responded to many critics, including those who have argued that it is not valid to make claims about writing achievement given the NAEP testing conditions (including the short time that students have for writing and the fact that they are writing for an artificial audience) and the way in which the writing is evaluated. Yet with each new version of its test, the NAEP has made improvements, such as lengthening the testing time, providing students with opportunities for prewriting, experimenting with the addition of a portfolio assessment system, and using varied kinds of scoring systems. Given this rich source of information, adult literacy educators should have a good foundation from which to address the inevitable question of how better to measure writing development in adult literacy programs for purposes of accountability.

The writing portfolio movement in K–12 settings is another valuable resource from which adult educators can draw to develop classroom-based assessment and to link classroom and large-scale assessment. Writing folders are particularly useful for revealing patterns in writing development over time and across different kinds of writing activities. For the adult literacy field, the inclusion of portfolio assessment would be one way to nudge teachers toward involving students in more significant amounts of and varied kinds of writing. It would also allow adult learners to take a more active role in their own assessment. However, to be effective, teachers would need clear guidelines related to "what writing is to be collected, under what conditions, for what purposes, and evaluated in what ways" (Freedman, 1991, p. 8).

Testing programs often exert a powerful influence over the nature of instruction and what "counts" as literacy. Since the ability to write in varied contexts for different kinds of purposes and audiences is not tested, writing does not "count" for many adult education teachers. This may well continue to be the case until portfolio assessment and possibly some form of performance-based writing assessment begin to "count" within the literacy field. Experience in the K–12 system shows, however, that if teachers are simply directed to ask students to submit work, called portfolios, without being given staff development related to the teaching of writing, the student writing submitted is often dismal indeed (Freedman, 1991, p. 15). The development of writing assessment processes needs to be introduced hand in hand with staff development. Writing tasks need to be focused on the most pressing writing demands that adults face in the workplace, family and civic life, and postsecondary education.

• *Support the dissemination of writing by and for adult literacy learners.* Perhaps one of the most exciting aspects of technology-based communication is its capacity to allow adult literacy learners entry into wider communities of discourse (Gee, 1989). Such communities represent more than a means for adult learners to publish their work. Each involves a group of people writing for a community of others, responding to one another's ideas, and building a knowledge base together. Discourse communities can provide a vehicle through which adult learners can write about and respond to issues of concern to them (Beaufort, 1997). Voice for Adult Literacy United for Education, the national organization formed in 1998 by and for adult literacy learners, has established a Web site (through the national LINCS system, at http://literacynet.org/value/) that has the potential to provide such a forum for adult literacy learners. Another example is the American Gateways Community Voice (http://gateways.unhny.org/). This site, funded by the American Gateways Technology Challenge Grant, provides adult learners with an avenue to share their stories of immigration. Teachers can support such forums by linking classroom activities to student participation, assisting students in revising their work for "publication" on the Web, and helping students see the value of sharing their viewpoints.

Up to now, adult literacy learners have far too often gone through years of schooling that involved only the reading of other people's words. Not enough opportunity has been provided for them to make words their own. In planning for the future of writing instruction in adult literacy, policymakers and program staff should consider James Boyd White's definition of literacy:

> Literacy is not merely the capacity to understand the conceptual content of writings and utterances, but the ability to participate fully in a set of social and intellectual practices. It is not passive, but active, not imitative but creative, for participation in the speaking and writing of language is participation in the activities that make it possible. Indeed it involves the perpetual remaking of both language and practice. [cited in Robinson, 1990, p. 158]

## References

Anderson, J. (1995). Journal writing: The promise and the reality. *Journal of Reading, 36*(4), 304–308.

Auerbach, E. (1992). *Making meaning, making change: Participatory curriculum development for adult ESL literacy.* Washington, DC: Center for Applied Linguistics and Delta Systems.

Bartholomae, D. (1980). The study of error. *College Composition and Communication, 31,* 253–269.

Bartholomae, D. (1985). Inventing the university. In E. Intgen, B. Kroll, & M. Rose (Eds.), *Perspectives on literacy* (pp. 273–285). Carbondale: Southern Illinois University Press.

Barton, D., & Hamilton, M. (1998). *Local literacies: Reading and writing in the community.* New York: Routledge.

Barton, D., & Ivanič, R. (Eds.). (1991). *Writing in the community.* Thousand Oaks, CA: Sage.

Barton, D., & Padmore, S. (1991). Roles, networks, and values in everyday writing. In D. Barton & R. Ivanič (Eds.), *Writing in the community* (pp. 58–77). Thousand Oaks, CA: Sage.

Bear, D. R., Truex, P., & Barone, D. (1989). Using children's spellings to group for word study and directed reading in the primary classroom. *Reading Psychology, 13,* 165–185.

Beaufort, A. (1997). Operationalizing the concept of discourse community: A case study of one institutional site of composing. *Research in the Teaching of English, 31*(4), 486–528.

Belzer, A. (1998). *Doing school and doing school differently: The perspective of five adult learners on their past and current educational experiences.* Unpublished doctoral dissertation, University of Pennsylvania, Philadelphia.

Bereiter, C., & Scardamalia, M. (1987). *The psychology of written composition.* Mahwah, NJ: Erlbaum.

Bereiter, C., & Scardamalia, M. (1993). *Surpassing ourselves: An inquiry into the nature and complications of expertise.* Chicago: Open Court Press.

Berninger, V. W., & Swanson, H. L. (1994). Modifying Hayes and Flowers' model of skilled writing to explain beginning and developing writing. In E. Butterfield (Ed.), *Children's writing: Toward a process theory of development of skilled writing* (pp. 57–81). Greenwich, CT: JAI Press.

Berninger, V. W., Vaughan, K., Abbott, R. D., Brooks, A. L., Abbott, S. P., Rogan, L., Reed, E., & Graham, S. (1998). Early intervention for spelling problems: Teaching functional spelling units of varying size with a multiple-connections framework. *Journal of Educational Psychology, 90(4),* 587–605.

Berninger, V. W., Vaughan, K. B, Abbott, R. D., Abbott, S. P., Rogan, L. W., Brooks, A., Reed, E., & Graham, S. (1997). Treatment of handwriting problems in beginning writers: Transfer from handwriting to composition. *Journal of Educational Psychology, 89(4),* 652–666.

Bizzell, P., & Herzberg, B. (1996). *Negotiating difference: Cultural case studies for composition.* New York: St. Martin's Press.

Blinn, C. (1995). Teaching cognitive skills to effect behavioral change through a writing program. *Journal of Correctional Education, 46(4),* 146–154.

Britton, J., Burgess, A., Martin, N., & Rosen, H. (1975). *Developing writing abilities 11–18.* New York: Macmillan.

Calkins, L. M. (1975). *Lessons from a child.* Portsmouth, NH: Heinemann.

Campbell, C. (1998). *Teaching second-language writing: Interacting with text.* Boston: Heinle & Heinle.

Cooper, S. E. (1998, Aug.). Remediation's end: Can New York educate the children of the "whole people"? *Academe,* 14–20.

Cumming, A. (1998). Theoretical perspectives on writing. *Annual Review of Applied Linguistics, 18,* 61–78.

Dauzat, S. V., & Dauzat, J. A. (1987). A new GED: Gearing up for change. *Lifelong Learning, 10(6),* 27–30.

Delpit, L. (1986). Skills and other dilemmas of a black progressive educator. *American Educator, 48,* 9–11.

Development Associates. (1994). *National evaluation of adult education programs: Final report.* Washington, DC: U.S. Department of Education.

Dyson, A., & Freedman, S. W. (1991). Writing. In J. Flood, J. Jensen, D. Lapp, & J. R. Squire (Eds.), *Handbook of research on teaching in the language arts* (pp. 754–774). New York: Macmillan.

Elley, W. B. (1994). Acquiring literacy in a second language: The effect of book-based programs. In A. H. Cumming (Ed.), *Bilingual performance in reading and writing* (pp. 331–366). Ann Arbor, MI: Research Club in Language Learning.

Emig, J. (1971). *The composing practices of twelfth graders.* Urbana, IL: National Council of Teachers of English.

Fadale, L. M., & Hammond, D. B. (1987). Intended learning outcomes: Teaching writing to adults. *Lifelong Learning, 11*(3), 8–10.

Fallon, D. (1995). Making a dialogue dialogic: A dialogic approach to adult literacy instruction. *Journal of Adult and Adolescent Literacy, 39*(2), 138–147.

Farr, M., & Guerra, J. C. (1995). Literacy in the community: A study of Mexican families in Chicago. *Discourse Processes, 19,* 7–19.

Ferris, D., & Hedgcock, J. (1998). *Teaching ESL composition: Purpose, process and practice.* Mahwah, NJ: Erlbaum.

Fingeret, H. A., & Danin, S. T. (1991). *"They really put a hurtin' on my brain": Learning in Literacy Volunteers of New York City.* Durham, NC: Literacy South.

Fingeret, H. A., & Drennon, C. (1997). *Literacy for life: Adult learners, new practices.* New York: Teachers College Press.

Flower, L. S. (1979). Writer-based prose: A cognitive basis for problems in writing. *College English, 41,* 19–37.

Flower, L. S. (1981). Revising writer-based prose. *Journal of Basic Writing, 3,* 62–74.

Flower, L. S. (1994). *The construction of negotiated meaning: A social cognitive theory of writing.* Carbondale: Southern Illinois University Press.

Flower, L. S., & Hayes, J. R. (1980). Identifying the organization of writing processes. In L. W. Gregg & E. R. Steinberg (Eds.), *Cognitive processes in writing* (pp. 31–50). Mahwah, NJ: Erlbaum.

Forester, A. D. (1988). Learning to read and write at 26. *Journal of Reading, 31*(7), 604–613.

Freedman, S. W. (1991*). Evaluating writing: Linking large-scale testing and classroom assessment* (Occasional Paper No. 27). Berkeley:

National Center for the Study of Writing, University of California at Berkeley.

Freedman, S. W., Flower, L., Hull, G. L., & Hayes, J. R. (1995). *Ten years of research: Achievements of the National Center for the Study of Writing and Literacy.* Berkeley, CA: National Center for the Study of Writing.

Frost, G., & Hoy, C. (1987). *Opening time: A writing resource pack written by students in basic education.* Manchester, England: Gatehouse Press.

Gaer, S. (1998). Learning more and teaching less. *Focus on Basics, 2*(D), 9–12.

Gardener, S. (1985). *Conversations with strangers: Ideas about writing for adult students.* London: Adult Literacy and Basic Skills Unit.

Gee, J. P. (1989). Literacy, discourse, and linguistics: An introduction. *Journal of Reading, 171*(1), 5–17.

Gillespie, M. (1991). *Becoming authors: The social context of literacy for adult beginning writers.* Unpublished doctoral dissertation, University of Massachusetts, Amherst.

Glasgow, J. N. (1994). Accommodating learning styles in prison writing classes. *Journal of Reading, 38*(3), 188–194.

Goethel, J. (1995, Nov.–Dec.). Writing: The golden thread in family learning. *Adult Learning,* 26–27.

Graff, H. J. (1987). *The legacies of literacy: Continuities and contradictions in Western culture and society.* Bloomington, IL: University of Illinois Press.

Graves, D. (1975). An examination of the writing processes of seven-year-old children. *Research in the Teaching of English, 9,* 227–241.

Guerra, J. C. (1996). "It is as if my story repeats itself." Life, language, and literacy in a Chicago comunidad. *Education and Urban Society, 29*(1), 35–53.

Halbrook, A. (1999). Formulaic writing: Blueprint for mediocrity. *GED Items, 3,* 8–9.

Hamilton, M., & Merrifield, J. (2000). Adult learning and literacy in the United Kingdom. In J. Comings, B. Garner, & C. Smith (Eds.), *The annual review of adult learning and literacy: Volume 1* (pp. 243–303). San Francisco: Jossey-Bass.

Hart-Landsberg, S., & Reder, S. (1997). Teamwork and literacy: Teaching and learning at Hardy Industries. In G. Hull (Ed.), *Changing work, changing workers: Critical perspectives on language, literacy, and skills* (pp. 351–381). Albany: State University of New York Press.

Hayes, J. R. (1996). A new framework for understanding cognition and affect in writing. In C. M. Levy & S. Ransdell (Eds.), *The science of*

*writing: Theories, methods, individual differences, and applications.*
Mahwah, NJ: Erlbaum.

Healy, M. K., & Barr, M. (1991). Language across the curriculum. In J.
Flood, J. Jensen, D. Lapp, & J. R. Squire (Eds.), *Handbook of research on teaching in the language arts* (pp. 820–826). New York: Macmillan.

Heath, S. B. (1983). *Ways with words: Language, life, and work in communities and classrooms.* Cambridge, England: Cambridge University Press.

Hedgcock, J., & Atkinson, D. (1993). Differing reading-writing relationships in L1 and L2 literacy development? *TESOL Quarterly, 30,* 329–333.

Heller, C. (1997). *Until we are strong together: Voices from the Tenderloin.* New York: Teachers College Press.

Himley, M., Madden, C., Hoffman, A., & Penrod, D. (1996). Answering the world: Adult literacy and co-authoring. *Written Communication, 13*(2), 163–189.

Hopey, C. E., Harvey-Morgan, J., & Rethemeyer, R. K. (1996). *Technology and adult literacy: Findings from a survey on technology use in adult literacy programs* (Report No. TR96–12). Philadelphia: University of Pennsylvania, National Center on Adult Literacy.

Hornberger, N. H., & Hardman, J. (1994). Literacy as cultural practice and cognitive skill: Biliteracy in an ESL class and a GED program. In D. Spener (Ed.), *Adult biliteracy in the United States* (pp. 147–169). McHenry, IL: Delta Systems and the Center for Applied Linguistics.

Hull, G. (Ed.). (1997). *Changing work, changing workers: Critical perspectives on language, literacy, and skills.* Albany: State University of New York Press.

Kazemek, F. (1984). "I want to be a tencra to help penp t_": Writing for adult beginning readers. *Journal of Reading, 27,* 614–619.

Kennedy Manzo, K. (2000, Mar. 15). NAEP drops long term writing data. *Education Week.*

Kent, T. (Ed.). (1999). *Post process theory: Beyond the writing-process paradigm.* Carbondale: Southern Illinois University Press.

Kerka, S. (1996). *Journal writing and adult learning.* Columbus, OH: ERIC Clearinghouse on Adult, Career, and Vocational Education, ERIC Digest Series.

Klassen, C. (1991). Bilingual language use by low-education Latin American newcomers. In D. Barton & R. Ivanič (Eds.), *Writing in the community* (pp. 38–57). Thousand Oaks, CA: Sage.

Langer, J., & Applebee, A. N. (1987). *How writing shapes thinking: A study of teaching and learning.* Urbana, IL: National Council of Teachers of English.

Leki, I. (1992). *Understanding ESL Writers: A guide for teachers.* Portsmouth, NH: Boynton/Cook.

Liberman, I. Y., Rubin, H., Duques, S., & Carlisle, J. (1985). Linguistic abilities and spelling proficiency in kindergartners and adult poor spellers. In D. B. Gray & J. F. Kavanagh (Eds.), *Biobehavioral measures of dyslexia* (pp. 163–176). Parkton, MD: York Press.

Lytle, S. L. (1990). Living literacy: Rethinking development in adulthood. *Linguistics and Education, 3,* 109–138.

Mace, J. (Ed.). (1995). *Literacy, language, and community publishing.* Clevedon, England: Multilingual Matters.

Marcel, T. (1980). Phonological awareness and phonological representation: Investigation of a specific spelling problem. In U. Frith (Ed.), *Cognitive processes in spelling* (pp. 373–403). Orlando, FL: Academic Press.

Matsuda, P. K. (1999). Composition studies and ESL writing: A disciplinary division of labor. *College Communication and Composition, 50*(4), 699–721.

McGrail, L. (1995). Memories of Mami in the family literacy class. In G. Weinstein & E. Quintero (Eds.), *Immigrant learners and their families* (pp. 77–89). McHenry, IL: Delta Systems and the Center for Applied Linguistics.

Merrifield, J. (2000). *Equipped for the future research report.* Washington, DC: National Institute for Literacy.

Merrifield, J., Bingman, M. B., Hemphill, D., & deMarrais, K. (1997). *Life at the margins: Literacy, language, and technology in everyday life.* New York: Teachers College Press.

Mezirow, J. (1991). *Transformative dimensions in adult learning.* San Francisco: Jossey-Bass.

Mikulecky, L. (1998). Adjusting school writing curricula to reflect extended workplace writing. In M. S. Garay & S. A. Bernhardt (Eds.), *Expanding literacies: English teaching and the workplace* (pp. 201–223). Albany: State University of New York Press.

Morley, D., & Worpole, K. (Eds.). (1982). *Republic of letters: Working class writing and local publishing.* London: Comedia Publishing Group.

Nash, A., Carson, A., Rhum, M., McGrail, L., & Gomez-Sanford, R. (1992). *Talking shop: A curriculum sourcebook for participatory adult ESL.* McHenry, IL: Delta Systems and the Center for Applied Linguistics.

National Assessment of Educational Progress. (1998). *Writing framework and specifications for the 1998 National Assessment of Educational Progress.* (ERIC Document and Reproduction Service ED 1.2:N Z1/10)

Norton, M., & Campbell, P. (1998). *Learning for our health: A resource for participatory literacy and health education.* Edmonton, Canada: Learning Centre Literacy Association.

Padak, G., & Padak, N. (1988). Writing instruction for adults: Present practice and future directions. *Lifelong Learning, 12*(3), 4–7.

Perl, S. (1979). The composing processes of unskilled college writers. *College Composition and Communication, 31,* 363–369.

Peyton, J. K. (1993). Listening to students' voices: Publishing students' writing for other students to read. In J. Crandall & J. K. Peyton (Eds.), *Approaches to adult ESL literacy instruction* (pp. 59–74). McHenry, IL: Delta Systems and the Center for Applied Linguistics.

Peyton, J. K., & Staton, J. (Eds.). (1991). *Writing our lives: Reflections on dialogue journal writing with adults learning English.* Englewood Cliffs, NJ: Prentice Hall.

Purcell-Gates, V. (1993). I ain't never read my *own* words before. *Journal of Reading, 37*(3), 210–219.

Purcell-Gates, V. (1995). *Other people's words: The cycle of low literacy.* Cambridge, MA: Harvard University Press.

Raimes, A. (1998). Teaching writing. *Annual Review of Applied Linguistics, 18,* 142–167.

Ramirez, J. D. (1992). Executive summary of the final report: Longitudinal study of structured English immersion strategy, early-exit and late-exit transitional bilingual education programs for language minority children. *Bilingual Research Journal, 16,* 1–62.

Rance-Roney, J. (1995). *Transitioning adult ESL learners to academic programs.* Washington, DC: Adjunct Clearinghouse for ESL Literacy Education. (ERIC Digest No. ED 385 173)

Read, C. (1975). *Children's categorizations of speech sounds in English.* Urbana, IL: National Council of Teachers in English.

Reder, S. (1987). Comparative aspects of functional literacy development: Three ethnic American communities. In D. Wagner (Ed.), *The future of literacy in a changing world* (pp. 250–270). New York: Pergamon Press.

Reder, S. (2000). Adult literacy and postsecondary education students: Overlapping populations and learning trajectories. In J. Comings,

B. Garner, & C. Smith (Eds.), *Annual review of adult learning and literacy: Volume 1* (pp. 111–157). San Francisco: Jossey-Bass.

Reid, J. M. (1993). *Teaching ESL writing.* Englewood Cliffs, NJ: Prentice Hall.

Rhoder, C. A., & French, J. N. (1995). Participant generated text: A vehicle for workplace literacy. *Journal of Adult and Adolescent Literacy, 39*(2), 110–118.

Robinson, J. (1990). *Conversations on the written word: Essays on language and literacy.* Portsmouth, NH: Boynton/Cook.

Rose, M. (1980). Rigid rules, inflexible plans, and the stifling of language: A cognitivist's analysis of writer's block. *College Composition and Communication, 34*(4), 398–400.

Rose, M. (1989). *Lives on the boundaries: The struggles and achievements of America's underprepared.* New York: Macmillan.

Rosen, D. (2000). Using electronic technology in adult literacy education. In J. Comings, B. Garner, & C. Smith (Eds.), *Annual review of adult learning and literacy: Volume 1* (pp. 304–316). San Francisco: Jossey-Bass.

Russell, M. (1999). The assumptions we make: How learners and teachers understand writing. *Focus on Basics, 3*(D), 20–23.

Scheffer, L. (1995). *Literacy development among homeless adults: Effects of participation in an electronic writing community.* Unpublished doctoral dissertation, University of Pennsylvania, Philadelphia.

Schneider, P. (Ed.). (1989). *In our own voices.* Amherst, MA: Amherst Writers and Artists Press.

Scribner, S., & Cole, M. (1981). *The psychology of literacy.* Cambridge, MA: Harvard University Press.

Shaughnessy, M. P. (1977). *Errors and expectations.* New York: Oxford University Press.

Silva, T., Leki, I., & Carson, J. (1997). Broadening the perspective of mainstream composition studies: Some thoughts from the margins. *Written Communication, 14,* 398–428.

Sommers, N. (1980). Revision strategies of student writers and experienced adult writers. *College Composition and Communication, 31,* 378–388.

Spack, R. (1997). The acquisition of academic literacy in a second language. *Written Communication, 14,* 3–62.

Stein, S. G. (1995). *Equipped for the Future: A customer-driven vision for adult literacy and lifelong learning.* Washington, DC: National Institute for Literacy.

Stein, S. G. (2000). *Equipped for the Future content standards.* Washington, DC: National Institute for Literacy.

Street, B. (1984). *Literacy in theory and practice.* London: Cambridge University Press.

Street, B. (1995). *Social literacies: Critical approaches to literacy in development, ethnography, and education.* Harlow, Essex, England: Longman.

Szwed, J. F. (1981). The ethnography of literacy. In N. F. Whitman (Ed.), *Writing: The nature, development, and teaching of written communication.* Mahwah, NJ: Erlbaum.

Taylor, D., & Dorsey-Gaines, C. (1988). *Growing up literate: Learning from inner-city families.* Portsmouth, NH: Heinemann.

Taylor, E. W. (1998). *The theory and practice of transformative learning: A critical review.* Columbus, OH: ERIC Clearinghouse on Adult, Career, and Vocational Education.

Taylor, K. K. (1987). Teaching writing in the GED program. *Lifelong Learning, 10*(4), 23–28.

Taylor, M. L. (1993). The language experience approach. In J. Crandall & J. K. Peyton (Eds.), *Approaches to adult ESL literacy instruction* (pp. 47–58). McHenry, IL: Delta Systems and the Center for Applied Linguistics.

Templeton, S., & Morris, D. (1999). Questions teachers ask about spelling. *Reading Research Quarterly, 34*(1), 102–112.

Tracy-Mumford, F. (2000). The year 1998 in review. In J. Comings, B. Garner, & C. Smith (Eds.), *Annual review of adult learning and literacy: Volume 1* (pp. 1–24). San Francisco: Jossey-Bass.

Van Duzer, C., & Berdan, R. (2000). Perspectives on assessment in adult ESOL instruction. In J. Comings, B. Garner, & C. Smith (Eds.), *Annual review of adult learning and literacy: Volume 1* (pp. 200–242). San Francisco: Jossey-Bass.

Viise, N. M. (1996). A study of the spelling development of adult literacy learners compared with that of classroom children. *Journal of Literacy Research, 28,* 561–587.

Wales, M. L. 1994. A language-experience approach (LEA) in adult immigrant literacy problems in Australia. *Journal of Reading, 38*(3), 200–208.

Weinstein, G. (1992). Literacy and social processes: A community in transition. In B. Street (Ed.), *Cross-cultural approaches to literacy* (pp. 279–293). Cambridge, England: Cambridge University Press.

Willinsky, J. (1990). *The new literacy: Redefining reading and writing in schools.* New York: Routledge.

Wolfram, W. (1994). Bidialectal literacy in the United States. In D. Spener, (Ed.), *Adult biliteracy in the United States* (pp. 71–98). McHenry, IL: Delta Systems and the Center for Applied Linguistics.

Worthy, M. J., & Viise, N. (1996). Morphological, phonological, and orthographic differences between the spelling of normally achieving children and basic literacy adults. *Reading and Writing: An Interdisciplinary Journal, 8,* 138–159.

Wrigley, H. S. (1998). Knowledge in action: The promise of project-based education. *Focus on Basics, 2*(D), 13–18.

Young, D. (1997). *Adult basic education: Literacy, learning, and instruction.* Unpublished doctoral dissertation, University of Michigan, Ann Arbor.

Zamel, V. (1997). Toward a model of transculturation. *TESOL Quarterly, 31,* 341–352.

# CHAPTER FOUR

# Time to Reframe Politics and Practices in Correctional Education

*Stefan LoBuglio*

> *We must accept the reality that to confine offenders*
> *behind walls without trying to change them is an expensive*
> *folly with short-term benefits—a "winning of battles*
> *while losing the war." . . . [We must] provide a decent*
> *setting for expanded educational and vocational training.*
>
> —Warren Burger, former chief justice
> of the U.S. Supreme Court

> *In the hectic pace of the world today, there is no time for*
> *meditation, or for deep thought. A prisoner has time that*
> *he can put to good use. I'd put prison second to college as*
> *the best place for a man to go if he needs to do some think-*
> *ing. If he's motivated, in prison he can change his life.*
>
> —Malcolm X

There is a compelling logic to provide expansive education and training programs for adults under correctional supervision. In theory, these programs can prepare an underused pool of workers at a time when the nation is facing significant labor shortages. Uniquely, correctional education programs hold the promise of addressing the poor education and literacy skills of a significant percentage of individuals, particularly young, black, and Hispanic adult males. By improving the opportunity for these individuals to secure and retain employment in better-paying jobs, society could reap huge long-term benefits in terms of greater family stability, lower rates of child poverty, reduced welfare payments, lowered crime rates, improved civic life, along with many social indicators of well-being. Correctional education programs have found advocates in such distinctly different leaders as Warren Burger, the conservative former chief justice of the Supreme Court, and Malcolm X, the militant civil rights leader, but the logic of offering these programs remains captive to the ever-changing and unpredictable forces of politics.[1]

In 1994, for example, Oregon voters overwhelmingly approved the Prison Reform and Inmate Work Act, a ballot measure amending the state constitution to require that inmates engage in "meaningful work or in workforce development activities" for a minimum of forty hours a week (Oregon Department of Corrections, 1998). This "get-tough" action has had the effect of rejuvenating education and other treatment programming in the state's correctional system over the past six years. In the same year, President Clinton signed the omnibus crime bill, which restricted state and federal inmates' eligibility to secure federal financial assistance in the form of Pell grants for college programs while residing in prison. A national survey published three years later found that "66 percent of the reporting correctional systems indicated that the loss of Pell grants eliminated most if not all of their college course opportunities for inmates" (*Corrections Compendium*, 1997).

This chapter, an overview of the politics and practices of adult correctional education programs, aims to explain why, after a two-decade spending spree on new prisons in this country, resources for correctional education programs have significantly lagged the rise in the inmate population, which has tripled in size (Maguire & Pastore, 1999) and serves longer sentences than before. It explores whether the public policy shift in correctional philosophy toward incapacitation (the belief that the main purpose of prisons are to remove dangerous individuals from the street) and away from a rehabilitative focus (which some contend never existed) represents an overreaction of political leaders to prevailing public attitudes. Public opinion polling over this same time period has documented strong support for both rehabilitation and incapacitation (Flanagan & Longmire, 1996). I argue that correctional education programs can garner new support when framed as part of an accountability strategy, similar to the Oregon experience, along with the traditional framing of these programs as issues of inmates' rights. Sustained support for correctional education programs will occur only with solid research that demonstrates that these programs reduce recidivism rates—that is, the probability that offenders will be arrested, convicted, or incarcerated for future crimes.

## A PRIMER ON CORRECTIONS AND ITS POPULATION

Corrections as a field is little noticed or understood by the general public. While most Americans are at least familiar with the workings of other criminal justice institutions, such as the police or the court system, comparatively few have direct contact with jails, prisons, probation, and parole, the exception being those in urban minority communities. Although the term *corrections* is often thought to be interchangeable with the term *prisons*, it actually refers to a variety of agencies and institutions that provide some form of court-mandated supervision of adults suspected or convicted of criminal offenses. These institutions include prisons and jails, which are both characterized by secure correctional facilities, and probation and parole, which are referred to as community corrections because these programs supervise convicted criminal offenders who reside and work outside correctional facilities. Intermediate sanctions, such as day reporting centers, are a form of community corrections that seek to bridge the gap between secure and community-based supervision programs and are a rapidly growing part of corrections.

Jails are typically short-term correctional facilities run locally by city and county correctional departments. They both detain individuals awaiting trial and incarcerate convicted offenders who have been sentenced to serve time in jail, are awaiting sentencing to prison, or are serving time for a parole or probation violation. Jails house approximately 70,000 inmates held under state and federal correctional jurisdictions. In addition, they perform other functions, such as temporarily holding juveniles or mentally ill people awaiting movement to appropriate facilities (Beck, 2000b). Time in detention in a jail can range from several hours to years. At the close of 1998, the nation's 3,400 jails held almost 600,000 inmates, and the number of total admissions to jails was 15 million (see Table 4.1). Most jails, owing to the short-term stay of their inmates, offer limited educational

| Correction Status | Total | By Gender | | By Racial and Ethnic Background | | | Released |
| | | Male | Female | White | Black | Hispanic[a] | |
|---|---|---|---|---|---|---|---|
| Probation | 3,418 | 2,700 | 718 | 2,187 | 1,196 | 513 | 1,555 |
| Parole | 705 | 620 | 85 | 388 | 310 | 148 | 424 |
| Prison | 1,233[b,c] | 1,149 | 84 | 592 | 604 | 222[d] | 546[e] |
| Jail | 592[b,c,f] | 530 | 62 | 248 | 248 | 94[a] | 15,000[g] |
| Total | 5,948 | 4,999 | 949 | 3,415 | 2,358 | 977 | N.A. |
| Percentage of total | 100 | 84 | 16 | 57 | 40 | 16 | |

Table 4.1. Adult Correctional Population, 1998 Estimates (in thousands).

*Sources:* Bonczar & Glaze, 1999; Beck & Mumola, 1999; Beck, 2000a, 2000b; Perkins, Stephan, & Beck, 1995.

[a]Hispanic numbers include those of Latino background who identify as both black and white racially except for the jail population statistics.

[b]In 1998 1,302,019 offenders were under state and federal prison authorities. Approximately 70,000 of these offenders were held in local jails.

[c]As of June 1999, 1,254,577 inmates in state and federal prisons; 605,943 in jail.

[d]The percentage of Hispanics incarcerated was taken from the year-end percentage for 1997 and applied to the 1998 population figures.

[e]Projected to rise to 585,400 in 2000.

[f]An additional 72,385 offenders were under the supervision of jail authorities held outside jail facilities.

[g]No release data could be found for jails. However, in 1993, more than 13 million individuals were admitted to jails across the country at a time when the jail inmate population was 459,804. Most are released to the community, while others are transferred to correctional agencies.

programs, if any at all. However, some jails do have excellent educational programs. The Orange County Jail in Florida has a comprehensive educational program, complete with vocational programs, for an inmate population with an average stay of only sixty days (Finn, 1997).

Prisons hold convicted prisoners for longer periods of time and serve different inmate populations with different security levels and specialized needs. Maximum-security prisons incarcerate the most violent and serious offenders and are fortified institutions with redundant security measures that carefully control all inmate movement within the facility. Minimum-security facilities typically house less serious offenders or offenders at the end of a longer sentence who have demonstrated good institutional behavior. These facilities may lack a perimeter security fence or wall and provide inmates with much discretion as to their whereabouts and activities. They can include work and education release programs that allow inmates to leave the facility in the morning and return in the late afternoon. Specialized prisons have unique functions, such as detaining inmates who will be deported or incarcerating inmates with special physical or mental medical needs.

At the close of 1998, the nation's estimated fifteen hundred prisons held more than 1.2 million individuals convicted of crimes; 546,000 offenders were released during that year (see Table 4.1). More than 90 percent of these inmates were incarcerated in state facilities. The Federal Bureau of Prisons (FBOP) runs ninety-six facilities and incarcerates about 140,000 inmates, fewer than each of the states of California and Texas. Nationally, the average expected length of time to be served for an inmate entering prison grew to forty-three months in 1997 (Beck & Mumola, 1999). In the FBOP, the median sentence is sixty-eight months.

Prisons provide the settings for the most fully developed education programs in corrections. Most correctional education programs fall into the following categories: enrichment programs (art, literature, creative writing), higher education academic programs (liberal arts), postsecondary vocational training programs, General Educational Development (GED) preparatory programs (a few offer alternative high school diploma programs), adult basic education/English for speakers of other languages (ABE/ESOL) programs, and life skills programs. (Life skills is a recent catch-all category that includes such short-term programs as parenting skills, job readiness, anger management, and cognitive skills, a psychoeducational program that attempts to address "thinking deficits.") The order of presentation of these categories reflects the relative degree of institutional and political support that these programs generally garner, enrichment programs enjoying the least and life skills enjoying the most.

Federal legislation in 1994 eliminated many higher education programs based in prisons. Subsequent legislation also restricts offenders convicted of certain drug offenses from receiving Pell grants even after their release from prison. Other important changes include mandatory literacy laws in twenty-six states and at the federal level and restrictions on the use of federal financial aid for offenders. Mandatory literacy laws generally require inmates entering a correctional system who read below a specific education threshold to participate in educational programming for a specified period of time or until they meet the threshold requirements. Most states have chosen the eighth grade as the literacy threshold. Finally, judicial action resulting from class action lawsuits filed on behalf of inmates has mandated a certain minimum level of programming in some correctional systems and individual prisons. The U.S. Supreme Court has generously interpreted Section 1983 of the U.S. Code to allow prisoners to sue correctional officials if prison conditions fail to meet "constitutional standards of physical security, adequate medical treatment, freedom of religious expression, and so forth. Section 1983 litigation is a major portion of the U.S. District Courts' civil caseloads. One in every ten civil lawsuits is a Section 1983 lawsuit" (Hanson & Daley, 1994).

The largest group of offenders under correctional supervision are those on probation, 3.4 million at the close of 1998, who reside outside prison and jail facilities. Although there is a federal system of probation, the vast majority of probationers are supervised by a state-level department of probation that is often tied to the court system. Probation is a sanction administered by a judge in addition to or in lieu of a sentence of incarceration. This program requires probationers to report regularly to an assigned probation officer about their progress in a prescribed treatment plan that usually involves employment. The duration of probation, frequency of reporting, and mode of reporting (in person or by telephone) depend on the offender's criminal offense and history. Drug testing and electronic monitoring devices that track individuals at all times are security measures frequently employed to ensure compliance with the plan, which is stipulated by the court. Failure to comply with any aspect of this plan results in a technical violation of probation and can lead to the surrender of the probationer for another appearance before the judge, who can then remand the individual for either more intensive probation or to a prison.

Parole is the most politically malleable of all correctional programs and the only one in which the relative share of the correctional population has decreased recently (Maguire & Pastore, 1999). Several states and the federal government have abolished parole (Tonry, 1999). This program, administered by a state parole board whose members are appointed directly by the governor, is offered to selected prisoners who have demonstrated exemplary institutional behavior and pose minimal risk to the public safety based on their criminal offense and history. Inmates who receive parole are allowed to serve the remainder of their sentence while residing in the community. At the close of 1998, more than 700,000 offenders were on parole supervision (see Table 4.1). The supervision process for parole is similar to that of probation.

Because of prison overcrowding, the dividing lines between institutional (prisons and jails) and community corrections (probation and parole) and among local, state, and federal systems has blurred, and many agencies have collaborated to create a host of intermediate sanctions that provide intensive supervision of offenders in the community (Flanagan & Longmire, 1996). These programs attempt to provide courts and correctional agencies with a sanction between prison, which is thought to be overly harsh and ineffective for some inmates, and standard probation and parole, which are considered lax. One example of such a sanction is the day reporting center, which allows offenders to live in the community but requires them to report to a central location every day for treatment programming as well as frequent drug testing. These centers divert offenders from prison and are used by probation departments for their high-risk probationers and by correctional agencies for their low-risk inmates. Over the next several years, intermediate-sanction programs are likely to grow rapidly as offenders with mandatory sentences continue to crowd out of prison nonviolent, nonhabituated offenders, many of whom have significant substance abuse problems.

Community corrections programs typically do not run their own education programs and rarely mandate education for those they supervise. Typically probation and parole officers require offenders to work and, based on the nature of the offense, to participate in a specified treatment program, such as substance abuse, anger management, or sex offender counseling. Supervising officers for these agencies explain that few judges are willing to remand an offender who is working and participating in specified treatment programs to prison for failure to attend an educational program. Furthermore, they express concern about "overprogramming" offenders who are not only required to work and attend treatment programs but to manage the day-to-day responsibilities of housing, transportation, and, sometimes, child care. The exceptions are younger probationers and parolees (under twenty-one years of age), who may be mandated to attend school. At the state level, departments of corrections, departments of probation, and the state parole boards are often different agencies that fall under different lines of authority. This fragmented system has a deleterious effect on correctional education programs as the correctional population moves among these institutions. An accused offender may begin his correctional experience in a local jail, wind up in a state prison after receiving a criminal conviction, and get parole for good behavior at the same time that he serves a sentence of probation, which might require him to attend a day reporting center. As offenders move within and between these institutions, they rarely are provided a consistent and uniform level of educational programming.

## Demographics

At the close of 1998, nearly 6 million offenders were under correctional supervision: almost 1.9 million inmates were in prison or jail, and more than 4 million offenders were on probation or parole (this figure increased to 6.3 million at the close of 1999, according to statistics released as this chapter was prepared for publication). Table 4.1 provides estimates of the corrections population at the close of 1998 by correctional status, race, Hispanic origin, and gender. Table 4.1 also lists the number of offenders released in a given year by correctional category to illustrate the huge number of inmates released from custody each year. Table 4.2 provides the latest inmate census, taken on June 30, 1999, of those incarcerated in the nation's prisons and jails by gender, race, Hispanic origin, and age grouping. It shows that almost 11 percent of black males, 4 percent of Hispanic males, and 1.5 percent of white males in their twenties and early thirties in the U.S. population were incarcerated on that day (Beck, 2000b). Almost one in three black males (32 percent) in the age group twenty to twenty-nine is currently under the supervision of some form of corrections (Sentencing Project, 1999), far more than the 649,000 black males aged fourteen to thirty-four who were enrolled in two- and four-year public and private institutions in 1998 (Snyder & Hoffman, 2000).

Also, Table 4.2 shows that black females in this same age group are also incarcerated at a much higher rate than white and Hispanic females. As a category, female offenders now constitute almost 16 percent of the correctional population, and their numbers have doubled since 1990. Those incarcerated are often parents who leave children behind in the care of family and foster care. In 1999, almost 2 million children had a parent or close relative in jail or prison, and an additional 5 million had had a parent incarcerated in a jail or prison in the past (Butterfield, 1999). Combined, these children make up a very large percentage of the estimated 14 million children in poverty in this country.

| Age | Male | | | | Female | | | |
|---|---|---|---|---|---|---|---|---|
| | Total[a] | White[b] | Black[b] | Hispanic | Total[a] | White[b] | Black[b] | Hispanic |
| Total | 1,261 | 630 | 4,617 | 1,802 | 106 | 53 | 375 | 142 |
| 18–19 | 1,868 | 885 | 5,787 | 2,524 | 92 | 63 | 224 | 94 |
| 20–24 | 3,130 | 1,462 | 10,407 | 4,141 | 205 | 121 | 524 | 284 |
| 25–29 | 3,363 | 1,535 | 12,334 | 4,220 | 303 | 154 | 956 | 357 |
| 30–34 | 3,193 | 1,674 | 11,225 | 3,844 | 370 | 185 | 1,362 | 372 |
| 35–39 | 2,474 | 1,302 | 9,548 | 2,898 | 257 | 128 | 940 | 308 |
| 40–44 | 1,699 | 897 | 6,224 | 2,746 | 144 | 73 | 512 | 203 |
| 45–54 | 896 | 522 | 3,399 | 1,521 | 63 | 33 | 214 | 133 |
| 55 and over | 193 | 129 | 611 | 460 | 8 | 5 | 27 | 11 |

Table 4.2. **Number of Inmates in State or Federal Prisons and Local Jails, per 100,000 Residents, as of June 30, 1999.**

*Source:* Beck, 2000b, Table 12.

*Note:* Based on estimates of the U.S. resident population on July 1, 1999, and adjusted for the 1990 census undercount.

[a]Includes American Indians, Alaska Natives, Asians, Native Hawaiians, and other Pacific Islanders.

[b]Excludes Hispanics.

## Literacy Needs of Offenders

The 1992 National Adult Literacy Survey (NALS) provides the most comprehensive assessment of the literacy skills and educational backgrounds of prisoners in state and federal prisons in the past twenty years. NALS researchers interviewed and assessed 1,150 inmates selected randomly from eighty state and federal prisons across the country as part of a nationwide survey to measure the literacy skills of the nation's general household population. Although detainees, probationers, and parolees were not surveyed, the results can be generalized with some caution to these other offender populations. The instruments used for the inmate interviews were the same as for the general population, although additional background information was collected from the inmates on their criminal history, participation in prison training and education programs, and prior work experience. Inmates' literacy skills were assessed using the now-familiar NALS rating system of five proficiency levels in each of three different scales: prose literacy, document literacy, and quantitative literacy (Haigler, O'Connor, & Campbell, 1994).

The NALS showed that about 51 percent of prisoners had their high school diplomas or equivalents, compared with 76 percent of the general population. Overall, 11 percent of inmates self-reported a learning disability compared with 3 percent of the general population. Seventy percent of prisoners performed in the two lowest levels on each of the three scales, performing most poorly on the quantitative literacy scale. This means that they demonstrated abilities to read and compute but could not apply these skills to situations calling for them to interpret a train schedule or write a letter to resolve a billing dispute. By comparison, approximately 50 percent of the general population performed at these two levels. Table 4.3 compares the performance of prison and general populations on the three literacy scales. In terms of education program participation, the percentage of inmates enrolled in basic adult education classes, 7 to 15 percent, is quite small compared with the percentage of inmates who, as demonstrated by NALS, could benefit from enrollment in such classes (National Institute for Literacy Web site; Haigler et al., 1994).

Most of the difference in literacy skills between the prison and the general population is explained by differences in sex, age, race and ethnic identification, and educational attainment. Prisoners are

| | | | Levels and Average Proficiency | | | | | |
|---|---|---|---|---|---|---|---|---|
| Literacy Scales by Population | n | WGT n (/1000) | Level 1 225 or lower RPCT (SE) | Level 2 226 to 275 RPCT (SE) | Level 3 276 to 325 RPCT (SE) | Level 4 326 to 375 RPCT (SE) | Level 5 376 or higher RPCT (SE) | Average Proficiency PROF (SE) |
| *Prose scale* | | | | | | | | |
| Prison | 1,147 | 766 | 31 (1.7) | 37 (2.0) | 26 (1.6) | 6 (0.8) | 0 (0.2) | 246 (1.9) |
| Household | 24,944 | 190,524 | 21 (0.4) | 27 (0.6) | 32 (0.7) | 17 (0.4) | 3 (0.2) | 273 (0.6) |
| *Document scale* | | | | | | | | |
| Prison | 1,147 | 766 | 33 (2.1) | 38 (2.1) | 25 (1.5) | 4 (0.9) | 0 (0.2) | 240 (2.2) |
| Household | 24,944 | 190,524 | 23 (0.4) | 28 (0.5) | 31 (0.5) | 15 (0.4) | 3 (0.2) | 267 (0.7) |
| *Quantitative scale* | | | | | | | | |
| Prison | 1,147 | 766 | 40 (1.9) | 32 (2.2) | 22 (1.9) | 6 (1.0) | 1 (0.4) | 236 (3.1) |
| Household | 24,944 | 190,524 | 22 (0.5) | 25 (0.6) | 31 (0.6) | 17 (0.3) | 4 (0.2) | 271 (0.7) |

Table 4.3. Prison and Household Populations, NALS Proficiencies.

Source: Haigler et al., 1994, p. 19, Table 2.3; *National Adult Literacy Survey,* 1992.

Note: n = sample size; WGT n = population size estimate per 1,000 (the sample sizes for subpopulations many not add up to the total sample sizes owing to missing data); RPCT = row percentage estimate; PROF = average proficiency estimate; (SE) = standard error of the estimate (the true population value can be said to be within 2 standard errors of the ample estimate with 95 percent certainty). Percentages less than 0.5 are rounded to 0.

overwhelmingly young, minority males with a higher percentage of high school dropouts and a lower percentage of college experience than the general population (Table 4.4). When these factors are taken into consideration, the "performance of the prison population on the three scales is comparable to that of the household population" (Haigler et al., 1994). (Table 4.3 shows the NALS scores for the inmate and the general household population tested.)

Inmates who reported having high school diplomas performed at lower literacy proficiencies than adults in the general population who reported having diplomas. By contrast, inmates and adults in the general population who reported having a GED demonstrated comparable literacy proficiencies (Haigler et al., 1994). Also, on average, white prisoners performed at higher proficiency levels than black inmates, who performed at higher levels than Hispanic inmates. Perhaps owing to the much larger percentages incarcerated relative to their population, black and Hispanic inmates performed at skill levels comparable to their counterparts in the general population, while white prisoners demonstrated lower skill proficiencies than the average white householder (Haigler et al., 1994). Finally, prisoners attained lower levels of education than their parents, and their parents attained lower levels of formal education than others in the general population.[2]

## ISSUES OF CONCERN IN CORRECTIONAL EDUCATION

In the national conversation about crime, the prevailing punitive attitude toward offenders obscures the long tradition that has considered the potential of prisons to reform individuals. The terms *corrections* and *penitentiaries* capture some of the religious and humanistic goals

| Characteristic | Inmate Population | General Household Population |
|---|---|---|
| Male | 94 percent | 48 percent |
| Minority | 65 percent | 24 percent |
| 35 years old and under | 65 percent | 40 percent |
| High school diploma/GED | 51 percent | 76 percent |
| Post–high school diploma education | 20 percent | 45 percent |

Table 4.4. Inmate and General Household Population Characteristics.

*Source:* Haigler, O'Connor, & Campbell, 1994, p. 18, Table 2.2.

of the earliest proponents of correctional education, such as William Rogers, a Quaker clergyman who began teaching prisoners at Philadelphia's Walnut Street Jail in 1789. The emergence of a more formalized correctional education program is often credited to Zebulon Brockway, the superintendent of the Elmira (New York) Reformatory in the 1880s and 1890s. He assembled a professional staff of artisans and teachers and provided individualized academic and vocational instructional plans and physical regimens to prepare his students to lead successful lives on release. This systemic approach to correctional education treatment was incorporated in Austin Mac-Cormick's 1929 book, *The Education of Adult Prisoners,* one of the seminal texts in the field. MacCormick was also the founder and first president of the field's professional organization, the Correctional Education Association (CEA).

These early advocates for correctional education subscribed to the medical model of corrections, which views individuals' engagement in criminal activity as a function of physical, environmental, mental, and vocational deficits. Viewed in this context, individual treatment plans that included correctional education and other rehabilitative programs would cure criminal behavior. An alternative view is "the balanced philosophy," which considers rehabilitation programming as one of four equally valuable correctional goals, the others being punishment, deterrence, and incapacitation. This approach recognizes that an inmate's ability to succeed after release is contingent on many factors beyond the control of treatment programs. It supports programs based on their ability to contribute to the orderliness of the institution by keeping inmates engaged in constructive activities while assisting inmates who have the motivation to change (Roberts, 1996).

At the risk of generalization, it does seem that in the 1970s many correctional systems, following the lead of the FBOP, the agency under the U.S. Department of Justice that administers the federal prison system, shifted toward the more pragmatic balanced philosophy that continues to reign to this day. This shift is ascribed to many factors, including the publication and wide dissemination of a 1974 report casting doubt on the effectiveness of prison rehabilitation treatment programs (Martinson, 1974) and a reaction to turbulent prison disturbances such as occurred in New York's Attica prison in 1971. Of course, this shift was part of the rise of social and fiscal conservatism in the nation during the 1970s, which was fueled by the distressed economic conditions, a reaction to the social disorder of the 1960s, and the perceived failures of the much touted Great Society programs of President Lyndon B. Johnson.

The most persistent and long-standing challenge that correctional education programs face is the significant decline in relative resources given the sixfold increase in the institutional correctional population since 1973 (Maguire & Pastore, 1998). In a 1994 survey, nearly half of the correctional systems claimed to have cut educational programming in the previous five years (Lillis, 1994). Three years later, a similar survey revealed a funding increase of only 7 percent, which did not keep pace with inflation or the growth of the inmate population.[3] While the nation's spending on corrections has soared, prison administrators are under great fiscal pressure to reduce the per diem cost to incarcerate inmates. Correctional education and rehabilitative programs are often seen as discretionary expenses that can be reduced. The correctional education programs that are in place are subject to the unique correctional environment. For instance, many programs lose students to other programs such as work details that might offer financial benefits or the opportunity to earn prisoners more time off their sentences for good behavior. Correctional education programs depend on the cooperation of correctional officers who let the inmates out of their living units and monitor classroom activities along with performing a host of other duties. Wardens and superintendents who value rehabilitative programs make sure that the incentives are properly structured and that correctional staff willingly and consistently ensure the smooth operation of these programs. Institutions that have top prison administrators who are indifferent to rehabilitation programs and are plagued by labor-management disputes often have poorly functioning programs that are cancelled for a variety of security reasons.

In corrections today, the fluidity of the offender population is also an obstacle to education. At the end of 1998, the country's state and federal prisons were operating at between 113 percent and 127 percent of their rated capacities (Beck & Mumola, 1999), and the scarcity of bed space has led to increased shuffling of inmates between different living units within facilities, between secure facilities within a correctional system, between secure and community correctional programs, and even between different correctional systems. In a much publicized case in 1997, the Massachusetts Department of Corrections flew 140 inmates in the dead of night to prisons in Texas, where there was a surplus of cell space. Although offenders are serving longer sentences—the average length of sentence for inmates released from state correctional facilities in 1997 was almost 25 percent higher (twenty-seven months) than that for those released from the system in 1990 (Beck & Mumola, 1999)—offenders are moving more frequently between institutions. This increased inmate movement has significantly impaired the ability of offenders to complete educational and vocational programs or even demonstrate progress. In a study commissioned in Texas in 1994, researchers found that the average offender did not have enough time remaining on his sentence to complete an adult educational or vocational program because of prior time served in a county jail waiting for a bed in the state prison (Criminal Justice Center, 1994).

Owing to increased inmate movement, substance abuse, anger management, and cognitive-behavioral programs have grown at the expense of basic literacy programs. These programs offer correctional administrators three attractive qualities: they appear to be more relevant to the immediate needs of the offender, they can be offered in relatively short periods of time (typically thirty to ninety days), and they are inexpensive and often taught by nonprofessional staff with minimal training (Fabiano, 1991; Gaes, Flanagan, Motiuk, & Stewart, 1998). The tendency to forgo traditional educational programs is particularly evident in the new intermediate-sanction programs, where offenders have much less time for treatment programming because of the employment requirements built into the programs.

Correctional education program content is also problematic when considered in the light of the changing needs of employers in the new service-oriented, technology-based economy. The national discussion about educational reform and the need to raise the skill levels of K–12 students and incumbent workers has almost completely bypassed corrections. While the skill levels required by employers for entry-level positions have increased markedly, the range of skills and credentials offered to offenders has actually narrowed with the elimination of many college and vocational programs. These programs gave inmates with secondary diplomas—approximately half of the total inmate population—the opportunity to develop the problem-solving, presentation, computer, high-level literacy, and numeracy skills that have been documented as necessary to succeed in today's economy (Murnane & Levy, 1996). Many correctional education programs have been pruned back to provide GED diploma preparation classes only and offer very little lower- or higher-level literacy instruction.

Exceptions to this trend are the correctional education systems in Ohio and Maryland, which have continued to fund college programs in spite of federal cutbacks.

The new service economy is also less hospitable to individuals with criminal histories. A job applicant's record of arrest, criminal conviction, and incarceration provides negative signals to a prospective employer that the individual may possess a host of undesirable attributes. As described in the economic literature on statistical discrimination (Spence, 1973), prospective employers might confer negative perceived group attributes for criminals on individual offenders for whom they have very little other information that might indicate true job potential at the time of screening. Increased tort liability concerns that penalize employers for hiring offenders, combined with greater access to and lowered costs of obtaining criminal records, have led increasing number of employers to conduct criminal checks and discriminate against offenders (Holzer, 1996; Boshier & Johnson, 1974; Albright & Furjen, 1996; Finn & Fontaine, 1985).

## POLITICS, PUBLIC PERCEPTIONS, AND RESEARCH

Efforts to reform the country's eighty-five thousand school districts have often been likened to the slow process of making course adjustments in a supertanker; political action in correctional education often takes the form of sinking the ship. In response to the mistaken perception that inmates were receiving federal financial aid for college at the expense of law-abiding adults, in 1994 Congress barred state and federal inmates from receiving Pell grants and thereby practically eliminated overnight the majority of prison-based higher education and vocational programs. Given that state correctional institutions supervise more than 95 percent of offenders, correctional education and other rehabilitation programs are particularly vulnerable to gubernatorial changes. In December 1996, Georgia's corrections commissioner fired most of the full-time correctional education staff and replaced them with contract instructors as a purported cost-saving measure, losing many programs in the exchange. In 1997, the Tennessee governor ordered cuts in the correctional education program after learning that it enjoyed smaller teacher-to-student ratios and a greater percentage of teachers with doctoral degrees than did the state's K–12 school systems.

It is not hard to explain the susceptibility of correctional education programs to such actions. Offenders represent the least powerful constituency; forty-seven states disenfranchise prisoners from voting, and many prohibit even released offenders from voting (Drinan, 2000). Moreover, offenders' chief basis of support lies within urban minority and white rural populations that exhibit irregular voting patterns and have limited political influence. Even nationally established minority advocate groups have been reluctant to embrace the issue for fear of perpetuating the view that most offenders belong to a minority group.

## Argument for a New Strategy: Inmate Accountability

Cullen and Gendreau (1989) and Flanagan and Longmire (1996) describe the paradoxical and changing public attitudes about crime and criminals. They argue that although the American public has become more punitive toward crime and less supportive of treatment programs since the 1960s, the overall support for rehabilitation programs remains surprisingly strong. Cullen and Gendreau posit that although the public favors lengthy prison terms, they will support interventions that hold the promise of returning offenders to society as law-abiding citizens. The researchers believe that most people reject the idea that nothing works (the philosophy that society should lock offenders up and throw away the key) but want assurances of safety. Furthermore, the two researchers indicate that legislators and other criminal justice policymakers overestimate the public's desire for punishment and underestimate its support for rehabilitation. Polling data from the 1995 National Opinion Survey on Crime and Justice seem to support this notion that there is considerable support for rehabilitation programs, particularly for juvenile offenders, when these programs are not posed as alternatives to incarceration (Flanagan & Longmire, 1996). Rather than pushing for rehabilitation as an alternative to the correctional goals of incapacitation and punishment or asserting the rights of inmates to these programs, supporters of correctional education might argue more effectively that inmates should be held responsible for a weekly regimen, comparable in time and energy with that of working citizens, and that this regimen will best prepare them to reintegrate into society. Correctional education and treatment programs can and should help "normalize" the correctional experience (Harer, 1995a) and teach socially productive skills.

# Does Correctional Education Reduce Recidivism?

For the past half-century, researchers in the field of adult treatment programs for offenders have attempted to find statistically significant and causal connections between treatment programming and reduced recidivism in literally thousands of studies. Although there has been some examination of other positive outcome measures for correctional treatment programs, such as their ability to improve offenders' institutional behavior and increase literacy and vocational skills, the search for lowered recidivism rates has been the field's holy grail. Political support for educational programs has been centered squarely on claims to reduce recidivism. Unfortunately, Gaes et al. (1998) explain that education and treatment programs have not been designed or optimized to reduce recidivism: "The design and delivery of educational programs has commonly violated many of the principles of effective correctional treatment. . . . Education programs in prison have not been directed to specific criminogenic needs of offenders, have not been part of a multimodal intervention strategy, have not considered responsivity effects, have not been tailored to address the needs of offenders in different risk classifications, and have not been adequately funded to permit the high doses of educational intervention that many offenders require."

If part of the explanation for the ambiguous findings linking programs to reduced recidivism rates is poorly and inadequately designed correctional education programs, another part is that most of the evaluations of these programs are methodologically flawed. The vast majority of studies are retrospective in nature. They examine programs that occurred in the past and have had no control over what data were collected. Information revealing the true quality of educational program design and the extent of the inmates' participation and progress is often lacking or available only for small numbers of inmates. Because many studies have been conducted by agencies administering the programs, there is also an inherent bias to publish positive findings. The fact sheet on the National Institute for Literacy Web site describes a Virginia study that claimed to find that out of a sample of three thousand inmates, 49 percent of those who did not participate in correctional education programs were reincarcerated compared with only 20 percent of those who did participate in these programs. Such dramatic reductions in recidivism are not found in more carefully conducted studies (National Institute for Literacy Web site). Most studies fail to consider the fact that educational programs may enroll inmates who are more predisposed to low recidivism rates. This problem makes it difficult for researchers to separate the effect of correctional education programs on recidivism rate reductions if more motivated and better prepared inmates self-select into programs.

The term *recidivism* itself is open to interpretation and makes the findings of studies difficult to compare. Some studies observe the criminal activity of offenders for only a matter of months following release from prison, and others for years. Some define recidivism to include any further involvement in the criminal justice system. Thus, an offender who technically violates his term of probation because of a failed drug test is statistically equivalent to an offender who commits a new and more serious crime. Other studies employ a narrow definition and include only offenders who are reincarcerated in the same correctional system; they exclude cases in which an offender may be incarcerated in another jurisdiction, a point that also raises the issue of the difficulty of obtaining accurate criminal history, education, and economic information on offenders after their release (Kling, 1999; Needels, 1996).

THREE NOTEWORTHY STUDIES. One of the most comprehensive and sophisticated correctional education studies conducted examined the recidivism rates of a representative sample of 1,205 FBOP inmates released during the first six months of 1987. The author of the study, Miles Harer (1995b), a senior researcher with the Office of Research and Evaluation for the FBOP, found that 41 percent of all offenders "recidivated," which he defined as being rearrested, reconvicted, or reincarcerated within three years of release. He found that recidivism rates were inversely related to participation in correctional education programs. The more education programs successfully completed for each six months of confinement, the lower the recidivism rate was. For inmates successfully completing one or more courses per each six months of their prison term, 35.5 percent recidivated compared with 44.0 percent of those who completed no courses during their prison term, controlling for other important predictors of recidivism, such as age and prior criminal history.

Harer found that the more years of schooling offenders had completed prior to imprisonment, the less likely they were to recidivate. Individuals with only some high school experience recidivated at a rate of 54.6 percent compared with 5.4 percent of college graduates.

Similarly, Harer found that offenders who were employed full time or had attended school for at least six months within two years before they entered prison had a recidivism rate of 25.6 percent compared with 60.2 percent for those who were not so engaged. This study, as the author noted, suffers from some of the methodological problems described previously. The focus on evaluating correctional education programs was ancillary to the study's main purpose to calibrate instruments used by the FBOP to predict recidivism. Nevertheless, this study serves as a model for other retrospective evaluations in the thoroughness of the data collection and the sophistication of the analysis.

A second correctional education study warranting special attention tracked fourteen thousand inmates released from Texas prisons between March 1991 and December 1992 and tallied those who recidivated on or before March 1994 (Criminal Justice Center, 1994). Although the study design suffers from inadequately matched control and treatment groups and an all-too-brief observational period, it uniquely captured the length of time offenders were exposed to education programs, information that was not available in Harer's study. The Criminal Justice Center found that inmates who had logged more than three hundred hours in programs had a recidivism rate of 16.6 percent, while those inmates with fewer than one hundred hours of exposure had a recidivism rate of 24.0 percent. Furthermore, the study found that programming had the greatest effect on inmates at the lower grade levels, though hours of program participation resulted in lower levels of reincarceration for inmates at all grade levels.

The most current research project in correctional education is an ongoing, two-phase, three-state recidivism study involving a cohort of one thousand inmates released in each of the state correctional facilities of Ohio, Maryland, and Minnesota in 1997. Funded by the U.S. Department of Education's Office of Correctional Education, the first phase of this study involves administering and analyzing a comprehensive education and background survey and educational test of the three thousand inmates. The survey gathered information on the educational, treatment, and other prison experiences of the inmates, along with some personal and family data. The Test of Adult Basic Education was used to gauge literacy levels in math and reading. The second phase of the project involves using state criminal history and probation and parole records to evaluate recidivism rates and labor market performance. According to one of the researchers, Stephen Steurer, early results from the Maryland data indicate that those participating in educational programs show an 8 percent differential in recidivism rates (Stephen Steurer, personal communication, Aug. 5, 2000). The final report from this study is expected in 2001.

Although these studies report rather modest recidivism rate differentials of 7.0 to 8.5 percent, a simple calculation demonstrates the significant potential return on investment for correctional education programs even at this level of reported success. The chief statistician of the Bureau of Justice Statistics estimates that 41 percent of the 546,000 inmates released in 1998 will have been reincarcerated within three years of release (Beck, 2000b). If this population recidivated at a lower differential rate of 8 percent, or 33 percent, as a result of correctional education programming, 43,680 fewer inmates would be reincarcerated over this period. Assuming the inmates diverted from prison by correctional education programming would have served the average sentence length of twenty-seven months at a cost of incarceration of $25,000 per inmate per year, the cost savings would amount to almost $2.46 billion per release cohort over three years. Factoring in the $1.36 billion estimated cost required to provide a quality correctional education programming investment for the 546,000 released inmates during their average prison sentence (assuming a cost of $1,000 per inmate per year on correctional education—a much higher figure than most systems' reported expenditures—and a twenty-seven-month average time served), correctional education programming would provide a return on investment of 81 percent over the first three years. These figures do not include the additional savings that would occur as a result of reduced welfare payments and other government transfer programs, as well as the income and sales taxes that these individuals diverted from prison would contribute to the general tax revenue.

LITERATURE REVIEW. A review of the literature on correctional education always begins with a review of more than two hundred treatment studies by Robert Martinson that was published in the journal *Public Interest* in 1974, which hung the skeptical "nothing works" placard over adult rehabilitative programs for offenders. Five years later Martinson changed his mind (Martinson, 1979). In a later series of literature reviews, other researchers found that treatment programs, when properly designed and implemented, did indeed show modestly lower recidivism rates (Andrews et al., 1990; Gendreau & Ross, 1983–1984, 1987; Cullen & Gendreau, 1989; Palmer, 1994).

A literature review of sixty correctional education programs by Gerber and Fritsch (Criminal Justice Center, 1994) also found evidence in support of such programs (see also Adams et al., 1994). The authors found credible studies that showed a lowered recidivism rate for participants in precollege adult basic education (ABE) programs and college education programs and found that offenders in vocational programs performed better on a variety of measures, including institutional behavior and employment patterns; in all cases participant behavior was contrasted with that of nonparticipants. Gerber and Fritsch nonetheless added this important caveat: "Other research has suggested that the most stable predictors of recidivism may be age at first arrest, age upon release, ethnicity, gender, living arrangements, family ties, current income, and history of drug and alcohol abuse. These latter factors are well beyond the control of prison educators. It may be therefore unrealistic to expect prison education to have a substantial effect on recidivism."

The most comprehensive review of the correctional treatment literature for adults and juveniles was commissioned in 1998 and is nearing completion. The CDATE project (Lipton, Pearson, Cleland, & Yee, 1998, cited in Gaes, Flanagan, Motiuk, & Stewart, 1998) is a meta-analysis, a literature review that uses statistical techniques to control for study differences. It aims to review more than fifteen hundred juvenile and adult correctional treatment studies. Based on the results of nine hundred studies in which recidivism is used as an outcome, the CDATE project has found a modest average effect size of .03 to .06 for adult treatment programs, including correctional education. This means that for a given population of offenders whose probability of recidivating is 60 percent, correctional education and other treatment programs can effect a lowering of this rate from 57 percent to 54 percent (Gaes et al., 1998).

## NOTEWORTHY PROGRAMS AND IDEAS

Although I have catalogued many of the challenges and problems the correctional education programs face, many excellent programs currently exist.[4]

## Maryland

The Maryland Department of Education, which runs the state department of corrections' educational program, deserves much credit for adopting a rigorous and comprehensive data collection system that allows the state to track overall performance by student, program, and prison. Steven Steurer, coordinator of correctional academic education in Maryland and executive director of the CEA, explained that his agency decided to implement the same reporting requirements applied to schools under Maryland's new K–12 school reform efforts to promote greater accountability. Steurer says that he has seen GED pass rates increase from 50 percent to 75 percent and seen more GEDs awarded overall now that the performance of individual prisons can be measured. The state superintendent of schools has also singled out the correctional education program's achievement (Steurer, personal communication, June 29, 2000).[5]

## Federal Bureau of Prisons

The FBOP has used a similar strategy to make wardens mindful that they are being held accountable for the performance of the educational programs within their specific institutions. This federal agency, an arm of the U.S. Department of Justice, is highly respected within the correctional field for many of its innovations, mostly related to its security and prison management practices. The FBOP has the distinction of being the only federal agency that has never had a politically appointed director from outside the agency. Correctional researchers have commented on the consistency in operations between the FBOP's nearly one hundred prisons located around the country compared with most systems operating in any one state. The FBOP has maintained a strong correctional education program in all of its facilities and offers vocational training in seventy-three skill areas. The vocational programs vary in depth from exploratory programs, intended to introduce students to an occupation, to marketable programs, intended to provide students with entry-level marketable skills, to the most intense apprenticeship programs, which are registered with the U.S. Department of Labor's Bureau of Apprenticeship and Training.

In 1996, the FBOP's Federal Prison Industries division established the Inmate Placement Bureau to provide inmates released from federal custody with more comprehensive job placement services (Federal Bureau of Prisons, 1998). The bureau has actively implemented mock job fairs within the federal penal system, where employers provide inmates with an opportunity to practice their interviewing and job-seeking skills. It is a mock or simulated job fair largely because inmates serving time in federal facilities typically return to different parts of the country; the employers recruited for the fair are located in the surrounding areas of the facility. The FBOP has also encouraged other state and local correctional systems to host job fairs. In Ohio, the Department of Corrections holds actual job fairs, and inmates interview with company representatives for actual position openings that may be available to them upon release. Taking the private-public partnership one step further, the FBOP's Federal Prison Industries plans to launch an initiative whereby employers can identify inmates who have the aptitude and interest to work with them on release and the federal agency will train and relocate these inmates to the federal facility nearest the company.

The FBOP is also the agency that best combines excellent programs with quality research. Its research division is among the most respected and strongest in the correctional field and has published important studies on the effectiveness of correctional education and prison work programs noted in this chapter.

## Oregon

The Oregon Department of Corrections, in an effort to comply with the 1994 Prison Reform and Inmate Work Act, overhauled its assessment, treatment planning, case management, and program incentive processes. This agency adopted an automated assessment process that efficiently identifies offenders' security issues, health problems, education and workforce development deficits, and treatment program needs and records the information in a database that is then used for effective incarceration and transition planning. These plans are developed and monitored throughout offenders' incarceration by institutional counselors. The counselors map out a sequence of daily education and treatment programming amounting to twenty hours a week, along with twenty hours a week of workforce development training for inmates' entire projected length of stay. The workforce training is cleverly structured in graduated steps from institutional jobs, to specific vocational training, to actual job training, and to prison industry positions and is timed to coincide with offenders' release dates (Oregon Department of Corrections, 1998).

In addition, Oregon implemented a reward system to encourage "prosocial" behavior in education, treatment, and work assignments. In the Performance Recognition and Award System, inmates earn points for successfully completing their plans and can use these points to earn canteen money and additional institutional privileges. Institutional misconduct or unsatisfactory program participation leads to the loss of points (Oregon Department of Corrections, 1998). Oregon is also conducting task force meetings involving other correctional agencies to develop the ability to share this information (Mary F. DeLateur, personal communication, March 28, 1999).

## Ohio

The correctional "school district" within the Ohio Department of Corrections runs perhaps the largest and most comprehensive correctional education program in the country relative to the size of the state's inmate population. To gain legislative support, those sponsoring the program have provided good data on its effectiveness, including a report finding that inmates in the state system who earned GEDs had lower recidivism rates than those who did not have the GED. Ohio is the clear leader nationwide in the use of technology for the delivery of distance-learning programs in corrections and has developed a sophisticated computer network linking all programs offered. The state has also used this technology to offer an excellent college program for inmates. Furthermore the state correctional system has devoted considerable resources to job readiness and prerelease programs and is developing programs that integrate training, industries, and education (TIE) programs. The so-called TIE model has been part of a comprehensive strategy to prepare inmates for the workforce and has involved the business community.

## Canada

The Correctional Services of Canada deserves special mention for the quality of its programs and research, particularly in the light of Canada's comparatively small inmate population. In Edmonton, Alberta, the Canadian correctional agency has developed a certificate of competence program for various vocational education programs, institutional work assignments, and prison industries that documents the skills demonstrated by students and accredits them through the Continuing Education Division of Concordia College (Correctional Education Association, 1997).

## Adult Basic Education Programs

Many correctional agencies across the country have introduced innovative curricula within their ABE correctional educational programs. At the Boston-based Suffolk County House of Correction, instructors have adapted the famous Nebraska's Boys' Town reading curriculum to an inmate population with very low literacy skills. This curriculum, taught in four levels (foundations, adventures, mastery, and exploration), teaches English proficiency by first introducing spelling and phoneme rules and then concentrating on vocabulary development and writing skills through the skillful use of quality literature and technology (personal interview with Debbie Cooper, Nov. 1999).

Reading programs in Milpitas, California, and the Massages program in Waterboro, Maine, are good examples of programs that have infused correctional education with up-to-date ideas circulating in ABE. They have introduced into the prison system the Equipped for the Future curriculum framework developed by the National Institute for Literacy to teach skills that adults need in their roles as workers, family members, and community residents (Lisa Levinson, e-mail communication, Dec. 13, 1999).

The California Department of Youth Authority introduced a mandatory high-skill and high-standard high school diploma as part of its "no diploma, no parole" program. This award-winning program provides strong incentives for youthful offenders to obtain a high school diploma as an alternative to the GED to prepare them better for the workforce and higher education opportunities (Innovations in American Government Program, 1999).

Inmates at the Minnesota Correctional Facility in Faribault are given incentives to attend ABE programs for full days, receiving wages comparable with those paid by industry assignments. In Texas, the Windham school system, which runs educational programs for the state's department of corrections, has attempted to integrate into its adult education and vocational education programming the skills identified in the Department of Labor's Secretary's Commission on Achieving Necessary Skills (SCANS), which identifies the minimum skills needed for entry-level workers in high-performance companies.

## Federal Legislation

At the federal level, the U.S. mandatory literacy law threshold was raised to the twelfth-grade level, and more recent legislation provided additional incentives to encourage inmates to participate in programs.

Inmates now must continue to enroll in ABE programs until they demonstrate competencies at the GED level in order to earn time off their sentences, so-called good time. Offenders are also eligible for pay raises in prison industry jobs only if they complete their GED (Federal Bureau of Prisons, 1998).

Mandatory literacy laws are mixed blessings. Although they can significantly increase inmate participation, they often serve as unfunded mandates for programs and provide no resources for additional programs. Even the Oregon law, which requires inmates to engage in forty hours of workforce development activities each week, provided very little money after its initial implementation, and program administrators continue to struggle to meet the objectives of the legislation. Nonetheless, as a statement of principle, these laws obligate institutions and inmates to offer and enroll in correctional education programs.

## Correctional Education Association

The CEA has developed and promulgated a set of correctional education standards that has been recognized by the American Correctional Association, the main accrediting body for correctional institutions. These standards have also been recommended by several government agencies in the U.S. Departments of Education and Justice. The CEA has also trained corrections professionals from around the country to conduct field audits to evaluate the compliance of educational programs with the seventy-eight standards covering all aspects of educational programming, including program budget, instructor compensation, and student assessment procedures, of which twenty-four are required standards. The CEA Standards Committee has continued to develop additional standards and recently issued forty-seven postsecondary education standards that have been used to accredit college-level courses in Ohio. This committee, soon to be called a commission, will shortly be considering additional standards focused on curriculum (Stephen Steurer, personal communication, Aug. 5, 2000).

## RECOMMENDATIONS FOR POLICY, PRACTICE, AND RESEARCH

Few of the nation's 6 million offenders under correctional supervision are adequately prepared to live productive and law-abiding lives on release from custody, as evidenced by the high recidivism rates of state prisoners—62 percent arrested within three years and 41 percent returned to prison—and parolees and probationers. Correctional education programs can and should play a significant role in helping offenders, who on average have poor educational backgrounds, to develop their literacy, academic, and vocational skills and to assist them in a successful transition back into their communities. Unfortunately, these programs now enroll a small percentage of the inmate population, and resources for these programs have significantly lagged the precipitous rise in the offender population, which on average is serving longer sentences. In addition, correctional education programs fail to provide offenders with a continuum of educational treatment services as the offenders journey between and within correctional agencies. These programs also rarely have significant links with ABE programs operating in the community. Finally, the curriculum and standards of correctional education need considerable updating in the light of the increasing skill demands in the nation's economy.

Inadequate resources, programs of inconsistent quality and effectiveness, high student attrition, poor coordination with other institutions, dearth of good data and research, mercurial political support: the litany of problems described in this chapter is not unique to correctional education. What distinguishes the challenges faced by correctional education are related primarily to the institutional settings and the demographics of the populations. By definition, these programs operate within agencies that traditionally view treatment programming as ancillary to their primary goals of care, custody, and control—the oft-quoted correctional mission triad. This gives rise to challenges that frustrate the enormous potential and possibilities of correctional education programs to intervene effectively with students, including a significant percentage of young black and Hispanic males, who have time on their hands, have fewer family responsibilities and face temptations to drop out of programming, and can be mandated to attend programs while under correctional supervision.

In his noted 1964 study, *The Effectiveness of a Prison and Parole System*, Daniel Glaser identified many of the same problems and challenges faced by correctional education in 1960, when he remarked, "American prisons, especially those for youthful inmates, have been distinctive for the extent of their investment in educational programs." Although the same statement could not have been made in the past twenty-five years, it is all the more remarkable that correctional education as a field has marched forward, through the efforts of thousands of dedicated practitioners and the leadership of numerous government and professional organizations in the face of political support shifting away from these programs. There are countless examples, many unpublicized, of well-designed and well-implemented programs operating around the country that are making differences in the lives of offenders every day and yielding significant societal benefits. Developing a new political constituency to support and promote effective programs, upgrading and expanding program offerings, and launching more and higher-quality research linking programs to reduced recidivism rates are three of the major challenges that must be addressed to reframe the politics and practices of correctional education if it is to serve a much larger percentage of the offender population with comprehensive educational programs more effectively. Following are specific recommendations on how such reframing might be accomplished.

## Policy

• *Develop a wider political constituency for correctional education programs.* Increased and long-term support for correctional education programs will not occur unless organizations representing those groups most affected by corrections—including African Americans, Hispanics, Native Americans, and the mentally ill—join other advocacy groups for prisoner rights and make this issue a priority for their members. The CEA, the Soros Foundation's Open Society Institute's Center on Crime, Communities, and Culture, the Urban Institute, and the Taskforce on Correctional Education, chaired by the board director of the FBOP, along with other groups, should collaborate to help build this political constituency. Given the significant labor shortages in the nation's economy, federal, state, and local business groups might be enticed to participate in this effort as well. Political leadership from individuals such as Arlen Specter, the Republican senator from Pennsylvania, who has been the single most effective legislator at the national level for correctional education, and U.S. Attorney General Janet Reno, who has recently raised the issue of the national need to prepare the more than one-half million inmates released from prison a year to reenter their communities, can and should be leveraged to build support for correctional education programs. Meetings and conferences would be helpful to educate these groups and policymakers about the scale of the problem and the potential solutions in the form of stronger and more effective correctional education programs.

• *Reframe correctional education as part of an inmate accountability strategy that encompasses education, work, and treatment.* Oregon's experience demonstrates the powerful effect of requiring inmates to engage in meaningful workforce development activities for a minimum of forty hours a week on both the correctional system's commitment to adult treatment programming and inmate participation. It also creates a model of correctional education founded on accountability that is much more acceptable politically than other models. Education, work, and treatment should form the foundation for inmate programming in correctional institutions and should be extensively linked. Heretofore, prison industries and correctional education have not been integrated. Each field has its own professional association, and institutionally these programs are typically operated by different departments (the exception is the federal system). Well-regarded studies demonstrate that participation in prison industry programs contributes to lower rates of recidivism. Prison industries and meaningful work assignments provide excellent experience in modeling the behavior and skills needed to obtain and retain employment. Similarly, better coordination between correctional education and substance abuse, anger management, and other treatment programming will strengthen the effectiveness of each of these programs.

• *Promote mandatory literacy laws with high standards.* Mandatory literacy laws have proven effective to increase the demand for correctional education programs in the twenty-six states that have implemented them. Unfortunately, they have often served as unfunded mandates for programs that have resulted in longer waiting lists instead of expanded services. Nonetheless, these laws establish an important principle for a correctional system about the importance of correctional education. Taking the lead from the federal system, the laws should require inmate participation in programs until a GED reading and math level is achieved and should tie other institutional incentives such as wages and time off sentence for good behavior to program participation.

• *Support increased funding for Specter grants and a relaxation of the age qualifications to age twenty-nine.* With the disappearance of Pell grants, fewer postsecondary opportunities are available to inmates. The Specter grants would be a more useful vehicle to replace these funds if they were larger and were available to offenders under the age of twenty-nine. Specter grants are now available only to offenders under twenty-five years of age, and the grant program totals $17 million for fiscal year 2001.

• *Support legislative and administrative efforts to decrease the barriers to employment for individuals with criminal histories.* The stigma of a criminal record has become more severe as the economy's service sector has markedly increased in size and as tort liability for harassment and injuries in workplaces has skyrocketed. Furthermore, some states prohibit the hiring of individuals for certain jobs. Correctional education advocates should advocate for programs that mitigate the financial liabilities of employers who hire offenders, such as the Federal Bonding program and the Work Opportunity Tax Credit (WOTC) program. The bonding program essentially insures the employer against any financial loss as the result of hiring an offender; the WOTC provides employers with tax credits to subsidize the employment of offenders during the initial year. Advocates for offenders should attempt to ensure that any laws restricting the hiring of offenders have a basis in public safety. Also, some academicians have recently raised the issue of providing a criminal history amnesty program for nonviolent first-time offenders who agree to participate in further education and treatment programming for a prescribed period of time.

• *Provide greater discharge planning and postrelease services for offenders.* Correctional education is an important and crucial element that helps offenders make the transition to the community. However, these and other treatment programs need to be coordinated as part of an overall discharge plan that addresses such issues as transportation, identifications (many inmates lose their IDs in prison), housing, and the like. It is crucial that resources be available to offenders postrelease from a correctional facility to continue to assist and support offenders as well as to allow them to continue educational programming.

## Practice

• *Update and upgrade correctional education programs.* Correctional education programs should aim to prepare and equip offenders with the knowledge and training needed to succeed in the current economy. Equipped for the Future and SCANS provide useful frameworks for developing relevant curriculum. Computer and other technology should be integrated into all programs. In addition, correctional education programs should offer transition, or bridge, programs that provide writing and numeracy classes beyond the GED level that prepare inmates for higher education opportunities. The GED, the mainstay of many correctional education programs, is slated for a significant revision and upgrading in 2002. Correctional education programs must consider the necessary pedagogical and curriculum changes needed to prepare students for the GED 2002, which promises to incorporate many of the new high school graduation skill requirements implemented across the country.

• *Encourage involvement of the business and private sector in the employment and training of offenders under correctional supervision.* Successful postrelease employment will largely determine the ability of offenders to continue educational and treatment programming and to prevent the resumption of criminal activity. Training programs set up in coordination with businesses that agree to hire offenders postrelease, job fairs, and other initiatives that help offenders gain entry into the labor market should be encouraged. These initiatives also serve a public relations benefit in demonstrating the eagerness of many offenders to work diligently and competently in jobs.

• *Provide more information about best practices in corrections, using the resources of the Internet.* Because of geographical and institutional isolation, correctional education programs often operate independently. The U.S. Office of Correctional Education, the CEA, and the National Institute for Literacy should jointly promote professionally managed listservs to develop a national discussion on correctional education issues (the CEA has listservs on its Web site). In addition, the Office of Correctional Education should include on its Web site information relating to national and state correctional education standards, descriptions of best practices in the field, and downloadable curriculum.

• *Promote CEA correctional education standards and incorporate additional performance criteria.* The current standards for correctional education promulgated by the CEA are an excellent starting point to ensure a basic level of performance by correctional education programs. More correctional institutions should be encouraged to adopt and receive certification on these standards. The efforts to expand these standards and add performance requirements with regard to the actual delivery of educational services should continue. Quality educational programs should meet specific performance requirements with regard to enrollment percentages, program offerings, program design, and data collection.

## Research

• *Support rigorously designed longitudinal studies of well-designed correctional education programs to demonstrate the effectiveness of correctional education in reducing recidivism.* The public and policymakers will dramatically increase support for correctional education only if evidence from scientifically valid studies demonstrates that these programs contribute to the public safety and save tax dollars by reducing the recidivism rate. The Office of Correctional Education, which is funding a three-state retrospective study, should consider funding prospective longitudinal studies of existing programs that have the potential—through solid design and implementation of services—to reduce recidivism. In addition, all correctional education programs should collect information that provides accurate information about the scope and quality of their services.

• *Establish extensive involvement in the preparations for the second NALS (the NAAL) in 2002.* The 2002 NAAL will serve as the definitive assessment of the literacy proficiencies of a national sampling of offenders in state corrections for the next decade. The 1992 NALS has proven extremely valuable in its literacy assessment of the prison population, as well as in the information collected on family backgrounds, criminal histories, work and education experience, and program participation of offenders. Representatives from the field should participate in developing the survey for the 2002 NAAL. In addition, both the survey and assessment instruments should be made available to correctional education programs to encourage them to align their data collection systems with the NAAL.

• *Provide greater support and research for correctional education programs in community corrections that are linked with programs in prisons and jails.* Correctional education programs for probationers, parolees, and those under conditional supervision in intermediate sanction are neither well developed nor well understood. Given that inmates in secure facilities often do not complete correctional education programs because of their frequent movement within the corrections system, there is a critical need to offer linked programs in community correctional settings that would allow offenders to continue their education. The Office of Correctional Education can and should play a role in funding initiatives in this area. This is a fruitful area for collaboration between ABE programs and corrections.

• *Fund a best practices survey in correctional education.* The National Institute of Justice, the National Institute of Corrections, and the U.S. Office of Correctional Education have collaborated on a series of publications highlighting best practices in offender job training, placement, and retention. The field would also benefit from more comprehensive and critical surveys of best practices in adult education correctional programs, vocational programming, and community correction programming. In addition, Oregon's initiatives to revamp correctional treatment programs merit a critical qualitative evaluation funded at the federal level.

## Notes

1. Sources of the opening quotes by Justice Warren Burger and Malcolm X are, respectively, *Vocational Education in Correctional Institutions,* a report based on hearings conducted by the National Advisory Council on Vocational Education, March 1981, referencing Burger's February 8, 1981, presentation to the American Bar Association, and *The Autobiography of Malcolm X,* written with the assistance of Alex Haley (New York: Grove Press, 1964), p. 396.
2. A complete analysis of the National Adult Literacy Survey of 1992 on prisoners is provided in Haigler et al. (1994) and in a subsequent article by Paul Barton, a senior researcher from the Educational Testing Service, the organization that conducted the survey (Barton & Coley, 1996). The only other national survey of the inmate population's educational background was administered in 1991 by the Bureau of Justice Statistics. A survey of fourteen thousand inmates found that only 34 percent had their high school diplomas, and another 25 percent had the GED. This survey did not assess literacy skills.
3. Correctional education is funded primarily through budget appropriations for state departments of corrections and inmate welfare and commissary funds. This latter funding source represents the profits from the sale of commissary items to inmates and, most important, a portion of the surcharges applied to inmates' use of telephones. In most jurisdictions, the fund is restricted to expenditures that directly benefit inmates, such as educational programming. Wyoming uses these funds for scholarships for postsecondary education programs. Texas uses state funds to establish loans to pay for postsecondary programs that prisoners must pay back on release. In the federal correctional system, the Federal

Bureau of Prisons uses some of the profits from the Federal Prison Industries to fund vocational and postsecondary educational programs.

Federal programs provide additional sources of funding for correctional programs. Under the original federal Adult Education Act, which was reauthorized in 1988 and amended to become the National Literacy Act of 1991, the U.S. Department of Education required states to set aside a minimum 10 percent of all federal adult education funds for corrections (Eliott, 1998). In 1998, Title II (Adult Education and Family Literacy Act) of the Workforce Investment Act (WIA) changed the 10 percent set-aside from a floor to a ceiling amount. This same act also changed the amount of funds set aside for vocational programming from a 1 percent minimum to a 1 percent cap, which has markedly reduced the amount of funds for training programs under the Carl D. Perkins Vocational and Applied Technology Education Act and Job Training Partnership Act. For fiscal year 2000, the WIA provided $450 million in federal funds to states for adult education programs, of which a maximum of $45 million can be allocated for correctional education programs.

Some states supplement these federal funds with a portion of their own state funding of adult education programming. In Massachusetts, the state Department of Education matches the WIA funds for corrections dollar for dollar. The Title I Neglected and Delinquent program provides a significant amount of funds for inmates under the age of twenty-two; the IDEA, Part B's Special Education programs, provides a smaller amount of money for inmates in the same age group who have documented special education needs (Stephen Steurer, personal communication, June 29, 2000). The Bureau of Justice Assistance also funds education programs through the Edward Byrne Memorial Formula Grant program administered at the state level. Showing a greater willingness to fund programs for younger offenders, Congress in 1998 authorized the Workplace and Community Transition Training for Incarcerated Youth Offenders. This program was introduced to provide opportunities for postsecondary education for offenders twenty-five years of age and younger who had been significantly impaired by the loss of Pell grant funding. Called Specter grants, after the chief congressional supporter of correctional education, Arlen Specter (R-Pennsylvania), they were funded for $14 million in fiscal year 2000 and $17 million in fiscal year 2001. Finally, the U.S. Department of Education's Office of Correctional Education administers a $5 million life skill reintegration program, which funds ten to thirteen competitively selected life skills programs at different institutions across the country for three years.

In the past several years, the Soros Foundation's Open Society Program has become a significant private funder of correctional education programs. It has funded an innovative higher education and training program for inmates in the Maryland Department of Corrections. The Maryland Department of Education, which runs the correctional education programs for the corrections department, has largely been able to sustain its higher education program through the use of Specter grants and Soros funds as a replacement for Pell grants. The Open Society Program has also funded a number of counselor positions to provide pre- and postrelease services (sometimes called reentry programs) for inmates leaving correctional facilities. Finally, the Department of Justice is considering a major $145 million initiative to fund reentry courts, which would serve as intermediate sanction programs. These courts would presumably promote correctional education and treatment programs.

In terms of budget appropriations, the Bureau of Justice Statistics reported that state expenditures in 1996 for inmate prison programs such as work activities (prison industries and facility support services), correctional educational, substance abuse treatment, and recreation activities amounted to $1.23 billion nationwide, or 6 percent of the nation's total state prison expenditures, with considerable variation by region. In the northeastern and western regions of the country, state correctional systems devoted 7 to 8 percent of their budget to these programs and spent on average $1,800 per inmate annually. By contrast, the Midwest and the South devoted only 4.3 percent and 4.1 percent, respectively, of total prison expenditures to such programs, which works out to $989 and $634, respectively, per inmate annually. The Bureau of Justice Statistics cautions that these figures may be seriously underreported owing to the inability of almost a quarter of the state correctional systems to break out program costs from general operating costs and to the failure to include costs expended by other state agencies for support programming (Stephan, 1999).

Estimates of the total amount of funding targeted for correctional education programs differ markedly by data source. The lower bound is provided by statistics gathered by the Division of Adult Education and Literacy of the U.S. Department of Education's Office of Vocational and Adult Education (Elliot, 1998). Its 1998 report indicates that the total correctional education expenditures for adult education programs increased from $9.1 million in 1986 to $45.3 million in 1994, with federal and state contributions amounting to $3.9 million and $5.2 million in 1986 and $28.2 million and $17.2 million in 1994, respectively (Elliot, 1998). Although these figures neither include the cost of vocational, life skill, and postsecondary programs nor account for inflation and the rise in the inmate population, they differ by an order of magnitude with those reported in a 1996 survey of forty-one correctional systems and the Federal Bureau of Prisons. The publication *Corrections Compendium* (1997) reported that $413 million was spent in 1996 by the U.S. prison system. These figures are more in line with a noted correctional education researcher's surveys conducted in 1983 and 1995 (Ryan, 1995; Ryan & Woodard, 1987). The disparity in the reported expenditures stems from the Bureau of Justice Statistics caution that many correctional systems track their budget for treatment programs independent of other operations.

4. Before describing some of these programs, I should say something about the way in which such "best practices" are determined in correctional education programs, which, unlike ABE programs, are difficult to visit. In 1998, the American Correctional Association published *Best Practices: Excellence in Corrections*, which highlighted five correctional education programs. While I do not dispute the quality of the programs selected, the selection process was arbitrary and solicited programs to submit written descriptions of their "best practices" for national competition, which few did. The Oregon Department of Corrections (1998) published a brochure about its rehabilitative treatment programs that the department itself actually titled *Best Practices*. Few programs are able to offer substantive and objective data that would bolster their claim as conducting the "best practices" in correctional education. Many simply provide program descriptions and goals and do not state whether these programs have been fully implemented or have attained their objectives. Nor do they provide information on program sustainability and longevity.

5. Maryland is also an example of the changing fortunes of correctional education programs. In 1991, the entire correctional education staff in the state received pink slips and faced dramatic reductions in their hours and programs. Through legislative lobbying efforts, the pink slips were rescinded after a considerable fight.

# References

Adams, K., Bennett, K., Flanagan, T., Marquart, J., Cuvelier, S., Fritsch, E., Longmire, D., & Burton, V. (1994). A large-scale multidimensional test of the effect of prison education programs on offenders' behavior. *Prison Journal, 4,* 433–449.

Albright, S., & Furjen, D. (1996). Employer attitudes towards hiring ex-offenders. *Prison Journal, 2,* 118–137.

Andrews, D. A., Zinger, I., Hoge, R. D., Bonta, J., Gendreau, P., & Cullen, F. T. (1990). Does correctional treatment work? A psychological informed meta-analysis. *Criminology, 28,* 369–404.

Barton, P., & Coley, R. (1996). *Captive students: Education and training in American prisons. Policy information report.* (ETS Publication No. BBB27038). Princeton, NJ: Educational Testing Service.

Beck, A. (2000a). *State and federal prisoners returning to the community: Findings from the Bureau of Justice Statistics.* Paper presented at the First Reentry Courts Initiative Cluster Meeting, Hotel Washington, DC, Apr. 13.

Beck, A. (2000b). *Prison and jail inmates at midyear 1999* (NCJ Publication No. 181643). Washington, DC: U.S. Department of Justice, Office of Justice Programs, Bureau of Justice Statistics.

Beck, A., & Mumola, C. (1999). *Prisoners in 1998* (NCJ Publication No. 175687). Washington, DC: U.S. Department of Justice, Office of Justice Programs, Bureau of Justice Statistics.

Bonczar, T., & Glaze, L. (1999). *Probation and parole in the United States, 1998.* (NCJ Publication No.178234). Washington, DC: U.S. Department of Justice, Office of Justice Programs, Bureau of Justice Statistics.

Boshier, R., & Johnson, D. (1974). Does conviction affect employment opportunities? *British Journal of Criminology, 14*(3), 264–268.

Butterfield, F. (1999, Apr. 7). Parents in prison: A special report. *New York Times,* p. 1.

Correctional Education Association. (1997). *Standards for adult and juvenile correctional education programs.* Washington, DC: Author.

*Corrections Compendium.* (1997, Sept.). Survey summary: Educational opportunities in correctional settings. *Corrections Compendium, 9,* 4–16.

Criminal Justice Center. (1994). *Prison education research project final report.* Huntsville, TX: Sam Houston State University.

Cullen, F. T., & Gendreau, P. (1989). The effectiveness of correctional rehabilitation: Reconsidering the "nothing works'" debate. In L. Goodstein & D. Mackenzie (Eds.), *The American prison: Issues in research and policy* (pp. 23–34). New York: Plenum Press 1989.

Drinan, R. (2000, Jul. 14). Let prisoners keep the right to vote. *Boston Globe.*

Elliot, B. (1998, Oct.). *Digest of adult education statistics—1998.* Washington, DC: U.S. Department of Education, Office of

Vocational and Adult Education, Division of Adult Education and Literacy.

Fabiano, E. (1991). How education can be correctional and how corrections can be educational. *Journal of Correctional Education, 2,* 100–106.

Federal Bureau of Prisons. (1998). *Education and recreation programs.* Washington, DC: Education Branch.

Finn, P. (1997). *The Orange County, Florida, jail educational and vocational programs* (NCJ Publication No. 166820). Washington, DC: National Institute of Justice.

Finn, R. H., & Fontaine, P. A. (1985). The association between selected characteristics and perceived employability of offenders. *Criminal Justice and Behavior, 12*(3), 353–365.

Flanagan, T., & Longmire, D. (Eds.). (1996). *Americans view crime and justice: A national public opinion survey.* Thousand Oaks, CA: Sage.

Gaes, G. G., Flanagan, T., Motiuk, L., & Stewart, L. (1998). Adult correctional treatment. Version 2, Sept. 17. Unpublished manuscript. Revised version appears in M. Tonry & J. Petersilia (Eds.), *Prisons: Crime and Justice* (vol. 26). Chicago: University of Chicago Press.

Gendreau, P., & Ross, R. (1983–1984). Correctional treatment: Some recommendations for effective intervention. *Juvenile and Family Court Journal, 34,* 31–39.

Gendreau, P., & Ross, R. (1987). Revivification of rehabilitation: Evidence from the 1980s. *Justice Quarterly, 4,* 349–407.

Glaser, D. (1964). *The effectiveness of a prison and parole system.* New York: Bobbs-Merrill.

Haigler, K. C., O'Connor, P., & Campbell, A. (1994). *Literacy behind prison walls: Profiles of the prison population from the National Adult Literacy Survey.* Princeton, NJ: Educational Testing Service.

Hanson, R., & Daley, H. (1994). *Challenging the conditions of prisons and jails: A report on Section 1983 litigation.* Washington, DC: Bureau of Justice Statistics, Office of Justice Programs, U.S. Department of Justice.

Harer, M. D. (1995a). *Prison education program participation and recidivism: A test of the normalization hypothesis.* Washington, DC: Federal Bureau of Prisons.

Harer, M. D. (1995b). Recidivism among federal prisoners released in 1987. *Journal of Correctional Education, 46*(3), 98–128.

Holzer, H. (1996). *What employers want: Job prospects for less-educated workers.* New York: Russell Sage Foundation.

Innovations in American Government Program. (1999, Aug.). For California youth offenders: "No diploma—no parole" [press release]. Cambridge, MA: Harvard University, JFK School of Government, Ford Foundation Awards Program.

Kling, J. R. (1999). *The effect of prison sentence length on the subsequent employment and earnings of criminal defendants* (Discussion Paper No. 208). Princeton, NJ: Princeton University and National Bureau of Economic Research.

Lillis, J. (1994). Prison education programs reduced survey—Education: Part 1. *Corrections Compendium, 3,* 1–11.

Maguire, K., & Pastore, A. (Eds.). (1998). *Sourcebook of criminal justice statistics—1997.* (NCJ Publication No. 171147). Washington, DC: Bureau of Justice Statistics.

Maguire, K., & Pastore, A. (Eds.). (1999). *Sourcebook of criminal justice Statistics—1998* (NCJ Publication No. 176356). Washington, DC: Bureau of Justice Statistics.

Martinson, R. (1974). What works? Questions and answers about prison reform. *Public Interest, 35,* 22–54.

Martinson, R. (1979). Symposium on sentencing: Part 2. New findings, new views: A note of caution regarding sentencing reform. *Hofstra Law Review, 7,* 243–258.

Murnane, R., & Levy, F. (1996). *Teaching the new basic skills.* New York: Free Press.

*National Adult Literacy Survey.* (1992). Washington, DC: U.S. Department of Education, National Center for Education Statistics.

National Institute for Literacy at http://www.nifl.gov/newworld/correct.htm.

Needels, K. E. (1996). Go directly to jail and do not collect? A long-term study of recidivism, employment, and earnings patterns among prison releases. *Journal of Research in Crime and Delinquency, 33*(4), 471–496.

Oregon Department of Corrections. (1998). *Best practices.* [brochure]. Correctional Programs Division.

Palmer, T. (1994). *A profile of correctional effectiveness and new directions for research.* Albany: State University of New York Press.

Perkins, C., Stephan, J., & Beck, A. (1995). *Jails and jail inmates, 1993–94* (NCJ Publication No. 151651). Washington, DC: U.S. Department of Justice, Office of Justice Programs, Bureau of Justice Statistics.

Roberts, J. (1996). Work, education, and public safety: A brief history of Federal Prison Industries. In A. Stephens (Ed.), *Factories with fences:*

*The history of Federal Prison Industries* (pp. 10–35). Washington, DC: Federal Prison Industries.

Ryan, T. A. (1995). Correctional education: Past is prologue to the future. *Journal of Correctional Education, 2,* 60–65.

Ryan, T. A., & Woodard, J. C. (1987). *Correctional education: A state of the art analysis.* Washington, DC: U.S. Department of Justice, National Institute of Corrections.

Sentencing Project. (1999, Oct.). *Facts about prisons and prisoners.* Briefing/Fact Sheet #1035 at www.sentencingproject.org.

Snyder, T., & Hoffman, C. (2000). *Digest of Education Statistics, 1999.* Washington, DC: National Center for Education Statistics.

Spence, A. M. (1973). Job market signaling. *Quarterly Journal of Economics, 87*(3), 355–374.

Stephan, J. (1999). *State prison expenditures, 1996* (NCJ Publication No. 172211). Washington, DC: Bureau of Justice Statistics.

Tonry, M. (1999). The fragmentation of sentencing and corrections in America. In *Sentencing and corrections: Issues for the 21st century* (NCJ Publication No. 175721). Washington, DC: U.S. Department of Justice, Office of Justice Programs, National Institute for Justice.

# CHAPTER FIVE

# Building Professional Development Systems in Adult Basic Education

## Lessons from the Field

*Alisa Belzer*
*Cassandra Drennon*
*Cristine Smith*

The practice of organizing professional development offerings through a system is relatively new in adult basic education (ABE), dating from the passage of the National Literacy Act (NLA) of 1991, under which all states were required to allocate a minimum of 15 percent of their ABE dollars to professional development and research. This mandate prompted many states to develop a system for providing teachers, tutors, administrators, and other adult literacy staff with continuing education opportunities. We define *system* in this chapter as an institutionalized set of processes and learning activities, sponsored by a state department of adult education or other state-level entity responsible for ABE, intended to provide ABE practitioners with professional development. The goal of such processes is to support and improve the practice of adult basic and literacy education. By and large, state professional development staff do not have much knowledge of other states' systems: how the systems were built, how they evolved, what has been learned along the way, how the current systems work, how they are alike and different, and what challenges they face. This chapter addresses this knowledge gap by examining the professional development systems in Idaho, Massachusetts, Ohio, Pennsylvania, and Virginia, each of which has now been in place for several years.

Lytle, Belzer, and Reumann, (1992, p. 1) say that "examining the assumptions that currently inform staff development for teachers, tutors, and administrators and constructing new conceptual frameworks for research and practice have become critical tasks for the field of adult literacy." This is true in terms of both specific professional development activities and the ways in which professional development is organized on a broad scale (that is, through systems). What is also critical is states' ability to share such information and learn from one another. Interviews with state-level professional development staff around the country indicate that they engage in little of such information sharing or collaborative problem solving. An important first step in improving professional development systems is making available such basic information on these systems and the challenges they face.

This is an especially good time to take a close look at state systems for professional development because the most recent federal legislation that funds ABE, the Workforce Investment Act of 1998, suggests the need for states to (re)examine their professional development system. On one hand, the legislation may implicitly undermine the importance of professional development because it eliminated the 1991 spending mandate (RMC Research Corporation, 1996). On the other hand, marked changes in the legislation, such as the establishment of a national reporting system, challenge state agencies to play a rapid game of catch-up to respond to a new performance-based system, therefore suggesting a pressing need for additional professional development. At this crucial time in the evolution of professional development in ABE, we explore key issues and challenges in the implementation of professional development systems as expressed by professionals in five states.

## HISTORY OF PROFESSIONAL DEVELOPMENT IN ABE

The history of professional development in ABE is tied strongly to the history of federal funding of ABE, which can be traced to the passage of the Adult Education Act in 1965 and its transfer to the U.S. Office of Education (USOE) (now the U.S. Department of Education) in 1966. Staff training was considered key to the successful implementation of the act (Rose, 1991). In these early years, the primary mode of professional development was conceptualized as baseline training aimed at full-time elementary and secondary school teachers who taught adults part time outside regular school hours. Then, as now, most practitioners entered the field with little or no formal training in how to teach adults. A series of two- to three-week summer institutes sponsored by the USOE was offered to practitioners around the country on the assumption that an accelerated program could be used to prepare ABE teachers. These early institutes, often university based, paid

> attention to the teaching of the academic areas of reading, math, and communications as well as life skills, including parenting, the utilization of community resources, civic responsibility, job-seeking and keeping skills, health and safety, and consumer skills. A majority of USOE institutes offered information relating to the psychological and sociological characteristics of the educationally disadvantaged adult, and some approached the problems that might arise because of the conflicting cultures, values, lifestyles, and communication patterns of predominately white, middle-class teachers and [minority, immigrant, and low-income] adult basic education students. [Leahy, 1986, p. 4]

The institutes grew in number, participants, and sophistication (Leahy, 1986). Although popular, they were criticized for several reasons. Some critics considered them to be "pedestrian in scope and execution" (Hoffman & Pagano, 1971, p. 17); little provision was made for the various levels of participant expertise and experience; the institutes were thought to be expensive, especially given the high rate of turnover in the field; and opportunities for organizers of one institute to learn from another were limited. Although each was required to produce a final report, the reports were submitted to the funder (USOE) and not widely disseminated.

Based in part on these criticisms, a shift in emphasis in professional development away from the use of institutes began in the late 1960s, and the institutes were discontinued in 1971. Beginning in 1969, the USOE supported a regional approach to staff development (Leahy, 1986). Ultimately, ten regional Adult Education Staff Development Projects were established. While regions (made up of several states) were expected to follow the same general guidelines, each also developed its own focus. For example, training programs and materials aimed at specific practitioners or populations were developed regionally. Money also began to flow into the development of graduate and undergraduate programs in adult education. By 1975, there were about one hundred postsecondary training programs in this area.

Next came an important shift in funding. Until the mid-1970s, the USOE had been deeply involved in reviewing and guiding the development of proposals for staff training and made the funding decisions (Rose, 1991). Beginning in 1975, federally controlled monies no longer contributed to an overall, broad-based national plan for training teachers. Instead, staff training funds were allocated on a project-by-project basis at the state level (Leahy, 1986). The states took over much of the responsibility for (and control of) ABE staff training and development (initially known as Section 310 and later as Section 353 money). It has been argued that this shift had negative consequences on two levels (Leahy, 1986). First, although many innovative approaches grew out of the special project money allocated to programs by the states, the piecemeal nature of the work made it very difficult to disseminate information, and there were few opportunities to develop a shared knowledge base built on project findings and experiences. Second, statewide staff development and teacher training efforts were often too general in scope and needed a great deal of adaptation for local implementation. Consequently, the impact of these efforts on staff development at the local level was often limited.

The early 1980s are remarkable in that they represent the only period since 1966 when funding for ABE did not rise. By 1988, however, a major influx of funds to the field was under way. At this time, Congress "discovered" adult literacy as "a solution to a wide range of problems in other federal programs with which it had been struggling for some time" (Chisman, 1990, p. 222). Along with the increase in funding came more specific goals for literacy education related to the employability of adults with low skills and the integration of immigrants into American society. The skills emphasized were thus not only reading and writing but also mathematics, communication, and problem solving. In many cases, programs did not have the capacity to address these broader goals (Chisman, 1990), and no additional funds were earmarked for staff training. Fingeret (1992) argued that because little attention had been paid to building an ABE infrastructure, the professional development systems that could address these broader goals had simply not been built. She blames this weakness of the field on federal funding policies formulated with short-term crisis management mentality. In general, dollars were appropriated to maximize operating funds rather than to build capacity, and "this thinking undermine[d] proponents of a more robust adult education system and development of a cadre of adult education professionals" (RMC Research Corporation, 1996, p. 20).

By the time ABE funding was reauthorized in 1991, the emphasis had begun to shift away from an approach that could be characterized as short-term crisis intervention to one based on long-term commitment to increasing the literacy levels of adults (Fingeret, 1992). For example, the NLA of 1991 mandated that all states allocate a minimum of 15 percent of their federal ABE dollars for professional development and research (at least two-thirds had to be used for teacher training), leading to a sharp increase in state-initiated professional development activities (Quigley, 1997). In many states, especially those receiving significant funding, this change encouraged the development of comprehensive statewide professional development delivery systems.

Title II of the Workforce Investment Act (WIA) of 1998, which superseded the 1991 NLA, eliminated the specific set-aside for professional development and research. Instead, a decreased set-aside of a maximum of 12.5 percent is allowed for state leadership funds (defined as a wide variety of support and coordination efforts among existing support services, occupational skill training and employers, and postsecondary educational institutions). Professional development is funded—but not mandated—within this section of the legislation, as are a multitude of other efforts, including incentives for program coordination and performance.[1] This cut in spending and the elimination of a specific spending mandate can be construed as a devaluation of the importance of professional development systems, which had earlier been encouraged to grow and develop. Despite the potential for decreased funding, professional development systems have become integral to the work of many states. Based on conversations with professional development professionals in the fifteen states we contacted for this chapter, professional development appears to be a front-burner issue. These respondents report that they will continue to strengthen their systems while creatively finding ways to streamline expenses and work around the funding constraints imposed by the latest legislation.

## SURVEY METHODS

We have synthesized the ways in which five states—Idaho, Massachusetts, Ohio, Pennsylvania, and Virginia—have implemented professional development systems. Each state is different in terms of local need, size, political context, ABE service provision, and federal allocation of dollars, and their systems reflect a response to these realities. To develop a set of lessons learned, we studied the systems of these states to make visible a variety of approaches to the challenges of providing professional development systematically.

Because selection of states based on the notion of "best practices" is problematic, we began the process by trying to identify those states that have clearly visible and well-established professional development systems (that is, institutionalized processes and learning activities for providing professional development).[2] To do this, we drew on our combined knowledge of various states' professional development systems to list some possibilities for focus. In addition, we solicited suggestions from several state directors and other leaders in the field. As a result, we collected through telephone interviews thumbnail sketches of professional development systems in fifteen states. From these, we selected five that were diverse in terms of size, location, and overall structure to feature here.

After selection, we contacted a key representative (state director or state staff person most responsible for professional development) to secure permission to include that state's system in this chapter. In all, six people from the five states assisted us in creating a detailed profile of their state's professional development system.[3] These representatives participated in a telephone interview in which they described their system's strengths and vulnerabilities, key challenges, and important learnings; answered clarifying questions regarding the description of the state's professional development system; and read and responded to a draft of this chapter. Our state profiles are also based on a variety of documents generated by the states to describe their systems: mission statements, brochures, proposals and final reports to funders, and forms related to professional development planning.

Once we had collected all of the information on the states, we analyzed it for presentation in the following categories: student and teacher demographics; thumbnail sketch, or overview, of the professional development system; significant features of the system; and common issues and challenges faced by each system. Based on the analysis, we identified implications for practice, research, and policy.

# ANALYSIS OF FIVE STATE SYSTEMS

Certain challenges are common to all efforts to establish professional development systems. The very existence of statewide professional development systems is unique to adult literacy education. Owing to the history of local funding and control at the K–12 level and the configuration of schools with more or less common elements, professional development in that realm is generally organized by schools or by districts rather than by states. Titzel (1998) points out that although public school teachers may face isolation as a result of long-held assumptions about the autonomy of teachers, K–12 teachers do work within structures that by their very nature create proximity among teachers and can engender a sense of community. The K–12 workforce is generally employed full time, and groups of teachers typically work at or near a common site. Furthermore, although K–12 teachers have different levels of experience and skill, they all have preservice training. In adult education, most teachers work part time, and many do not have preservice training in an area of K–12, much less in adult education. ABE practitioners must also often overcome geographic isolation if they are to participate in training that fosters the development of learning communities.

Additional challenges of common concern to providers of ABE professional development services include inadequate funding;[4] a nagging belief by many that professional development takes money away from direct services to learners; multiple funding streams that make it difficult for programs to establish standardized policies on release time to allow staff to participate in professional development activities; a relative lack of models for statewide systems; a lack of information on how to adapt existing models to the needs of a particular state; a history of poor professional development that has contributed to practitioner apathy; and demands from state agencies that training focus on content that may not match practitioner interests. At the same time, each state also faces challenges unique to its structure, stakeholders, and history.

## ABE Student and Teacher Demographics

Idaho, Massachusetts, Ohio, Pennsylvania, and Virginia have some important statistical similarities and differences that are worth noting (see Table 5.1). They represent five regions of the country (the Northwest, New England, the Midwest, the mid-Atlantic states, and

| State | 1998 Federal and State Allocation | | Enrollment | | | | Personnel | | | |
|---|---|---|---|---|---|---|---|---|---|---|
| | | | Total | Adult Basic Education | English for Speakers of Other Languages | Adult Secondary Education | Total | Part Time | Full Time | Volunteer |
| Idaho | Federal: | $1,334,468 | 10,472 | 5,721 | 2,677 | 2,074 | 537 | 149 | 12 | 376 |
| | State: | $496,400 | | | | | | | | |
| | Total: | $1,830,868 | | | | | | | | |
| Massachusetts | Federal: | $6,758,226 | 13,295 | 4,174 | 6,531 | 2,590 | 2,977 | 668 | 553 | 1,756 |
| | State: | $19,545,465 | | | | | | | | |
| | Total: | $26,303,691 | | | | | | | | |
| Ohio | Federal: | $14,103,969 | 107,701 | 78,352 | 11,928 | 17,421 | 7,803 | 1,712 | 221 | 5,870 |
| | State: | $9,151,480 | | | | | | | | |
| | Total: | $23,255,449 | | | | | | | | |
| Pennsylvania | Federal: | $15,898,856 | 51,938 | 23,945 | 11,038 | 16,955 | 9,662 | 1,869 | 659 | 7,134 |
| | State: | $12,059,000 | | | | | | | | |
| | Total: | $27,957,856 | | | | | | | | |
| Virginia | Federal: | $8,255,055 | 25,410 | 11,030 | 6,273 | 8,107 | 1,535 | 1,209 | 179 | 147 |
| | State: | $3,500,000 | | | | | | | | |
| | Total: | $11,755,055 | | | | | | | | |

**Table 5.1. Quantitative Comparison of Five States.**

*Source:* Based on information provided by the U.S. Department of Education, Office of Vocational and Adult Education, Division of Adult Education and Literacy, Aug. 1999.

the South), and their state and ABE populations range considerably in size. While Idaho has a student enrollment of 10,472, Ohio serves more than ten times that number. Although a simple division of federal and state dollars by number of students enrolled does not account for other funding sources, reflect how dollars are actually allocated, or indicate quality of services, it can indicate differences in the distribution of resources. For example, Massachusetts receives a particularly large state allocation for ABE that allows it to spend more than ten times as much per student ($1,978) as Idaho does, which has the lowest possible dollar amount spent per student ($175) of the five states. Pennsylvania and Virginia, similar to each other in spending per student ($538 and $463, respectively), fall in between Idaho and Ohio ($216) at the low end of the spectrum and Massachusetts at the high end.

States also differ in the type of students they serve. The categories used by the Office of Vocational and Adult Education at the U.S. Department of Education to describe the adult learners served by federal dollars are adult basic education (ABE), English as a second language (ESL), and adult secondary education (ASE). (ESL is also referred to as ESOL, English for speakers of other languages.)[5] In Idaho and Pennsylvania, ABE students make up about half of the total adult student population. In Massachusetts, the ABE population makes up only about one-third of the adult student population; more than half of those served are in ESOL programs. This is a far greater proportion of ESOL to ABE and ASE students than in any other of the four states. Proportionally, Pennsylvania and Virginia serve significantly more ASE students than the other three states.

Because our focus is on professional development, it is even more relevant to compare demographic information related to the personnel data for these five states. The student-to-staff ratio varies greatly.[6] Idaho, Ohio, and Virginia all have ratios that average around 16 to 1. Pennsylvania and Massachusetts show an average student-to-staff ratio of around 5 to 1. This difference may be an indication of greater emphasis on classroom and group instruction versus one-to-one and small group learning contexts. One might infer that a higher ratio of students to staff indicates a larger percentage of paid staff (assuming that classes are usually taught by paid staff and that one-to-one and small group tutoring is done by volunteers). While it is true that Virginia, with one of the highest student-to-staff ratios (16.6 to 1), has the highest percentage of paid staff (90 percent), the statistics are somewhat inconsistent. Massachusetts has the lowest student-to-staff ratio (4.5 to 1) and the second highest percentage of paid staff (41 percent). While Pennsylvania and Ohio have roughly the same percentage of paid staff (26 percent and 25 percent, respectively), the student-to-staff ratio is quite different—5.3 to 1 in Pennsylvania and 13.8 to 1 in Ohio.

Another distinction can be found in the percentage of volunteers to total staff. Here, Virginia stands out with a workforce that is only 10 percent volunteer. The other states range from 60 to 75 percent, with most in the upper part of this range. Finally, the statistics indicate that in most cases, only a minuscule proportion of staff work full time in the field.[7] In Idaho and Ohio, fewer than 5 percent of the staff work full time. Pennsylvania does only slightly better at 7 percent. Virginia is in the middle of the range, with a 12 percent full-time workforce. Massachusetts is an outlier at 19 percent. Even this relatively high percentage indicates a workforce with very little full-time representation. Unfortunately, there is no information available on how much states spend on professional development.

A number of other features differentiate the contexts of service delivery in these five states, and they illustrate the many ways in which systems can vary while still working to accomplish similar aims. At a general level of structure, these distinctions include whether and what kind of certification is required for practitioners, the number of funded programs in the state, and the mode of service delivery (for example, services may be offered through postsecondary institutions, school districts, community-based organizations, literacy councils, or an eclectic mix). More specifically related to professional development, contextual distinctions include the existence and role of the state literacy resource center (or some similar state-level entity); the ways in which volunteers are trained and supported over time; the availability of stipends, travel expenses, and program-based professional development funds; and the ways in which professional development systems are staffed. Table 5.2 provides a brief synopsis of these contextual features in the five states under discussion here.

## Thumbnail Sketches

These sketches of the five states set the scene for the discussion that follows. Following the descriptions of each state, we present a more in-depth, cross-state analysis to illustrate what certain aspects of professional development systems look like in practice.[8]

| | Required Practitioner Credential | Number of Programs Receiving Federal Funds | Primary Mode of Service Delivery | State Literacy Resource Center/ Central PD Entity | PD Staffing and Location | Individual PD Requirements (State Level) | PD Support |
|---|---|---|---|---|---|---|---|
| Idaho | None. | 6 (The Idaho Migrant Council and Department of Corrections also receive funds.) | State postsecondary institutions. | Member of the Northwest Regional Literacy Resource Center consortium. | State ABE staff development coordinator subcontracted with University of Idaho. | None. | Programs receive a training budget to cover travel, lodging, per diem, and salary. Some trainings offer reimbursement directly from the state. |
| Massachusetts | None (voluntary certification being developed). | About 200 (about 125 additional unfunded programs). | Varied. | Five regional centers and a central resource center. | World Education contracted to be the Central Resource Center; five community colleges have grants to be regional support centers. The DOE has a liaison to SABES. | Full-time staff, fifty hours per year; part-time staff, fifteen hours per year. | Full-time staff receive up to fifty hours paid release time; part-time staff receive a minimum of fifteen hours per year. New staff receive fifteen-hour orientation. |

Table 5.2. Teacher Requirements, Service Delivery, and Organization of Professional Development in Five States.

| | Required Practitioner Credential | Number of Programs Receiving Federal Funds | Primary Mode of Service Delivery | State Literacy Resource Center/ Central PD Entity | PD Staffing and Location | Individual PD Requirements (State Level) | PD Support |
|---|---|---|---|---|---|---|---|
| Ohio | Certification, based on Ohio revised code required in school district programs. Certification recommended but not required in others. | 158 | Varied. | Resource Center Network: Ohio Literacy Resource Center and four ABLE Regional Resource Centers. | Each regional state consultant supervises one center; one is also assigned to oversee administration of PD system (in addition to other responsibilities) and coordinate resource center network activities. | Completion of an individual PD plan. Two activities per year required for those who work seven or more hours per week; one activity required for those who work fewer hours. | Stipends and expense reimbursement for at least two activities a year for those who work seven or more hours per week; one for those who work fewer hours. Additional activities supported pending availability of funds. |
| Pennsylvania | None. | 221 | Varied. | State literacy resource center functions as a materials resource to the PD system, programs, and practitioners. | Six regional PD centers (situated in a variety of contexts) contracted to provide services. ABLE bureau staff person supervises. | Program requirements to participate in program improvement, technology, and assessment training. No individual requirements. | Stipends and travel reimbursement for some activities. |

| Virginia | K–12 certification required but waived when certified personnel are not available. | 66 (about 88 volunteer-based programs receive some support but no federal funds). | Primarily public school districts and a few community colleges. | AELC. | The AELC houses the Center for Professional Development and the Resource Center subcontracted to Virginia Commonwealth University. The system also includes the Virginia Adult Institute for Lifelong Learning (regional and topical conferences), the Virginia Adult Education Research Network, and the *Progress Newsletter*. Each activity is contracted separately. | Professional development plans. | Programs are required to allocate money to cover teacher salary for ten hours per year of PD (twenty hours per year for new teachers). |

**Table 5.2. Teacher Requirements, Service Delivery, and Organization of Professional Development in Five States (*continued*).**

*Note:* PD = professional development; DOE = U.S. Department of Education; SABES = System for Adult Basic Education Support;

ABLE = Adult Basic and Literacy Education; AELC = Adult Education and Literacy Centers.

**IDAHO.** Idaho's professional development system is based on a learning organization model defined in the state plan as an organization that supports "systemic organizational learning." The system is envisioned to "create continuous learning opportunities, promote inquiry and dialogue, encourage collaboration and team learning, establish systems to capture and share learning, empower people toward a collective vision, and connect the organization to its environment."[9] The system serves six regionalized literacy service providers that operate multiple learning sites around the state. Professional development leadership is provided by the state director and a staff person who works, under a subcontract, for the University of Idaho. As a member state of the Northwest Regional Literacy Resource Center (NWRLRC),[10] Idaho was involved in the development of and has implemented a series of fourteen professional development modules of twelve to fourteen hours each with the following features: presession preparation, introduction of theory, demonstration, practice, structured feedback, application, and reflection and evaluation. The topics covered include adults as learners, communicative English for speakers of other languages (ESOL), cooperative learning, teaching the reading process, and math as problem solving. The professional development system uses practitioners as trainers and an incentive system that certifies participants as advanced and master-level instructors on completion of a specified number of modules. In addition to this form of professional development, aimed at individuals, the state staff has implemented a process of continuous program improvement that requires programs to integrate professional development plans into their funding proposals. A third part of the system funds special projects. Special staff development projects have focused on statewide needs (such as the development of a management information system) and the piloting and implementation of initiatives such as the Crossroads Café, a video-based, distance-learning ESOL curriculum. Grants that fund these latter activities are usually awarded by the state on a regional basis and go to one of the six provider organizations.

**MASSACHUSETTS.** The System for Adult Basic Education Support (SABES) has been in existence for nearly ten years. Organized geographically, the Massachusetts professional development system has five regional centers and a Central Resource Center. Each regional center has limited flexible funds to provide a menu of training, teacher sharing, practitioner research, and other activities. Representatives from each center meet regularly, along with staff from the state's

Department of Education, to plan professional development activities and work toward integrating these with program and system development. SABES encourages the identification of and response to local needs and supports field-based, local professional development leadership. It is also responsible for implementing state-level initiatives, such as the development of a voluntary teacher certification plan. Thus, SABES strives to balance field-driven and funder-driven needs. Full-time practitioners in Massachusetts receive up to fifty hours of paid staff release time to participate in professional development; part-time staff receive a minimum of fifteen hours.

OHIO. The professional development system in Ohio is shaped by input from the field. Each of the state's four regional resource centers develops a calendar of professional development activities based on annual submissions from all funded programs in their areas of a document called the Program Professional Development Plan. This plan is designed to encourage individual and programwide reflection on and planning of professional development needs based on annual program performance reports. Although the resource centers operate somewhat autonomously, they are guided by a common set of goals and objectives. A statewide literacy resource center and an evaluation design team are responsible for research and implementation of initiatives with state and national connections, implications, and applications. These include work on Equipped for the Future (EFF), ABLE LINK (Ohio's management information system), and leadership development. In addition, the evaluation design team is working on developing connections among the program review process, ABLE LINK, and local program evaluation and continuous improvement efforts. Practitioners who work seven or more hours per week in funded programs are required to participate in at least two professional development activities a year. Those who work fewer than seven hours are required to participate in one.

PENNSYLVANIA. Six regional professional development centers (PDCs) provide the majority of professional development in Pennsylvania. Although intended to be responsive to local needs, the PDCs spend a lot of time coordinating local trainings of centrally planned professional development activities. Many of these centrally planned activities are developed (with significant input from the field) in the service of an overall program improvement agenda envisioned by the ABE state director. Some PDCs, as well as other entities (universities, for instance), receive additional funds to develop and provide statewide professional development activities related to special initiatives; these activities may include training modules, workshops on learning differences, technology training, and practitioner inquiry and action research. Although there are no individual requirements for participation in professional development, all funded programs are required to have representatives take part in centrally planned training related to assessment, management information, and program improvement strategies. Participants range from program administrators to volunteers, depending on activity offered, individual and program interests, and time commitment involved.

VIRGINIA. The hallmark of Virginia's professional development system is its requirement that all practitioners working in funded programs develop (with the support of a local learning plan facilitator), individually or in collaboration with others, a yearly professional development plan. The centralized Adult Education and Literacy Centers, which house the Resource Center and the Center for Professional Development, act as the hub of the system by developing and analyzing a database of all of these plans. These efforts generate professional development activities and help to connect practitioners with similar interests. Other regionally or centrally planned efforts support implementation of the plans. These include regional conferences, a research network, and a quarterly newsletter. Larger urban adult learning programs are assumed by the state to have internal mechanisms for providing professional development in response to site-based needs, and no additional provisions are made to support their efforts locally. However, rural areas are supported by regional adult education specialists, whose key responsibilities include providing instructional assistance and professional development opportunities for the practitioners in their regions.

## Professional Development System Features Close-Up

The thumbnail sketches begin to illustrate some features that are similar in the implementation of professional development across these five states. These include what we have termed scope, cooperative leadership, coherence, and accessibility. In fact, these characteristics are so evident across all five state systems that we propose them as key features of ABE professional development systems.

This section details the ways in which the five states are acting to implement these features as a way to better illustrate how they function as systems.

We begin by defining these features based on our understanding of the systems we studied. By *scope* we mean that the system accommodates and serves the full range of practitioners from program managers to volunteer tutors—regardless of role, level of experience and training, and interests; makes professional development available in varying degrees of intensity and duration throughout the year; and provides professional development activities and offerings in a wide range of formats and topics. By *cooperative leadership,* we mean that state-level staff take clear responsibility for management of the system but often work with practitioners to develop a vision for the system and its implementation. While there is a high level of collaboration, state-level staff usually have a leading role in shaping the system and setting policy and have more responsibility for its maintenance than do practitioners in the field. *Coherence* signifies that there is a logical relationship among the various activities and an overall alignment across individual and program development needs as well as state and national system reforms. It also involves the development of structures and activities that are based on needs assessment that is demand driven (as articulated by practitioners and programs or by competencies and standards established through legislation, state and federal policy, and a field-driven process of feedback and input). *Accessibility* implies that the professional development system makes training available at varied times and locations so that as many practitioners as possible can participate. Distance learning technology is being used increasingly to facilitate accessibility.

SCOPE. The scope of the five professional development systems described here is evident in their offerings. Each of the five states is making a systematic effort to reach out to practitioners who fill all types of job responsibilities and have a wide range of years of experience. For example, Ohio and Pennsylvania offer professional development activities aimed specifically at administrators and program managers. All five ABE departments fund statewide and, in some cases, local tutor training and ongoing support. Massachusetts has a required fifteen-hour orientation for new adult education staff that practitioners must attend during their first year in the field.

Activities occur throughout the year. For example, although the model of summer institutes developed in the 1960s still exists, it has been altered in a variety of ways. Often much shorter (three or four days), institutes now may focus on a particular topic or be aimed at a specific group of practitioners. They are not always held in the summer and sometimes include either face-to-face follow-up or ongoing support through the use of technology. Meanwhile, a wealth of other activities are available throughout the entire year, during the day or evening and during the week or on weekends.

The range of activities being carried out in each state is wide: technical assistance, minicourses, research teams, minigrant projects, peer observations, classroom visitations, mentoring activities, curriculum development teams, inquiry groups and action research, training modules, workshops, conferences, focus groups, publication of newsletters, network building, and college courses. These activities vary greatly in terms of duration (from three hours to a year of ongoing meetings or class sessions) and intensity. They also make very different demands of participants, from simple attendance and participation to completion of research reports and other kinds of final products. These states also have resource centers that provide access to a variety of print materials available for individual reading and research. The varying formats and requirements employ a range of pedagogical approaches, from learner centered, participatory, and constructivist to knowledge transmission.

Similarly, the range of topics is far-reaching, organized around such general educational areas as adult learning and cognition; practice-based topics such as multilevel classroom teaching, project-based learning, and math as a problem-solving skill; programmatic issues such as data management, recruitment, and retention; and broader issues and initiatives in the field such as Equipped for the Future (EFF), SCANS, and technology use.

COOPERATIVE LEADERSHIP. The very existence of a state-level system for professional development may lead some to assume a relatively traditional hierarchical planning process in which notions of authority and control lead to top-heavy leadership practices. In fact, at least some of the states report that they have recently chosen to try to implement a more centrally driven system after many years of local autonomy and little central leadership or direction. For example, in Idaho, programs were given funds for professional development to use as they saw fit. In Ohio, regional centers were funded and became operational before much central planning had taken place. As a result, each of these centers implemented some unique professional development approaches and strategies. Similarly, Pennsylvania had nine regional professional development providers that for the most part functioned independently and often created programs that were unique but sometimes inconsistent from one to another. Cheryl Keenan, Pennsylvania state director, explained that while professional development offerings in several regions might be on a similar topic, the information presented might vary considerably and could be contradictory from one region to another. The movement toward more centralized planning and uniformity is related to a need to monitor the quantity and quality of offerings more consciously so that more effective links among professional development, practice, and program improvement can be made. Such efforts also assist in the development of overall system coherence. Ultimately such centralized leadership may have been instituted in anticipation of or in response to the demands of WIA for performance-based accountability. Thus, while the state-level agencies are demanding more accountability— owing at least in part to WIA—they are also offering program strategies to cope with these requirements and improve services for learners. Although there may be drawbacks associated with taking greater control, these changes are leading to systems that increasingly are more coherent and linked, evidently as a result of more centralized planning and leadership.

State-level leadership has begun to exert more control over professional development offerings and participation in three ways: (1) requirements, (2) incentives or encouragement to participate, and (3) implementation of statewide professional development initiatives. Requirements include mandated planning strategies (such as the individual or program professional development plans found in Virginia and Ohio), the amount of time practitioners must spend in professional development activities (Ohio and Massachusetts), and the type of professional development activities in which practitioners participate (Pennsylvania requires all funded programs to send representatives to three different professional development activities; Massachusetts requires new teachers to participate in a specially designed training). Idaho and Massachusetts are using strategies that encourage voluntary use of the professional development system. Massachusetts funds a significant number of hours of participation, while Idaho rewards practitioners by creating titles ("advanced instructor" and "master instructor") that signify a certain level of participation in the professional development system. Another strategy that comes from the top down is the planning and implementation of uniform activities offered statewide, often in multiple venues to maximize accessibility. Training modules used in Pennsylvania and Idaho are good examples of this approach to centralized professional development.

While state-level staff take the lead in many aspects of design and implementation, practitioners help shape systems through various means: participation in planning committees and task forces, design and facilitation of professional development activities, and expression of their professional development needs through participation in individual and program planning procedures. For example, SABES in Massachusetts selects professional development topics in three ways: regional centers conduct ongoing needs assessment with teachers and other program staff to decide on the content and type of staff development activities; discussions between staff at regional centers and at the Central Resource Center help to identify topics of interest to many practitioners across regions; and staff and program development is organized through yearly work plans developed through negotiation among the state department of education, the CRC, and the regional center SABES staff. Such a structure allows for balancing the needs of the ABE system as a whole with those of individuals and programs.

Practitioners participate actively in all of these states as professional development leaders. The SABES system, for instance, is built on the assumption that practitioners best understand their own needs and have the skills and knowledge to support and enable the strengthening of the field. They are frequently involved in task forces and planning groups that help to shape professional development mission statements for the system, set and define policy, and develop implementation strategies. They also frequently function as trainers, facilitators, curriculum developers, conference presenters, and newsletter writers and editors.

The advantages of this high level of involvement are easy to articulate. For example, practitioner participation helps to make the system field driven, it grounds professional development activities in the day-to-day realities of practitioners' work, and it helps create a sense of personal investment and buy-in. Nevertheless, the data from our interviews with state-level professional development staff suggest that when systems depend both philosophically and practically on practitioners for help in developing and maintaining system activities, there may be a constant struggle to find individuals who have the time and energy to take on leadership responsibilities.

COHERENCE. All five states have worked diligently to establish logical relationships in the range of their professional development offerings to ensure internal coherence across activities. Such coherence creates systems that are simultaneously aligned with program improvement goals (such as management and accountability systems, which contribute to whole system reform), self-identified program and individual practitioner professional development needs, and national initiatives and legislation (EFF, the WIA, and welfare reform, for example).

In each of the five states, the state-level leadership is working to make such alignment more possible by implementing management information systems that can provide programs with useful data about their programs' strengths and weaknesses and to train program staff to analyze and use this information effectively. Ohio, Pennsylvania, Idaho, and Massachusetts have established processes designed to match programwide challenges and needs with professional development through the systematic collection and analysis of program data. In Idaho, the state ABE director and the staff development coordinator visit each funded program at least once during the year for what they call a results-based reporting discussion. In this discussion, program staff are "encouraged to integrate their annual reports into their strategic planning process and to look at the annual report as both a statistical report and a planning tool to support learning gains" (*Idaho Adult Basic Education Five-Year State Plan,* 1999). Massachusetts, using the integrated program staff development process, engages in a similar activity to encourage program-level planning. Professional development, then, is based on goals developed through a process of continuous program improvement, and program data are used as a planning tool.

Pennsylvania has engaged in a three-year project to train staff at all of its 221 funded programs in a process of program improvement called Educational Quality for Adult Literacy. This process begins with program self-evaluation. Program improvement teams (made up of agency staff) then collect program data in response to a question they have generated regarding program structure, operation, or service provision that emerges from the self-study. Finally, the team develops a plan for professional development that addresses the program and individual practitioner needs identified through this process.

In Ohio, each program is directed to work as a team to complete a needs analysis using local annual performance report data. During this process, each staff member translates program goals into what is called an Individual Professional Development Plan. These plans are approved by the local program administrator and subsequently summarized in a Program Professional Development Plan. As part of this document, the administrator states whether local professional development is available to address this need or if assistance is needed from the regional resource center. Thus, when planning documents from programs throughout a region are forwarded to the regional resource center, staff can use them as a key source in setting priorities and planning the professional development offerings for the year. For instance, technology training may be planned if it emerges as a commonly stated need at the program level.

Each of these centrally planned and locally implemented strategies for linking professional development with program improvement uses competencies, standards, or other indicators of quality as part of the process. For example, Pennsylvania's self-evaluation is based on the state's program performance standards, which focus on administrative reporting, enrollment, retention, pre- and posttesting, and educational gains.[11]

Another way in which professional development providers strive to create coherence in their systems is to serve as a clearinghouse, connecting programs and practitioners with the resources and information they need to obtain their goals. Ohio, for example, makes a systematic effort to link individual and program development needs with the state-level staff who can address those needs. Virginia requires all practitioners to submit annual professional development plans and maintains an extensive database that catalogues these plans. The plans help practitioners focus their professional development activities for the year and give the central organization (the Center for Professional Development) a look at professional development needs around the state. Staff at the center use the individual practitioner plans to identify trends and common issues. The professional development staff pass the information along to professional development conference planners or newsletter editors, make matches between individual practitioners and existing professional development offerings, connect practitioners from around the state who have expressed similar interests, and recommend other resources through which practitioners might address specific professional development needs and interests. One example of how this works is evidenced in a call for proposals put out by the Adult Education and Literacy Centers workshops that will be listed in its annual *Professional Development Catalogue.* The catalogue is based in part on an analysis of the professional development plans submitted in the previous year.

Yet another way in which professional development providers have built coherence into their professional development systems is by acting as a bridge between programs and broad national initiatives and legislation. Each of the five states is using its professional development system to meet requirements related to the WIA. Although the WIA requirements are aimed at state agencies, professional development systems are being used so that programs can help their state agencies meet their requirements. Although such professional development may be an example of the tail wagging the dog, these activities can benefit programs, practitioners, and learners.

For example, all states need to implement a management information system to address the accountability section of this legislation. Idaho and Pennsylvania began implementing a management information system before the legislation was passed and then established professional development activities that enabled programs to meet their federal reporting requirements and better use data to inform program improvement. States are providing professional development related to program standards and teacher competencies. While it may be possible to critique the particulars of some of these initiatives, the overall intent of linking professional development to program improvement in response to federal legislation creates coherence in the system.

Another example of a national initiative is EFF, a content framework for adult literacy standards. Pennsylvania is using the EFF framework as a program improvement–related instructional strategy in the context of its program improvement initiative and is providing professional development to support this process. Ohio has encouraged programs to pilot EFF through its quality enhancement grant program and has supported these efforts through ongoing training and support provided by national EFF staff and Ohio-based experts.

ACCESSIBILITY. Because widespread participation is a key element in ensuring that professional development systems fulfill their potential, working to maximize accessibility is viewed as critical in all five states. Accessibility to professional development takes a variety of forms.

Bringing professional development as close as possible to the practitioner (rather than centralizing the offerings in one location) is a practical and common strategy that cuts down on travel expenses and the time spent away from classrooms and programs.

To bring the training to the practitioner, four of the five states studied have developed a regional system for delivering professional development, although each of these regionalized structures is different. Some salient differences concern what type of entity houses regional centers, how the centers are staffed, how they relate to each other and to a central planning body that may be inside or outside the state agency, and how autonomous they are. Regardless of the differences, a regional structure has the advantage of making professional development more accessible than centrally implemented activities and provides a potential for cross-program fertilization and exchange of ideas.

The staff in the five states studied did not discuss the use of technology in relation to the goal of improving accessibility to professional development activities. However, technology is becoming an increasingly important vehicle for communication, data management (as in Virginia's use of a database to analyze and respond to professional development plans for multiple purposes), service provision (distance-learning strategies such as downlinking teleconferences and on-line courses), and problem solving (often using listservs). Most states now have Web sites, many with a link to the state-level entity responsible for ABE, and more and more practitioners have access to e-mail. From the interviews we conducted and our personal experiences, we have found that technology that seemed rare and exotic just a few years ago is now available to professional developers and participants alike. However, the challenges as to how best to use technology for professional development remain. These include how to create learning communities and networks in the face of physical (if not virtual) distance, how to overcome the unequal distribution of technology, and how best to match the range of professional development content and delivery formats with available technology.

## Common Issues, Challenges, and Lessons Learned

Each of the five states has a well-defined, coherent professional development system, but each also faces challenges that are to a large extent rooted in the structure of the ABE workforce, which is largely part time and has a high rate of attrition. In the five states studied, only

7 percent of the combined workforce are employed full time, and 68 percent are volunteers. This type of employment structure leads to a high turnover rate and extremely limited time on the part of practitioners for professional development. Sally Waldron, the director of the SABES Central Resource Center, asked, "Is there hope for real capacity building given the essential nature of part-time staff? Would you ever try to educate kids with people who work six hours a week without benefits? Is it folly to try to build a strong system of professional development on a delivery system with such an essential flaw?" In addition, because credentialing of any kind is still rare, practitioners enter the field with diverse experiences, often underdeveloped teaching skills, and no background in adult education, thus taxing the capacity of staff development systems to offer training that is relevant to their varying needs and abilities. In large states with an eclectic combination of programs providing ABE, program support needs are as varied as those of practitioners. Waldron summarizes the issue well:

> When professional development is statewide, and you're trying to reach everyone, you've got a huge range of strengths and needs and experience. The range never gets smaller. There are always new people on the one hand and you have to get them initially trained. On the other hand, there are always really experienced, strong practitioners who need opportunities for in-depth staff development. And then there's everyone in between. Since one of the features of the system is a belief in the need to integrate program development with staff development, the system also faces a challenge in meeting the wide range of program types and needs, which are as varied as practitioners' needs.

Not only does the nature of the workforce complicate efforts to make professional development accessible and appropriate, it also complicates efforts to involve the field in planning, decision making, and implementation. For example, a necessary ingredient of involvement in professional development planning and leadership may be attendance at frequent and lengthy meetings, sometimes quite distant from the workplace. Only the small pool of full-time practitioners are likely able to attend with any consistency. Moreover, while such opportunities may eventually serve as springboards for upward career movement, limited opportunities for state-level responsibilities and leadership make such advancement more of a promise than a reality.

In our conversations with state staff, we noted several challenges that all of the five state professional development systems face:

- *Spearheading change* by functioning as visionaries responsible for implementing overall reform and growth of the professional development system
- *Working to balance top-down and bottom-up needs and interests* by involving stakeholders at all levels of the system in planning and implementation while maintaining the basic vision
- *Building a shared vision of a professional development system* among multiple stakeholders, including professional development staff, program administrators, teachers, and tutors

While these challenges are most related to the problem of establishing coherence in professional development systems and we have compartmentalized them for the sake of discussion, they are all in fact interrelated.

SPEARHEADING CHANGE. Many of the state staff members interviewed talked about spearheading change: taking the lead in building, shaping, and reforming the professional development system in their states. Cheryl Engel, Idaho staff development coordinator, and Shirley Spencer, Idaho ABE state director, discussed the challenge of moving from a relatively autonomous, field-driven system to one with internal coherence that links professional development to program improvement and learner outcomes. Engel and Spencer focused on the challenges of spearheading change, restructuring, and initiating reform from the top down in an environment that has often espoused a collaborative and participatory philosophy. They see their task as moving slowly and incrementally toward change, all the while ensuring that local programs can see the benefit of a new system. This is a particularly tricky task given that program directors are losing some local control in the process. "If you're going to shift something, it had better be for a good reason," Engel stated. More important, she explained, the rationale for change must be clearly and consistently communicated to make sure it is thoroughly understood at the local level. Change should also be implemented at a slow and steady pace, according to Spencer. "One of the things that I've found with all this is that you do have to allow time and you have to keep cultivating and nurturing what you're trying to do and altering it in small pieces. You don't get where you want to be as quickly as you want to. It takes time to develop a real system and it takes time for it to be recognized as a system—unless you want to be very directive and authoritarian."

Engel and Spencer discussed the approach they have employed to support centrally planned change. Understanding the program managers' points of view is important, they agreed. "You don't want your managers too ruffled," Engel explained,

> but I don't think that every decision about what you're going to do as a system can rest in each program manager's hands. But that's a hard line to walk. Sometimes it feels like the net is not close enough. You really have to handle with care. In fairness, my job is to help them elevate professional development to a place in their program where it becomes more of a priority. They have so many things they're trying to juggle that professional development has been relegated to a back burner.

Engel seems to combine a sensitivity to the difficulty of change (especially when it involves ceding control) with a very strong message about its importance (for instance, by requiring that program professional development plans be submitted as part of a program's grant application). "Not to hold a stick over them, but it does imply that it's going to be important," adds Spencer.

This sort of approach to instituting change is also favored by Cheryl Keenan, Pennsylvania state director of the Bureau for Adult Basic and Literacy Education, who, following her appointment as state director, restructured the professional development system initiated by her predecessor. Keenan found ways to nudge change along at the level of implementation by adjusting some structural procedures. For example, she had regional professional development centers submit bids for funding after having received funding for several years without competitive bidding. As part of that process, she altered the proposal guidelines. Submitted proposals now had to reflect the system's newly developed Guiding Principles for Professional Development. By insisting that professional development centers' goals and objectives be consistent with these principles, she was trying to build commitment to the principles, as well as consistency between the system's overall mission and its actual implementation. She noted the importance of developing and building on field-based expertise in the implementation of various centrally planned but locally implemented initiatives: "This makes a difference in terms of acceptance of new ideas."

STRIKING A BALANCE IN COOPERATIVE LEADERSHIP. The concerns expressed about making changes from the top down may indicate a commitment on the part of professional development staff to find an appropriate and comfortable way of balancing top-down leadership with direction and input from the field; all of the state staff members we talked to discussed the challenge of balancing professional development offerings and requirements that are implemented in response to funding legislation with practitioner needs for ongoing training. Sally Waldron, for example, observes that Massachusetts has experienced a tremendous amount of innovation and change owing to centrally planned strategic initiatives. Although she believes that many program staff see these changes as positive and may ultimately have made some of them anyway, the sheer volume of initiatives is overwhelming:

> Programs do want to work on program strengthening, but they can only do so much. This presents two major challenges to the professional development system. First, people in programs are overwhelmed by initiatives, so they are much less focused on their individual professional development needs given the little time available to reflect on those needs. Meanwhile, the technical assistance people are overwhelmed trying to help programs with what they need to respond to these initiatives. Also, this presents a challenge to the field-driven nature of the system, since it is being initiated by the state department of education rather than the balanced field- and funder-driven system that is the vision of both SABES and the state ABE agency.

Cheryl Keenan too talked about the difficulty of responding to the demands for accountability, which have become such a dominant part of the ABE climate, when the philosophical underpinnings of the system (as stated in Pennsylvania's professional development "Guiding Principles") is of a more learner- and program-centered philosophy. "When I see how people respond to the standards, I'm afraid that the pressing demands of numbers contradicts the philosophy of learning that we're trying to put into place. It's the tail wagging the dog situation. Accountability is here to stay, but it's creating a tension."

Susan Joyner, director of the Virginia Adult Education and Literacy Centers, echoed these concerns. She noted tension in a system that positions itself as driven by teachers' questions about practice when there is a gap between "where practitioners are"—that is, what they identify as their professional development needs—and "where larger trends suggest that they—and programs—need to be." She continued, "The system's impulse to honor teachers' questions and the need to respond effectively to larger trends in the field represent a tension within inquiry-based staff development." In a more general sense, she, like others, is discussing the difficulty of walking the fine line between a commitment to collaboration and responsiveness and the need to implement a particular vision (not necessarily derived through inter-action with practitioners) of professional development (and, more generally, ABE service provision). This dilemma, expressed with regard to professional development, parallels one that is inherent in learner-centered education in any context. That is, it raises the questions of where the lines of authority and control should be drawn and how they can best be negotiated when the intent is to put the learner (in this case, the practitioner) in charge of his or her own learning.

The ongoing struggle over what and who should drive the system reflects a learning philosophy that respects the knowledge and experience of practitioners and the challenges of their work. However, there are no easy answers. From a policy perspective, the challenges discussed here reflect the fact that the requirements of the funder (the federal and state governments) are sometimes putting professional development system staff in the middle of the competing interests of practitioners and state and federal policy makers. Although everyone seems to be developing their system from this position, it is not necessarily a comfortable place to be.

Despite the discomfort, state professional development staff are cognizant of the importance of buy-in from the field when professional development requirements and expectations are changed from the top. They believe that the extent of practitioners' commitment to change (no matter where the drive to change comes from) will be determined to a large degree by their perceptions of its usefulness. Keenan explained, "I hope that once people have experienced the process and the 'I have to do this' attitude, they'll see that they got something valuable out of it. This change in mindset might pave the way to more conscious, thoughtful professional development choices in the future."

Joyner too stresses how important it is for practitioners to realize that professional development can support their needs rather than merely add to their workload. "It remains a challenge for people to see the staff development system as a means of tackling large new initiatives like EFF or welfare reform. Too often people see professional development as separate from, rather than integral to, these initiatives."

BUILDING A SHARED VISION. Denise Pottmeyer, Ohio ABLE LINK supervisor, talked about the challenges of communicating across a system that is striving for but not always achieving coherence—of how hard it can be for the right hand to know (and build on) what the left hand is doing. Because of the way in which professional development is staffed and special projects are funded in Ohio, communication is difficult, and opportunities for professional development staff to benefit from one another's projects are sometimes missed, she reported. Given the structure that is in place, she said, it is very easy for efforts to become fragmented. "We're getting better at this, but it is still difficult." She notes that improving communication among the various parts of the professional development system is key to addressing this problem, which is amplified by the fact that members of the professional development staff are spread out across the state and are often pursuing special (and unique) areas of interest and expertise.

Although Massachusetts and Ohio have on the surface a similar structure for service delivery, Waldron did not share Pottmeyer's concerns about fragmentation. She feels, for the most part, that diverse efforts are well coordinated and that roles and responsibilities are clear. Waldron noted that a collaborative and participatory structure requires concerted effort to ensure the continuation of a shared vision by professional development staff, the composition of which periodically changes as a result of system growth and, to a lesser extent, staff turnover. Such effort, she explained, includes paying regular attention to decision making and communication structures. Massachusetts professional development staff spend an extraordinary amount of time in face-to-face meetings to clarify and coordinate efforts. According to Waldron, these extra efforts at communication do address some of the issues that Pottmeyer raised.

For Susan Joyner, a related challenge is that of ensuring that professional development staff have truly integrated the guiding philosophy of Virginia's professional development system into their own work: "One of the biggest challenges is keeping the original principles in the minds of people who plan and support staff development activities while at the same time allowing the principles to be open to critique and change." In general, concerns about keeping everyone "on the same page" are exacerbated by the pressures of the work. Everyone seems to feel a tremendous pressure to keep up with rapid change, which can conflict with the need to reflect on, restate, and continually revise the vision for professional development among state and regional professional development staff.

Finally, a number of those interviewed expressed concern about assessing the quality of the professional development offerings in their states. As Joyner explained, now that putting in the requisite hours is no longer enough when it comes to the accountability of the professional development system, there is a gaping hole in the knowledge base related to the evaluation of professional development. Keenan said that since Pennsylvania has put in place a fully functioning professional development system, she is faced with the question, "How good is it, and how well does it really align with, for example, needs and research? Is it internally consistent?" Similarly, members of the Idaho staff wonder how others are measuring the outcomes of professional development and deciding what is useful.

## IMPLICATIONS FOR PRACTICE, RESEARCH, AND POLICY

All staff members in each of the five states expressed great interest in learning from each other. The desire to acquire knowledge of other states' systems and activities seems driven by an interest in doing the best job possible in the most efficient manner. Not surprisingly, questions of best practice arose, indicating a pressing need for more research, not only on what constitutes "best practice" but on how particular learning theories and approaches to professional development translate into statewide delivery systems. For example, Joyner stated that while there is now a growing literature on inquiry-based professional development on the individual level (Drennon, 1994, 1997; Sherman & Green 1997), little information is available on how to translate its principles into a statewide system. Equally important is a curiosity about how other states organize their systems and what content they have developed that could be adopted or adapted. Limited funds, overstretched staffs, rapidly changing requirements, and an extremely diverse workforce in the field compel professional development staff in all the states to learn from each other.

## Practice

One key implication for practice is a call to find ways to involve practitioners more fully in shaping the vision and mission of professional development at the system level. Almost everyone we interviewed expressed a sense of frustration in their struggle to balance the sometimes competing interests of the overall system with local program and individual practitioner needs. Part of the problem may be the point at which practitioners are called in to contribute to the development and implementation of the system. Their role is often more reactive than proactive, being played out mostly at the level of implementation. For instance, when they are called in to collaborate with state- or regional-level professional development staff, it is often to make decisions about professional development offerings within a predetermined system context; they are then invited to make decisions about how practitioners could be involved as developers and facilitators, but only within that particular set of professional development needs. Practitioners need to enter into the important planning and policy conversations at all levels (local, regional, state, and federal) as they are taking place, not after the fact.

Just as practitioners in the field need meaningful opportunities to come together to share information and raise concerns about their work, so do state-level professional development staff. Although this kind of exchange is occurring to some degree within and across states, it is not taking place in a systematic or broad-based fashion. Such exchanges would provide professional development opportunities for the professional developers and contribute to both efficiency and innovation. Staff also need opportunities to learn more about research and policy so that they can more effectively participate in discussions in these areas and assist practitioners in developing their understanding of new requirements, how they may play out at the state, local, and program levels, and what they can do to shape adaptation and response (M. Drew Hohn, personal communication, June 2, 2000). Opportunities for face-to-face and electronic communication, sharing, and problem solving need to be organized nationally, and financial resources for information sharing are needed to support it.

## Research

A clear set of research implications emerges from our analysis of the professional development systems. Perhaps most pressing is the need to develop ways to assess professional development outcomes. A lack of consensus on what counts as success and how to measure it on the learner level complicates evaluations of professional development. Many people would like to identify a causal link between professional development and learner outcomes. Research done in Pennsylvania (Belzer, 1999), however, suggests that defining the impact of professional development in broader terms is an important first step in understanding its potential outcome.[12] Until we define impact and outcome, questions related to the quality of professional development will remain relatively unanswerable.

Another question to explore is what happens when cooperative leadership structures that have an implicit or explicit commitment to collaboration and shared decision making bump up against policies that are written by funders. Research could help develop knowledge in the field about "reconciliation" between what are basically divergent paradigms when they must coexist. Research could look outside the field for models of reconciliation that do not exclude the voice of practitioners. Meanwhile, certain tensions are inherent in cooperative leadership even when it is not buffeted by outside forces (Cervero & Wilson, 1994, 1998). When leadership is shared but not equal, as we see in the five states, stakeholders may need additional strategies and tools for mediating competing interests and resolving difficulties related to power and authority. Descriptive research that seeks to understand the multiple perspectives on roles and responsibility, leadership, and decision making that exist in the field may shed light on what shapes both positive and negative interactions among professional development staff, state ABE staff, and practitioners. Such findings could help all involved find more comfortable places from which to plan and implement activities with each other within the limitations and restraints in the system.

Finally, there are research questions related to professional development system structures. The different system structures in these five states raise a number of questions that merit further inquiry. We do not know in what ways participation rates, learner-to-practitioner ratios, employment status of practitioners, and other particulars of the state context influence professional development system structures. What are the critical factors in shaping professional development systems? In what ways are unique system elements serving a purpose relevant to a particular state's context (for instance, the geography, practitioner or learner characteristics, or the program delivery system)? In what ways do differences in system structures influence quality of professional development and, ultimately, learner outcomes?

Furthermore, it seems likely that contextual features, such as where ABE is placed in a state bureaucracy and how it is staffed, have an influence on professional development systems. Improving our understanding of these relationships may help professional development staff make more purposeful choices regarding the ongoing evolution and development of professional development systems.

## Policy

There are at least two important implications for policy. First, it is important for policymakers to understand that professional development systems are critical vehicles for putting policy into practice. Policymakers should make these systems an integral part of any policy implementation plan and make the funding of these systems a priority. Policy will likely fail unless policymakers recognize that professional development is crucial to any strategy intent on instituting change. The more communication and collaboration that take place among policymakers, funders, legislators, state directors, and professional development staff, the better that professional development systems can help programs and practitioners respond effectively to policy changes. Such cooperation can open up channels that may better allow the field to influence policy. Without making such connections, changes are more likely to be resisted, to be transitory, and to occur in chaotic and destabilizing environments. What must also be kept in focus here is the importance of addressing professional development needs as expressed by local programs and individuals. It will be important to find ways to moderate the impact of change initiated at the policy level so that professional development systems can remain responsive to the needs expressed at the individual and program level.

Second, it is important to recognize that while professional development systems need participatory leadership from stakeholders at all levels (including program managers, teachers, and tutors), such involvement by practitioners is undermined by employment structures that do not reward it. Until there are more full-time positions for practitioners and more paid positions for those who choose to move into professional development, the potential for a professional development system that is field driven will be limited. Similarly, the potential of professional development to have a positive influence on practice, program improvement, and policy implementation will be limited as long as the predominant employment model in ABE is a part-time and underpaid workforce with limited time and incentives to participate in professional development.

## Notes

1. The U.S. Department of Education, Office of Vocational and Adult Education, Division of Adult Education and Literacy differentiates adult education funding related to professional development in 1991 and 1998 as follows. In 1991 the legislation required that states "use not less than 10 percent of allotment for teacher training and must use an additional 5 percent for demonstration projects of teacher training." Based on the 1998 legislation, "states must use 12.5 percent of allotment for State Leadership activities which may include not only teacher training but also technical assistance, support for networks of resource centers, program evaluation, incentives, curriculum development, coordination, linking literacy and occupational training, linkages to postsecondary institutions and other projects of Statewide significance."

2. Although the intent of *The Annual Review of Adult Learning and Literacy* is to focus on best practices, this is a problematic goal with regard to professional development systems because so little research has been done in this area. In a review of the literature, Titzel (1998) identified twelve principles of effective staff development based on research in K–12 in a variety of contexts. The principles include such concepts as change takes time; staff development must be connected to a larger, coherent vision of reform and change; variety is needed in content and format; and student learning should be a central focus of the effort. However, these principles have not been studied empirically in ABE at the individual, program, or system level. We know little about the relationship between the application of these principles, for example, and the improvement of learner outcomes. A few states have conducted, or are in the process of conducting, evaluations of their professional development systems, but none has yet focused comprehensively on the impact of professional development (although this is under way in Pennsylvania). Nor are there studies in which one system is compared with another. In developing this chapter, we hoped that the selected state systems could serve as illustrative models. Given the paucity of empirical data, however, we could not choose state systems based on identification of best practices in the implementation

of professional development systems. In fact, the whole notion of best practices is problematic not only because professional development in adult literacy is underresearched but also because it is underconceptualized. In a field that lacks consensus on instructional goals and methods (Imel, 1998), a lack of consensus as to the best way for practitioners to do their jobs and the best way in which they should be trained is unavoidable.

3. Interview participants were Cheryl Engel, staff development coordinator, and Shirley Spencer, ABE state director, Idaho; Sally Waldron, director of the SABES Central Resource Center and of the Literacy Division at World Education of Massachusetts; Denise Pottmeyer, ABLE supervisor of Ohio; Cheryl Keenan, ABLE state director of Pennsylvania; and Susan Joyner, director of the Adult Education and Literacy Centers of Virginia. Each of these respondents holds a position of key responsibility for professional development in her state.

4. Federal funding to states is based on population. Therefore, each state's available resources for professional development vary greatly depending on the size of the state. While it is true that serving fewer people costs less money, it is also true that there are certain baseline costs associated with developing and maintaining a system that are similar no matter the size of the client base. These expenses include communicating with practitioners about professional development offerings, setting up a body that can organize professional development activities, maintaining a database of practitioners, and conducting needs assessments.

5. English as a second language (ESL) is the term used by the U.S. Department of Education. Gaining more currency in the ABE community is English for speakers of other languages (ESOL), the term used in the balance of this chapter.

6. It is important to note that figures on volunteer data reflect numbers of volunteers in federally funded programs only. Volunteer programs that do not receive such funding are not counted in any of the statistics provided by the Office of Vocational and Adult Education, Division of Adult Education and Literacy.

7. The term *full time* is not defined in the statistical information made available by the U.S. Department of Education, Office of Vocational and Adult Education, Division of Adult Education and Literacy, Aug. 1999.

8. These descriptions are based on data collected in spring 1999. These professional development systems are undergoing constant change, but

we believe that the brief sketches are timely enough to capture the spirit of these five states' efforts.

9. *Idaho Adult Basic Education Five-Year State Plan (Draft)* (1999).
10. The NWRLRC also provides other kinds of professional development support related to both technology and print resources.
11. *Pennsylvania Performance Standards for Adult Basic and Literacy Education Programs* (Sept. 1999).
12. By asking a broad range of practitioners in Pennsylvania to define impact with regard to professional development, Belzer identified five kinds of impact: changes in practice, changes in thinking, changes in professional attitude, changes in program structures, and changes in the broader field. She suggested that different kinds of professional development activities have different kinds of impact and that there should not be an expectation that all professional development will have a direct impact on learner outcomes in a measurable way.

## References

Belzer, A. (1999). *ABE professional development system evaluation report, year 1.* Harrisburg, PA: Pennsylvania Department of Education, Bureau of Adult Basic and Literacy Education.

Cervero, R., & Wilson, A. (1994). *Planning responsibly for adult education: A guide to negotiating power and interests.* San Francisco: Jossey-Bass.

Cervero, R., & Wilson, A. L. (1998). Working the planning table: The political practice of adult education. *Studies in Continuing Education, 20,* 5–21.

Chisman, F. P. (1990). The federal role in developing an effective adult literacy system. In F. P. Chisman & Associates (Eds.), *Leadership for literacy: The agenda for the 1990s.* San Francisco: Jossey-Bass.

Drennon, C. (1994). *Inquiry and action: Implementation guide for program administrators and staff development facilitators.* (ERIC Document No. 371 237)

Drennon, C. (Ed.). (1997). *Practitioner inquiry review.* Athens, GA: University of Georgia, Department of Adult Education, Adult Literacy Staff Development Project.

Fingeret, H. A. (1992). *Adult literacy education: Current and future directions. An update* (Information Series No. 355). Columbus, OH: ERIC Clearinghouse on Adult, Career, and Vocational Education, Center on Education and Training for Employment.

Hoffman, H., & Pagano, J. (1971). *ABE staff training: A new conceptual model for adult basic education staff training with application to corrections, new careers, and migrant education.* Washington, DC: Adult Education Association of the U.S.A.

*Idaho Adult Basic Education Five-Year State Plan (Draft).* (1999). Boise, ID: Idaho Department of Education/Adult Basic Education Office.

Imel, S. (1998). *Using adult learning principles in adult basic education: Practice application brief.* Columbus, OH: ERIC Clearinghouse on Adult, Career, and Vocational Education.

Leahy, M. (1986). *Recommendations for expanding and enhancing adult education staff development in Pennsylvania.* Harrisburg, PA: Pennsylvania Department of Education, Bureau of Adult Basic and Literacy Education. (ERIC Document No. 352 852)

Lytle, S., Belzer, A., & Reumann, R. (1992). *Invitations to inquiry: Rethinking staff development in adult literacy education* (Report No. TR92–2). Philadelphia: National Center on Adult Literacy.

Quigley, B. A. (1997). *Rethinking literacy education: The critical need for practice-based change.* San Francisco: Jossey-Bass.

RMC Research Corporation. (1996). *National evaluation of the Section 353 set-aside for teacher training and innovation in adult education, summary report.* Portsmouth, NH: RMC Research Corporation.

Rose, A. D. (1991). *Ends or means: An overview of the history of the Adult Education Act* (Information Series No. 346). Columbus, OH: ERIC Clearinghouse on Adult, Career, and Vocational Education, Center on Education and Training for Employment.

Sherman, R., & Green, K. (1997). *Inquiry/research compendium.* Washington, DC: Pelavin Research Institute.

Titzel, J. (1998). *Catalyst teacher research report.* Unpublished manuscript, World Education Literacy Division, Boston.

# CHAPTER SIX

# Adult Learning and Literacy in Canada

*Linda Shohet*

C anada is a vast country stretching millions of square miles with a population of only 30.5 million as of 1999. With the move from rural to urban centers during this century, the population has clustered around major cities but remains strung out across the continent, situated mostly within a hundred miles of the U.S.-Canada border. The physical distances between communities and the generally sparse population have contributed to strong regional identities, which in some parts of the country, such as Quebec and to a lesser extent some western provinces, can surpass national loyalties. These regional identities have shaped Canada's culture and forms of government and policies, including those pertaining to education. Thus, it is not possible to talk about a *single* system of service provision regarding adult learning and literacy. Each of the ten provinces and three territories has its own constitutionally guaranteed system, any of which may differ from one another as much as do the systems in two different countries.

The varied terminology used to refer to adult learning and literacy across Canada is perhaps a reflection of the jurisdiction of the provinces and territories over education. Across Canada, the terms *adult basic education* (ABE) and *literacy education* are not necessarily defined in the same way, nor are they defined in the same way that they are in the United States. *ABE* is generally used to describe education for adults at the high school level, while *literacy education* usually refers to education for adults up to grade 9. Nonetheless, the term *literacy* is increasingly being used interchangeably with *ABE* in many provincial documents. The difficulty of separating these terms is evident in the definitions of literacy in current use in three provinces. The government of Alberta supports a definition formulated in the International Adult Literacy Survey (IALS), conducted in 1994 and sponsored by the Canadian government and Organization for Economic Cooperation and Development (OECD): "[Literacy is] the ability to understand and employ printed information in daily activities at home, at work and in the community—to achieve one's goals and to develop one's knowledge and potential." Alberta officials supplement this with additional definitions of "essential skills" and "employability skills." Quebec defines literacy education as follows: "Literacy services are designed to enable an adult to increase his functional abilities through the acquisition of listening, oral expression, reading, writing and arithmetic skills based on his everyday activities and needs and, when applicable, to make it possible for him to pursue further studies" (Ministry of Education of Quebec, 1994). Newfoundland, sensitive to the complexity and relativity of the concept of literacy, does not work from a single definition. For the purposes of this chapter, I will use the terms *adult basic education* and *literacy education* interchangeably, in keeping with their use in the other chapters. When a distinction in the grade-level equivalency is necessary, I will indicate it.

## CULTURAL HISTORY

Like the United States, Canada is a country of immigrants carved out of land taken from its native inhabitants. After colonial battles between the British and French from the sixteenth to the eighteenth centuries, the British won final control in 1759. Unlike the United States, Canada was not created by means of a galvanizing ideology or momentous event such as the American Revolution. The country was built slowly, and often reluctantly, through negotiation and compromise, reflecting the distinct ethnic origins and geography of the provinces (Francis, Jones, & Smith, 1992; McConnell, 1977).

### "Two Solitudes"

Canada has had from its beginning two official languages. The title of a famous Canadian novel, *Two Solitudes,* has become a recognized metaphor for the relationship between the English and French communities in Canada. Until the 1960s, they had developed separate ways of life that rarely crossed except in dramatic circumstances, such as conscription during the two world wars.

Following the British conquest, in 1763 the British accorded the French guarantees of language and religion as a way of keeping peace with a minimal military presence. Quebec became and has remained the place where a majority of French-speaking Canadians (today called francophones) live. Small communities of francophones continued to live in other parts of Canada, especially Nova Scotia, New Brunswick, Ontario, and Manitoba. The French language survived because its use was institutionalized in the federal parliament, the Quebec legislature, and both federal and provincial courts. However, by the early twentieth century, the use of and official support for French had waned; two provinces had abolished official bilingualism, and some had limited the teaching of French. By the 1960s such teaching was almost nonexistent outside Quebec (Wagner, 1990), where strong nationalist feelings were mounting as part of a "Quiet Revolution." This term, coined by a Toronto-based reporter, became a shorthand way to describe a new political and cultural reality that was peacefully transforming Quebec socially and economically from a closed Catholic society to a province with modern business and government structures. Simultaneously, Quebec politicians were stoking a sense of "national" pride based on their French language and heritage. (In Canada, the word *national* means Canadian or federal; in Quebec, it refers to Quebec.) The motto of the newly elected provincial government in 1960 was "*Maîtres chez nous*" ("Masters in our home"). The federal government, fearing a polarization of Canada and Quebec, responded with dramatic new legislation that sought to reentrench bilingualism in all of Canada.

In 1963, the federal Commission on Bilingualism and Biculturalism recommended a charter for the official languages of Canada that was implemented in 1969 with the Official Languages Act. It gave people the right to federal government services in the "official" language of their choice and gave preferential treatment to bilingual public servants. In protecting "minority language rights," it also gave parents the right to request education in one of the two official languages for students in grades K–12, where numbers warranted. The term *minority language* applies to French outside the province of Quebec and to English inside Quebec. It does not apply to other languages. The Official Languages Act was enshrined in the 1982 Charter of Rights and Freedoms. This charter is increasingly being invoked in Canada's courts to claim individual rights and is seen by many groups across the country as vital to language rights.

The 1969 Official Languages Act, while not well received everywhere in Canada, did lead several provinces to implement their own language policies. The province of Quebec in 1977 passed Bill 101, the Charter of the French Language, making French the official language in Quebec, restricting access to education in English, and limiting the use of languages other than French on public signs.

Under the umbrella of Official Languages, Heritage Canada, a department of the federal government, still annually transfers millions of dollars to provincial and territorial governments and to community groups for language teaching and cultural education. More than $250 million (Canadian)[1] has been given out each year since 1993. Some of this money finds its way to ABE and literacy through various routes, including formal (or accredited) English as a second language/French as a second language (ESL/FSL) programs as well as volunteer and community-based projects and activities.[2] Very little second-language funding shows up in provincial reports on ABE and literacy, complicating the possibility of producing an accurate account of annual spending on these dossiers.

## "Cultural Mosaic"

Four main cultural groupings are distinguished in Canadian policy. Predominant are the "two founding nations," Anglo-Saxon and French. Another is Native cultures, those of the "First Nations," who were here before the colonizers arrived. The fourth comprises all the other ethnic groups, representing many races and nationalities, who have immigrated to Canada since the nineteenth century, but in greatest numbers since World War II.

This immigration has changed the face of the country. Since the 1960s, Canada has represented itself as both a bilingual and a multicultural country that the federal government prefers to call a "cultural mosaic" rather than a "melting pot." The metaphor is meant to support the idea of ethnic and cultural diversity, expressing the fact that the different immigrant communities maintain many traditions and often continue to speak the languages of their country of origin while also becoming "Canadian" (Hawkins, 1988).

The concepts of "two founding nations" and "cultural mosaic" coexist with tension. The term *multiculturalism* arose in the 1960s, partly in response to criticism that *biculturalism* unfairly favored French. The federal government formalized a policy in 1971 that recognized the diversity of Canada's ethnic and cultural groups and supported programs to maintain the distinctions and foster mutual respect and equality. This policy was viewed with hostility by those who feared its potential to undermine bicultural policies and weaken the status of the French language (Palmer, 1975).

During this period, policies supporting the teaching of "heritage languages" (the mother tongues of immigrant groups) were implemented by the federal Department of Secretary of State (today part of Heritage Canada). While these policies were formulated with the children of immigrants in mind, funding streams such as the Newcomers Language/Orientation Classes (NLOC) allowed some creative community-based adult educators the opportunity to offer mother tongue literacy to immigrants who were not literate in their mother tongue and, it was argued, could not easily learn English as a second language. St. Christopher House and several other community-based organizations in Toronto, Ontario, ran mother tongue literacy programs for immigrants into the 1980s. These initiatives laid the foundation for some current models of literacy provision. For example, NLOC services in the 1960s were expanded to include a mother and preschooler program encouraging reading to the child in the mother tongue; this component was later adapted by family literacy programs without the mother tongue emphasis (Larimer, 1999).

During the 1970s, concerns about the literacy of adults who had not completed at least the ninth grade began to emerge from the larger discussion about adult training and ABE. This was also a time when concerns related to second-language learning first became an issue in urban areas with large immigrant populations. Immigrants in Quebec today are accommodated in FSL classes; immigrants in the rest of Canada learn ESL. The overlap in instruction for adults in a second language and in literacy is problematic in many places in part because funding for literacy and for second-language services comes from different sources. Teaching methodology is also a concern, as methods appropriate for immigrant students who are highly literate in their mother tongue are not suited to students with limited or no mother tongue literacy. Both types of immigrant student are sometimes placed in the same class with Canadian-born ABE students.

Native communities have unique literacy problems. (The term *Native* is used to refer to the Indian tribes across the country, the Inuit people in the far North, and the Métis in the western prairie provinces. The Métis are the descendants of Indian-French inter-marriage who were not accepted into either community.) Among multiple injustices committed against Native peoples was forced res-idential schooling for children, who were taken from their parents and placed in schools where they were forbidden to speak their mother tongue and compelled to learn English or French. This pol-icy persisted into the 1950s. Not only were many Native languages lost, but family life was destroyed. Native children in these schools experienced neither Native nor Canadian parenting, and many suf-fered physical and sexual abuse, which led to lasting psychological damage. On another front, Native land claims are being heard in several provincial courts, such as British Columbia's, resulting in mil-lions of square miles of territory being returned to the communities from which they were taken. But compensation and territory cannot respond adequately to the legacy of problems these communities face from alcohol, drugs, violence, suicide, a high incidence of disease (including diabetes and high blood pressure), and enduring racism. Not surprisingly, rates of low literacy, undereducation, and incarcer-ation are significantly higher in Native communities than anywhere else in Canada. Although these communities were not included in the 1994 IALS (or in a significant earlier nationwide study, the 1989 Survey of Literacy Skills Used in Daily Activities), the issue of Native literacy has been studied and acknowledged at provincial and federal levels over the past decade (Rodriguez & Sawyer, 1990; Canada Standing Committee on Aboriginal Affairs, 1990; Darling, 1993; George, 1997).

Native literacy issues vary across Canada. In some western provinces and in the territories, Native students comprise the major-ity or all of the ABE/literacy students. The Northwest Territories have eleven official languages: English, French, and nine Native languages. Some communities, such as the Mohawk, are attempting to revive dying languages through immersion schools for children, encourag-ing adults to learn as well. They are addressing mother tongue and

English-language literacy simultaneously. Communities in the far North have been more likely than those in the South to keep their mother tongues, but these languages were passed on as part of an oral, not written, tradition. Through formal schooling today, they are passing on a recently written language that was not part of their ancestry. In the past decade, many outstanding Native literacy materials (see, for example, Parkland Regional College, 1998) have been created, often incorporating audio and video components in recognition of the oral traditions. Native resource centers have been established. British Columbia did some of the earliest work on Native literacy in the 1980s. AlphaPlus, the Ontario Resource Centre, has a fully staffed Native section, and clearinghouses such as Ningwakwe, in northern Ontario, publish, collect, and disseminate materials. These are only a few examples of the initiatives developing wherever Native communities reside. Native literacy in Canada today is guided and created by Native practitioners and reflects a holistic philosophy characteristic of their cultures; literacy is addressed in the context of traditional practices and contemporary community concerns. The work to date is only a beginning; Native leaders know it will take generations to address all the challenges (George, 1997).

Yet another example of the differences between the pieces in Canada's cultural mosaic is the province of Newfoundland. See Exhibit 6.1 for details.

## EDUCATION: NO ONE SYSTEM

When Newfoundland joined Canada in 1949, it brought the number of provinces to its current ten. All ten have jurisdictional control of education. In addition, there are three territories in the North: the Northwest Territories, Yukon Territory, and Nunavut. The Nunavut, created in April 1999, is a primarily Inuit territory of twenty-seven thousand citizens. Because the territories lack sufficient population or political maturity to warrant provincial status, they are under the jurisdiction of the federal government. In certain areas, however, including education, authority is delegated to the territorial governments. The federal government sits in Ottawa.

Canada became a country through the confederation of four colonies in 1867 and added provinces and territories slowly. Union was not always popular, and in some cases was achieved by a bare majority vote or through political sleight-of-hand (Lower, 1977).

The influence of ethnic origin and geography is quite evident in Newfoundland. Newfoundlanders have traditionally been fishermen who, living in tiny coastal communities on this island in the Atlantic Ocean, have fairly homogeneous Anglo-Irish ancestry and speak a dialect of English understood only on the island. Education was not a central value of a culture that honored self-reliant seamen—until a moratorium was placed on cod fishing in the early 1990s in response to the depletion of the North Atlantic fish stocks. Literacy then emerged as an urgent issue, as Newfoundland had the lowest levels of literacy in Canada as measured by the 1989 national survey as well as the greatest need for retraining. The ABE programs put in place to meet this need were paid for through federal transfer dollars as part of the Atlantic Groundfish Strategy (TAGS), which was intended to retool the local economy and retrain the fishermen to run it. Two former ABE students express some of the conflict Newfoundlanders in the 1990s experienced about the merits of obtaining a formal education:

### BOOK LEARNIN'

I knew what it was to don
warm, wet boots and hairnet
to walk up to the table and lay
cold fish fillets
atop each other
and have a place in my world
where I was not just a drain on
the taxpayer.

But, those with book learnin'
Said the fish are gone.
The harbours and bays rich
with cod.

Now they want me to sell out
and get book learnin'.

    —Jeanette Winsor

### SLACKER

When he quit school at age sixteen
to work at the local fish plant
his friends ridiculed him
calling him a slacker
too lazy to learn.
Fifteen years later
when he took leave from work
to return to school
his friends once again ridiculed him
calling him a slacker
too lazy to work.

Six years and two degrees later
his friends call him Boss.

    —Thomas Pierce

Exhibit 6.1.  A Changing Way of Life in Newfoundland.

Some of the early resistance has been carried over to the present day, manifesting itself in grassroots disaffection and power struggles between federal and provincial governments. At its most extreme, it has led to the separatist movement in Quebec, where the elected government is committed to creating its own country. Concurrently the federal government is preoccupied with maintaining national unity and renewing federalism.

Canada has no federal department of education, and although the federal government has tried since World War II to carve out a niche for itself in the education sector, it has done so gingerly, with extreme concern about upsetting the provinces, which fiercely guard their jurisdictional powers. The federal government maintained control of workforce, or manpower, training, as distinguished from education, until 1997. It thus had a legitimate role in adult education, with much of the workforce training money allocated for high school equivalency training. In 1997, the workforce training jurisdiction devolved to the provinces, raising the prospect that training systems across the country may now become as diverse as the country's education systems.

Amid this complex of forces, ABE policies and provision in Canada are played out. In the formal (accredited) education sector, this provision is institutional and generally leads to certification; it may be offered at secondary schools, community colleges, or work sites. In the informal sector, which is usually community based and nonaccredited, provision can be as varied as providers are innovative; it can be through volunteer one-on-one tutoring, participatory popular education, or other group methodologies, and it may be offered through the workplace, church, libraries, community-based organizations, cultural communities, family centers, health centers, and others.

The differences in secondary education systems in the provinces and territories have their greatest impact on ABE provision at the formal level in programs offered through local school boards or community colleges. For example, in most provinces, students attend high school only until grade 12, but in some others they must attend through grade 13. In still other provinces, grade 13 is optional, while high school in Quebec ends at grade 11. Thus, there is a difference between provinces of up to two years in the time required to complete high school, covering comparable curriculum. Canadian universities have had to decide on admission equivalencies. A few provinces, such as Alberta and British Columbia, offer the certificate of General Educational Development (GED), but it has little status anywhere in Canada, even in provinces where it is offered, and it does not drive the ABE sector as it does in the United States. Since the 1960s, community colleges in all provinces and territories have offered technical and vocational certification. There are more than 140 colleges across Canada, but these also have diverse systems. In every province except Quebec, colleges play some role in ABE provision; in the northern regions of Ontario, Manitoba, Saskatchewan, Alberta, and British Columbia, colleges are the primary providers. This is also the case in the three territories. British Columbia recently created a hybrid system of university-colleges that can confer degrees. In Quebec, meanwhile, the college system is a hybrid of two-year preuniversity institutions, compulsory for anyone seeking admission to a Quebec university, and of three-year technical-professional institutions leading directly to the job market. These technical programs include dozens of options, such as nursing, engineering technology, and computer science; the curriculum is closer to that of an American technical B.A. or B.S. program than to the certificate programs at other Canadian community colleges. Students in the preuniversity and technical streams take a common general education core. Quebec colleges are not mandated to offer ABE/literacy. To date, there exists no formal agreement that accreditation achieved at any level of the education system, from ABE to postgraduate, in one province will necessarily be recognized in another.

The provision of ABE/literacy services is not statutory in all provinces and has generally operated on the fringe of the education sector, even in provinces that claim it is statutory. In 1999, more than eight hundred formal and nonformal programs were involved in literacy in some way across Canada, yet access remains uneven, since in many parts of the country, students cannot find a program appropriate to their needs, and much of the provision remains short term and unstable (Barker, 1999; Hoddinott, 1998).

Despite this diversity, provincial ministers of education meet regularly through the Council of Ministers of Education of Canada (CMEC), founded in 1967. They exchange information and try to work from common principles, but the council has no power. In 1988, the CMEC published a major study of adult illiteracy (see Cairns, 1988), comparing need and provision in the provinces and recommending new directions. That report identified a "lack of consensus" among the provinces on definitions of literacy and on "the validity and reliability of data," while acknowledging "considerable analysis of illiteracy in Canada" over the previous fifteen years (p. 14). In the 1990s, the CMEC began to do some "national" testing on reading, writing, and math for students ages nine, thirteen, and sixteen across several provinces but did not include a sample of those over sixteen, since adult literacy was being surveyed through Statistics Canada, the country's central statistical agency. In 1998, the CMEC commissioned another study that placed literacy among the "essential skills for the workplace" best addressed through a paradigm of lifelong learning (MacLeod, 1998); however, no joint action among ministers regarding ABE has yet been taken.

Since 1988, Statistics Canada has conducted two national adult literacy surveys. The 1989 Survey of Literacy Skills Used in Daily Activities (LSUDA) and the 1994 International Adult Literacy Survey have produced the only comparable data on adult literacy across provinces. The LSUDA, based on such earlier work in the United States as the 1985 Young Adult Literacy Survey, was conducted in both English and French and measured the literacy and numeracy skills of more than nine thousand adults ages sixteen to sixty-nine (Statistics Canada, 1991). It became the touchstone for literacy programs across the country and, with the imprimatur of Statistics Canada, provided credible empirical evidence that Canada required a national response to an issue that threatened the economic future of the country. The IALS was undertaken in seven industrialized countries by Statistics Canada and the OECD on the assumptions that adult literacy is "crucial to the economic performance of industrialized nations" and that "inadequate levels of literacy among a broad section of the population potentially threaten the strength of economies and the social cohesion of nations" (Organization for Economic Cooperation and Development, 1995, p. 13). The seven participating countries were Canada, Germany, the Netherlands, Poland, Sweden, Switzerland, and the United States. Expanding on the methodology used in the LSUDA and the 1993 U.S. National Adult Literacy Survey (NALS), the IALS provided an updated profile of Canada's adult literacy skills, with better data on some subpopulations, and promoted a broader concept of literacy that had been evolving over the past decade. It presented literacy not as "a simple dichotomy that distinguishes those who have it from those who do not. Rather, it is a continuous distribution of abilities that depends on the type of information and the complexity of the tasks presented" (Statistics Canada, 1996, p. 15). Although IALS data have been open to dispute, they serve as the most recent comparable data across the country and have been used extensively by the literacy community and the NLS to lobby for continued and expanded support from all levels of government and the corporate sector. Some of the IALS and LSUDA data are presented in the following section on demographics. (For a brief history of the legislation and organizations concerned with adult learning and literacy in Canada, see Appendix A. See Appendix B for contact information of relevant organizations today.)

## DEMOGRAPHICS OF ADULT LEARNERS

In the past few years, the United Nations Educational, Scientific, and Cultural Organization (UNESCO) has several times named Canada as the most desirable country in the world in which to live. The country has a strong social safety net that guarantees unemployment insurance, universal health care, and low-cost public education from kindergarten through postgraduate university levels. Canadians are, however, among the most highly taxed in the world. And with the increasing globalization of trade, passage of the North American Free Trade Act, and the advent of new technologies, the social benefits long taken for granted have come under attack. Canada's unemployment rate averaged close to 10 percent throughout the 1990s, unevenly distributed across provinces; only in November 1999 did the rate drop to a national average of 7.2 percent. Canada has an accumulated national debt of more than $576 billion and massive provincial debts. Under these circumstances, there has been a political shift to the right with calls for lower taxes, fewer social supports, more accountability, more targeted training for employment, and less "coddling" of "freeloaders." This has led to more short-term, narrowly focused skills training for specific jobs, has diverted funds from longer-term general education programs, and has forced some students out of ABE programs. Conversely, welfare-to-work policies have been implemented in many provinces, driving some reluctant students into literacy classes. These policy shifts have changed the profile of ABE provision over the past several years (Smith, 1997, 1998) and have caused fear among social activists that the neediest of the undereducated will be left out because they cannot be made employable quickly enough or because they may never be employable in the new economy.

While ABE and literacy have traditionally been the subject of little research, since the mid-1970s a series of researchers have dedicated themselves to the task (Hautecoeur, 1978; Thomas, 1976, 1983; Cairns, 1988; Wagner, 1990; Darville, 1992; Barker, 1992, 1999; Hoddinott, 1998). The caveat when conducting any sort of educational research in Canada is that there is no consistency of government data across provinces. Since funding comes from so many different streams and ministries, federal and provincial, reporting is fragmented, and similar kinds of provision are called by different names, making it almost impossible to come up with accurate figures on participation or costs. Much of what has passed for research from the field is memoir, anecdote, or, more recently, public relations documents written by participants, program developers, or government representatives. These can be invaluable sources of information, but they cannot be relied on to present a complete or objective picture. The university-based research that does exist has usually been based on short-term studies of limited samples. Researchers generally have only provincial government documents and figures as primary sources for studies and reports that have shaped policy. The most recent profile (1995–1996) of literacy activities and budgets in all the provinces and territories (Godin, 1996) illustrates the difficulty of conducting comparative analyses of activities in the provinces and territories.

The 1989 LSUDA and 1994 IALS do, however, offer comparable demographic data by region in a range of categories, including the gender, age, education, linguistic background, and immigration status of adults in each of the levels of literacy measured.[3] The IALS measured three literacy domains:

> *Prose*—the knowledge and skills needed to understand and use information from texts, including editorials, news stories, poems, and fiction

> *Document*—the knowledge and skills needed to locate and use information contained in various formats, including job applications, payroll forms, transportation schedules, and maps

> *Quantitative*—the knowledge and skills required to apply arithmetic operations to numbers embedded in printed materials, such as balancing a checkbook or figuring out a tip (Statistics Canada, 1996)

Table 6.1 shows the sample size of the IALS broken down by region and age group. Today, francophones make up just under 25 percent of

| | Sample Size | Population Ages Sixteen and Above |
|---|---|---|
| *Region* | | |
| Atlantic provinces[a] | 1,535 | 1,786,424 |
| Quebec | 794 | 5,431,033 |
| Ontario | 1,925 | 8,004,546 |
| Western provinces[b] | 1,406 | 6,085,890 |
| Canada | 5,660 | 21,307,893 |
| *Age group* | | |
| 16 to 24 | 1,193 | 3,369,904 |
| 25 to 44 | 2,006 | 9,080,575 |
| 45 to 64 | 1,212 | 5,749,886 |
| 65 and over | 1,249 | 3,107,529 |
| Canada | 5,660 | 21,307,893 |

Table 6.1. IALS Sample Size by Region and Age Group.

*Source:* Statistics Canada (1996, p. 17).

[a]New Brunswick, Newfoundland, Nova Scotia, and Prince Edward Island.

[b]Alberta, British Columbia, Manitoba, and Saskatchewan.

the Canadian population but 82 percent of Quebec's. In many parts of the country, they have assimilated into the English-speaking population; in Quebec, under the mandate of Bill 101, francophones are flourishing, but they remain worried about living in a North American "sea of English."

A further complication with the IALS data is that residents of the territories, prison inmates, persons living on Indian reserves, and full-time members of the Canadian armed forces were excluded. The number of Native Canadians living off reserves was too small for separate analysis (Statistics Canada, 1996, p. 18). Although the Northwest Territories, where Native Canadians make up 61 percent of the population, was not surveyed in the 1989 LSUDA or the 1994 IALS, a 1994 Northwest Territories labor force survey indicated that the Native population has the lowest literacy rate in Canada, with more than one in three residents over the age of fourteen having an educational level of grade 9 or lower (Godin, 1996).

Table 6.2 compares the findings of the 1989 LSUDA and 1994 IALS. The LSUDA measured across four levels of proficiency, with levels 1 and 2 considered to be less than functionally literate and level 3 to be merely functional; the population had 7 percent, 9 percent, and 22 percent, respectively, in each of these three categories (Jones, 1993). The IALS collapsed the LSUDA levels 1 and 2 into level 1 and replaced

|  | IALS Levels | | | |
| Scale | 1 | 2 | 3 | 4/5 |
| --- | --- | --- | --- | --- |
| Prose | 18 | 26 | 35 | 22 |
| Document | 19 | 25 | 32 | 24 |
| Quantitative | 18 | 26 | 34 | 22 |

|  | LSUDA Levels | | | |
| Scale | 1 | 2 | 3 | 4 |
| --- | --- | --- | --- | --- |
| Reading | 7 | 9 | 22 | 62 |

Table 6.2.  Distribution of Literacy on IALS and LSUDA Scales, Canadian Adults Ages Sixteen to Sixty-Nine (percentage of respondents).
*Source:* Statistics Canada (1996, p. 21).

level 4 with three new levels: 3, 4, and 5. The IALS shows 47 percent of the population in levels 1 and 2, both defined as below functional literacy for an industrialized society; 22 percent fell into level 1. Since the 1970s, regardless of the measures used or the programs implemented in various provinces, the estimate of those in the lowest levels has not diminished. In fact, it has increased, prompting some critics to suggest that the cut-off points for the different levels are not scientifically valid (Sticht, 1999).

Table 6.3 shows the relationship between literacy and education as measured by the IALS. While earlier studies stressed the relationship between low education and literacy, this survey offered a more nuanced commentary. The relationship between literacy and education was interpreted as strong but "far from perfect. Many individuals did not fit the general pattern. One-third of Canadians who had not completed secondary school were at level 3 or above; a quarter or more of those who had completed a community college program were at level 1 or 2" (Statistics Canada, 1996). The authors of the IALS hypothesized that literacy skills require maintenance over time and can be enhanced through use at home or on the job or lost through lack of use.

Distribution by gender (Table 6.4) was interpreted to show that differences between men and women mirrored differences in school-based assessments in both Canada and the United States. Women scored higher on the prose scale, but men scored higher on the document and quantitative scales.

|                               | Prose Scale |         |         |           |
| ----------------------------- | ----------- | ------- | ------- | --------- |
| Highest Level of Education    | Level 1     | Level 2 | Level 3 | Level 4/5 |
| Less than grade 8             | 89          | 9       | —       | —         |
| Completed primary school      | 59          | 29      | 12      | —         |
| Some secondary school         | 25          | 36      | 32      | 7         |
| Secondary school graduate     | 12          | 31      | 40      | 18        |
| Community college graduate    | 7           | 23      | 45      | 25        |
| University graduate           | —           | 11      | 33      | 56        |

Table 6.3.  IALS Distribution of Literacy by Highest Level of Educational Attainment, Canadian Adults Ages Sixteen and Above (percentage of respondents).

*Source:* Statistics Canada (1996, p. 24).

*Note:* A cell without a number indicates that the sample size was too small to produce reliable estimates.

|       | Prose Scale |         |         |           |
| ----- | ----------- | ------- | ------- | --------- |
|       | Level 1     | Level 2 | Level 3 | Level 4/5 |
| Women | 20          | 25      | 31      | 24        |
| Men   | 23          | 27      | 35      | 16        |

Table 6.4.  IALS Distribution of Literacy by Gender, Canadian Adults Ages Sixteen and Above (percentage of respondents).

*Source:* Statistics Canada (1996, p. 30).

Adults participating in the IALS could choose to complete the survey in English or French. The data show that francophones have more serious literacy problems than do English Canadians. The differences inside and outside Quebec reflect the lack of access to French schooling outside Quebec until recent years. Inside Quebec, the numbers in level 4 reflect the fact that access to postsecondary education did not become widely available in the province until the late 1960s. (See Table 6.5.)

The literacy levels of immigrants (Table 6.6) are anomalous. While the proportion of immigrants in level 1 is larger than the proportion of those born in Canada, Canada was unique among the seven countries surveyed in having such a large proportion in level 4/5. In its analysis, the IALS assumed that this reflects the Canadian policy of selecting skilled immigrants. However, the large numbers in level 1 should raise concern about the ESL/FSL/literacy overlap.

|  | Prose Scale | | | |
| Test Language | Level 1 | Level 2 | Level 3 | Level 4/5 |
|---|---|---|---|---|
| English | 19 | 26 | 31 | 24 |
| French | 28 | 26 | 38 | 9 |
|   Quebec | 27 | 25 | 39 | 9 |
|   Outside Quebec | 33 | 30 | 25 | — |

Table 6.5. IALS Distribution of Literacy by Language of Test, Canadian Adults Ages Sixteen and Above (percentage of respondents).
*Source:* Statistics Canada (1996, p. 31).
*Note:* A cell without a number indicates that the sample size was too small to produce reliable estimates.

|  | Prose Scale | | | |
| | Level 1 | Level 2 | Level 3 | Level 4/5 |
|---|---|---|---|---|
| Born in Canada? | | | | |
|   Yes | 18 | 27 | 37 | 19 |
|   No | 36 | 23 | 19 | 22 |

Table 6.6. IALS Distribution of Literacy by Immigration Status, Canadian Adults Ages Sixteen and Above (percentage of respondents).
*Source:* Statistics Canada (1996, p. 36).

# NATIONAL SUPPORT FOR ADULT LEARNING AND LITERACY

While most educators in the field of adult literacy agree that the most direct route to improving services for students is through the provinces and territories that are mandated to provide those services, a portrait of ABE provision would be incomplete without an overview of federal involvement. The most commanding agency in literacy in Canada is the National Literacy Secretariat (NLS). The NLS also recognizes as national and offers funding support for six nongovernment organizations.

## National Literacy Secretariat

The creation of the NLS by the federal government in 1987 was prompted by a number of government studies and independent reports on adult literacy in the preceding decade and a survey commissioned by the Southam newspaper chain and published earlier that year. The creation of the NLS was also timed to plan for International Literacy Year activities in Canada in 1990; its mandate allowed it to raise public awareness, develop learning materials, carry out research, improve student access and outreach, and improve coordination and information sharing among practitioners. The NLS is restricted from directing any of its funds to the actual teaching of ABE students. To maintain the arms-length relation to education demanded by jurisdictional divisions, the secretariat has worked through partnerships with a range of organizations, including local and regional literacy organizations, school boards, colleges, business groups, labor unions, and national organizations specializing in issues other than literacy, such as women's issues, health, criminal justice, and taxation. It also works with each province through Federal-Provincial/Territorial Initiatives, a mechanism whereby representatives from the provincial government and local agencies and groups work with an NLS project officer to identify literacy needs in that province and negotiate matched funding for projects to address them. These are separate from project proposals worked out independently by provincial groups or organizations for submission to the NLS.

The NLS has been housed in several different federal departments, and its movement over the decade reflects shifts in government thinking about literacy. Initially the NLS was located in the Department of the Secretary of State and Multiculturalism Canada. At that point, rather than focusing on the economic costs of illiteracy or on failures of the education system to teach young people, many of those interested in the issue of literacy viewed it as a fundamental human right for citizens of all ethnic groups (Miller, 1990). Literacy advocates were concerned with the human and social costs to a democratic society if citizens could not read and write well enough to know or exercise their rights as voters, as workers, as tenants, or in any of the other multiple roles every citizen plays. In 1987, this emphasis was a convenient point of entry for a federal agency that did not have the jurisdictional right to engage directly in education. Since then, the NLS has been moved twice and is now located in Human Resources Development Canada (HRDC) as part of a Literacy and Learning Directorate that includes several other agencies, such as the Office of Learning Technologies. This move is in line with a general international trend to locate literacy as a workforce training and economic issue. The NLS has attempted to balance the social justice motive for literacy with the economic.

Small in size if not in stature (the NLS has ranged in number from sixteen to twenty-six project officers) and located within huge departments (HRDC has twenty-six thousand employees), the NLS is the antithesis of a faceless bureaucracy. Project officers have made a point of meeting the field on the ground and, through continuing relationships with stakeholders, have developed a strong understanding of the way things work politically and logistically at the local level in every part of the country. They have also had a profile disproportionate to their size. For several years during the 1990s, until 1997, the government named a special minister responsible for literacy, with signing authority for the secretariat, an unprecedented appointment.[4]

Since its founding in 1987, the NLS has funded more than forty-five hundred projects across Canada (information on most of these projects can be found on the NLS Web site at www.nald.ca/nls/aboutnls/activ.htm). From 1987 to 1997 it distributed $22.5 million per year; in the February 1997 budget, its allocation was raised to $30 million annually, making it the only federal agency to receive an increase in funding in 1997, a year in which massive reductions in spending were made across the board to reduce the national deficit. The increase was seen as a sign that the federal government remained committed to literacy. In allocating the increase, however, the government also tightened its control, targeting the additional money to family literacy, workplace literacy, and new technology. The funding level has been maintained as of the year 2000, with greater emphasis on research. There is also more focus on evaluating the results, or outcomes, of funded projects. The NLS support for research is part of its original mandate. It sponsored the 1989 LSUDA and cosponsored the 1994 IALS.

In the academic arena, in 1998, in cooperation with the Social Sciences and Humanities Research Council, the NLS launched a new program, Valuing Literacy in Canada: A New Research Agenda, to fund strategic research. This program will make available $2.5 million over five years, a large amount by Canadian standards. It supports three-year projects that link university and community-based researchers in an effort to connect theory and practice through credible research models. One of the first proposals to be funded was an ethnographic study of several successful Canadian workplace literacy programs. As another piece of the research agenda, the NLS has funded the Centre for Research on Literacy at the University of Alberta, where the first task was to create a directory of all literacy research conducted and ongoing in Canada since 1994; each entry in the directory summarizes the project and its findings, and research reports are to be available for downloading in their entirety. (Although it is not yet complete, the directory can be visited at www.nald.ca/crd/start.htm.) Besides these few examples, the NLS has also funded original research on women and literacy through independent researchers (see Horsman, 1999) and through the Canadian Congress on Learning Opportunities for Women, a nongovernmental organization.

Since its inception, the NLS has been critical to the field, responsible for the creation of infrastructure such as provincial resource centers and the electronic links of the National Adult Literacy Database (NALD) as well as some provincial communication networks. Canada's NALD, one of the six literacy organizations in the country referred to as "nationals" (discussed later), is a database of information on all Canadian adult literacy programs, resources, services, and activities; it has also created and organized more than one hundred Web sites for literacy organizations across Canada and maintains them. Resource centers now exist in almost every province and territory. Functioning as libraries and technology centers, the resource centers have collections of materials for practitioners, students, and any other interested users; they are often repositories for locally developed materials never previously catalogued. Unfortunately, the resource centers are funded differently in different provinces. Some are supported by both the province and the NLS, and some by the NLS alone; some have additional support from a local library, and some, as in New Brunswick, have no support at all. Consequently, each resource center has developed independently and chosen various systems for organizing its collection. The NLS is funding a project to find a way to share resources through electronic links in a Web-based environment. This promises more equitable distribution of literacy resources and expertise across the country. To enable systematic cataloguing of literacy materials by resource centers, the NLS funded the Canadian Library Association in 1993 to undertake a bilingual Canadian Literacy Thesaurus Project, which collected and continues to update descriptors and key words that allow librarians to assign subject headings familiar to literacy practitioners. The thesaurus makes more precise distinctions between terms than the widely used U.S. Library of Congress system, which offers "adult literacy" as a catch-all subheading of "adult education." The Canadian Literacy Thesaurus is promoted by UNESCO and served as a model when the U.S. National Institute for Literacy developed its on-line thesaurus.

Another form of infrastructure supported by the NLS is the creation or expansion of literacy coalitions in almost every province and territory. These coalitions are not uniform in structure, but they all serve as meeting places for many, if not most, of the organizations involved in literacy in their province. They engage in awareness-raising activities, support practitioners, research the impact of various social policies, such as welfare reform, on the provision of literacy services, and represent their constituents in other forums. One coalition from each province and territory has a seat on the board of the Movement for Canadian Literacy, another of the six nationals. This organization plays a role in keeping literacy on the agenda at the federal level.

The NLS can also take credit for continually bringing literacy to the attention of other parts of the federal government. For example, it supported an internationally recognized national health and literacy program with the Canadian Public Health Association (CPHA) that has encouraged more than twenty national medical associations to promote the connections between literacy and health to their membership. In spring 2000, CPHA held its first International Conference on Literacy and Health. Ongoing NLS-funded projects with the Learning Disabilities Association of Canada have produced manuals on adult literacy and learning disabilities and related pilot workshops in prisons across Canada. NLS-supported plain-language initiatives at Revenue Canada and Health Canada have resulted in public documents and forms being rewritten in easy-to-read English and French.

Although precise figures are impossible to pin down, a careful examination of project-by-project funding reveals that the NLS provides a substantial portion of the financial resources put into adult literacy projects in some provinces and territories; in the smallest ones, the NLS funds entire projects. Even some provincial projects that appear to have diversified sources of funds have at least some money that can be traced back to the NLS. It would be difficult to find a literacy project or program in Canada today that did not receive some portion of its funding from the NLS. If the secretariat were to close, many literacy organizations and programs would be in danger of disappearing or at minimum reducing their activities.

All of its accomplishments notwithstanding, the NLS has not gone without its critics. It has funded some arguably weak projects and initially conducted insufficient strategic funding or evaluation. In the past three years it has been tightening its funding criteria and monitoring progress more carefully. More important, since 1989, it has underwritten wholly or in part much of the best in all of the efforts intended to improve adult literacy throughout Canada. The list, long and impressive, demonstrates ABE's unhealthy dependency on a single supplier of funds.

Another weakness of the NLS is its project funding model, which fosters short-term thinking and drives organizations to behave in ways they would not if they had secure funding with accountability. It has also encouraged duplication of effort. For example, in the mid-1990s, three unrelated organizations in three provinces were funded to survey literacy programs across Canada about the software they used. In addition, project funding has created competition between the six national organizations and members of local and regional groups across the country, who perceive that some of the nationals, which no longer received core funding in the late 1990s, are receiving or soliciting project funds that should go directly to the regions. Project funding is not peculiar to literacy; all federal funding programs work through this model. It can, however, be dangerous, as demonstrated by the closing of many strong Canadian women's organizations in the 1990s when support from their funding body in the federal government, Status of Women Canada, diminished. As is the case with research, there is currently a move at the NLS to guarantee funding for more than one year where warranted, as in maintaining infrastructure, such as the National Adult Literacy Database. The project model nonetheless remains in place.

Politically, the NLS has not been as effective as it might have been in making its role or its accomplishments clear to members of Parliament, many of whom still think about literacy in simplistic terms connected only to numbers of adults learning to read. The NLS is under considerable political pressure because the 1994 IALS data showed no improvement in literacy levels from the 1989 LSUDA data, and there is no empirical evidence of any further change today. Since the NLS was never in a jurisdictional position to provide students with direct services, there is some irony in the fact that it should be held accountable for something it is not allowed to do. What the NLS has done is to lay the groundwork and begin to create an infrastructure such that first-class services could be provided if all the provinces were able to fulfill their responsibilities for adult education.

## Six National Literacy Organizations

When the NLS was created in 1987, it tried to respect and build on preexisting organizational structures to facilitate its work. Frontier College, the Movement for Canadian Literacy, and Laubach Literacy of Canada predated the NLS and had national mandates. The NLS therefore chose to confer on them the special status of national literacy organization. At the time, this meant they were eligible for core funding, while other organizations could only apply for project grants. Since then, the formula has changed, and the "nationals," as they are known, must also submit project proposals for their annual funding rounds, although this policy is to be revisited. Within two years of its creation, the NLS funded three additional organizations designated "national" because of the nature of their mandates: the National Adult Literacy Database, ABC Canada, and the Fédération canadienne pour l'alphabétisation en français (FCAF). The six, all non-governmental, nonprofit organizations, remain the only literacy organizations entitled to call themselves nationals. Because of this special status, organization representatives are frequently called on to speak at national political and media events to represent the literacy community.

The nationals engender some distrust and resentment among provincial organizations, whose representatives argue that the nationals sometimes compete with provincial and local groups for similar project grants and that occasionally a "national" project carried out in locations across the country comes into conflict with local projects. Over time, the nationals are becoming somewhat more effective at defining their mandates, more sensitive about respecting boundaries, and more cooperative among themselves. The nationals are described in more detail in Exhibit 6.2.

## CHALLENGES AHEAD, PROMISING EFFORTS TO MEET THEM

Recent trends in Canada have been contradictory. As practitioners have broadened their understanding and practice of literacy education, policymakers have been tightening the definition of what counts

*Frontier College*
Initially called the Canadian Reading Camp Movement when it was founded in
1899 by a Presbyterian minister, this organization sent instructors to the wilderness
to bring literature to railroad, lumber, and mining workers. In 1922, the name of
the organization was changed to Frontier College to reflect the nature of its work—
teaching literacy and ABE to marginalized people—and the site of its work in
remote regions of the country. Frontier College, based in Toronto, is now a Canada-
wide literacy organization that relies on volunteers (fifty-five hundred in 1999) to
teach people in diverse, often difficult circumstances to read and write. It has
created ABE programs for the prison system, for the homeless, and for migrant
workers and is the nation's oldest literacy organization.

*Laubach Literacy of Canada*
Laubach Literacy of Canada (LLC) is committed to raising the literacy level of
Canadian society through volunteer-based, one-on-one tutoring. Its motto is
"Each one teach one." Founded in 1970 as an outgrowth of the American-based
National Affiliation for Literacy Advance, LLC was established in its own right in
1981; it has no connection with the U.S.-based Laubach Action. Using the
phonics-based approach to reading developed by Frank Laubach for teaching
English in the Philippines in the 1930s, LLC trains volunteer tutors to improve
students' basic skills in reading, writing, speaking, listening, and numeracy as well
as working on life skills, such as parenting and conducting a job search. In the
past decade, LLC has diversified its approach and incorporated some training on
whole language, learning disabilities, and ESL. In the past three to four years, LLC
has concentrated on family literacy and workplace literacy in some parts of the
country. Training, materials, and organizational support are available through
154 local Laubach reading councils across the country.

*Movement for Canadian Literacy*
The Movement for Canadian Literacy is a "coalition of coalitions" of literacy
organizations from every province and territory. Founded in 1977, MCL initially
worked to support research, awareness, and lobbying activities. Early on it had
difficulty trying to create a common voice among groups with divergent
philosophies, but it was a signatory to the 1986 Cedar Glen Declaration, which
marked the first time national groups in the volunteer sector had taken a common
public position on adult literacy. By the 1990s, MCL became the site where one
coalition from each province and territory can share information and common
concerns. MCL is committed to student leadership, and its board includes
current and former ABE students. MCL now focuses primarily on public and
government awareness of the need for literacy education.

*National Adult Literacy Database*
The National Adult Literacy Database was founded with the goal of establishing a
database of all college-based adult literacy programs across Canada. NALD was
federally incorporated in 1992 as a nonprofit service organization, and it is now a
vital part of ABE across Canada. It has evolved into a single-source, comprehensive,
and accessible database of Canadian adult literacy programs, resources, services,
and activities available in both English and French. Located in Fredericton,
New Brunswick, NALD links electronically with major organizations and advocacy

**Exhibit 6.2. The "Nationals."**

groups in communities, schools, and local governments across the country. It supports an electronic infrastructure for literacy by hosting Web sites for more than one hundred Canadian organizations; facilitating board management for many of these groups; and giving users access to the experience and expertise of contacts and programs involved in adult basic education and English and French as second languages across Canada and around the world on the Internet. It provides data, referrals, program models, and sites through which students, practitioners, and administrators can share ideas and information, and it has a downloadable library of documents. NALD also houses the Web site for the National Literacy Secretariat and for IALS data. For anyone wanting an overview of literacy in Canada, NALD is the place to start. (It can be accessed on the Web at www.nald.ca.)

*ABC Canada*
The ABC Canada Literacy Foundation is a national registered charitable organization consisting of a partnership of business, labor, education, and government. It is the national organization with the closest links to business, filling a role similar to that played in the early 1990s by the Business Council for Effective Literacy in the United States. In the early 1990s, it focused on workplace literacy and established the national Workplace Education Centre. By 1998, the WEC had closed, and ABC Canada concentrated its efforts on its other programs, such as the national LEARN campaign, which sponsors listings in the Yellow Pages across Canada for local ABE and literacy services. Television, radio, and print advertisements in every part of Canada end with the message: "Look under LEARN in your Yellow Pages." As an advocate for literacy in the corporate sector, ABC Canada does a significant amount of fundraising. Its golf tournaments for literacy have raised more than $2 million in the last ten years.

*Fédération canadienne pour l'alphabétisation en français*
The Fédération canadienne pour l'alphabétisation en français (FCAF) promotes access to French literacy services throughout Canada. Because of the history and politics of the two founding nations, French teaching was not accessible anywhere except in Quebec for generations, which resulted in English assimilation and significantly lower levels of mother tongue literacy among francophones. The FCAF represents the interests of francophones to the federal government and to national English literacy organizations. The FCAF advocates for mother tongue literacy as a prerequisite for second-language learning. The group argues that strong French literacy for francophones enhances their ability to learn English as a second language, recognizing that most francophones outside Quebec, apart from those in scattered, predominantly French communities, must use English at work and in other aspects of daily life.

Exhibit 6.2. The "Nationals" (*continued*).

as literacy and what outcomes are acceptable. Several provinces are involving the entire field in an examination of practice to identify outcomes that will respect learners' needs and providers' values; the provinces will present their findings to policymakers as alternatives to the more rigid assessment indicators. While these outcomes projects hold great promise, they also demonstrate that all the shifts in thinking about literacy will require a reexamination of curricula, retraining of personnel, and an increase in the dialogue between the formal and community-based sectors. A shift in the definition, or boundaries, of literacy is intertwined with most of the other challenges facing the Canadian literacy community today; these include the impact of technology, the roles and training of volunteers and practitioners, the increasing support for family and workplace literacy, the promotion of partnership models, and the ESL/FSL/literacy interface. The greatest challenge is to create a sustainable ABE system in the midst of jurisdictional circumstances that inherently work against it.

## Redefining the Boundaries of Literacy

Until the early 1990s, the focus of Canadian (as well as international) studies of adult literacy was illiteracy. *Literacy,* understood to be a continuum of skills rather than a great divide between haves and have-nots, is now the term and topic of choice. Although the definition of literacy has been broadened, the official understanding of the term as reflected in its use in government surveys and other documents acknowledges mainly reading and writing print information. Some literacy organizations talk about "new literacies" and "multiple literacies," but many practitioners, as well as members of the public, remain fixed on the idea of literacy strictly as a print-based concept.

Redefining the boundaries means looking beyond the medium of literacy to the reasons that adults seek out literacy programs and the outcomes that may result. In addition to enrolling in programs for the purpose of job upgrading, adults enroll in these programs to broaden their general education, help their children succeed in school, or make social connections. Besides learning to read and write, students report increased self-esteem and confidence and an awareness of the ability to learn. Whether programs focus on academic or school-based literacy or on the practices related to the uses of literacy for daily living, the question of boundaries persists. The boundary issues ultimately determine the scope of literacy programming eligible for funding.[5]

One organization that promotes continued questioning about the boundaries of literacy is the Centre for Literacy of Quebec, an NLS-funded resource center. Created in 1989 from a college-based professional development program, it offers a working definition of literacy as "a complex set of abilities to understand and use the dominant symbol systems of a culture for personal and community development . . . [including] the media and electronic text in addition to alphabets and numbers." Practitioners, researchers, and policymakers from across the country and internationally meet at the center each summer for an institute on literacy and technologies. While the center's vision was perceived by most practitioners as being on the fringe in the early 1990s, the currently increasing number of visitors to the "definition" and media/technology pages of its Web site (http://www.nald.ca/litcent.htm) may indicate a growing interest in expanding the concept of literacy. The center's semiannual newsletter, *Literacy Across the CurriculuMedia Focus*, examines the interfaces of literacy, media, and technology.

## Integrating New Technologies

Canada has developed some state-of-the-art uses of technologies for learning in K–12, university, and adult distance education, but until recently, few of them were used in ABE. Broadcasting has a long history in Canadian community-based education. Because of the vast distances separating sparse populations, radio was used in the 1930s to link the country from coast to coast, just as the railways had done a century earlier. Radio was used for adult education from the 1930s to the 1960s with programming such as citizenship forums and farm broadcasts. The Canadian Broadcasting Corporation (CBC), Canada's public broadcaster, identified education as a priority in its mandate and consistently produced high-quality radio and then television programming for adult learners well into the 1960s. In recent years, the CBC has been more committed to children's education. Other than these early uses, however, radio has been overlooked and television has not been used widely for adult literacy instruction in Canada, even though adults with the lowest levels of literacy watch more television than those with higher levels and use it as their primary source of information about the world. The cost of developing and sustaining high-quality television has worked against its being used to its full potential for literacy instruction, although its value for raising public awareness has been recognized (see ABC Canada in Exhibit 6.2).

An innovative use of low-cost television is a Newfoundland community video project that has involved citizens with limited education living in remote communities being trained to videotape town hall meetings on local issues and broadcast them to other communities to initiate dialogue and action. Growing out of an acclaimed 1960s project by the National Film Board, the Fogo Island Project, this participatory form of production continues today. Although the project is not referred to as a kind of literacy or adult basic education, it engages participants in the activities of scripting, filming, editing, and producing video documentaries that lead to community action.

A different use of television for basic skills education has been developed by the Open Learning Agency (OLA) in British Columbia. The OLA is a postsecondary institution adapted from Britain's Open University model that uses distance learning, including television, to reach adult learners. Working with industry, the OLA has created some basic skills upgrading programs for workers. One example is Skill Plan B.C., which was developed with employers and unions of the B.C. Construction Industry Skills Improvement Council. Skill Plan brings flexible learning to thousands of construction workers in the province; it allows participants to work from a personalized program that combines one-on-one instruction, workshops, peer counseling, and computer-assisted training. As early as 1993, the OLA began to use communications software and modems to give workers at remote construction sites access to training (Godin, 1996).

Unfortunately, neither the Newfoundland community video nor the OLA model of targeted distance ABE programming is well known or replicated in other parts of Canada, and funders and program developers across the country have decided that computers and the Internet are the best way of reaching ABE students. Many unrealistic claims are being made for these technologies without sufficient attention to the teaching and support components.

Ontario's AlphaPlus embodies a new way of linking physical and virtual resources. Created in 1998 through the amalgamation of Alpha Ontario, the provincial literacy resource library, and AlphaCom, a provincial electronic communication system for literacy practitioners, AlphaPlus is the first and most firmly established such system in Canada. Since the early 1990s, AlphaCom had maintained an electronic link between practitioners from the southern urban core of

Ontario and the scattered northern communities near the Arctic Circle. Its on-line discussions and support of special interest spurred professional development and more coherent literacy provision across the huge province. AlphaPlus serves the four cultural communities recognized in Ontario literacy programming: English, French, Native, and hearing impaired. AlphaPlus also houses a large collection of ESL materials, serving as a bridge between the ESL and literacy communities in the province that receives the most immigrants in Canada. AlphaPlus staff are currently developing AlphaRoute, a resource that will eventually offer a supported on-line system of literacy instruction to students in a Web-based environment.

The four western provinces have linked their provincial literacy organizations through the First Class conferencing system, which allows them to communicate across provincial lines, a positive sign in Canada. The provinces anticipate using the system increasingly for professional development activities.

Nationally, the NLS has actively promoted the use of new technologies and sponsored seminars and consultations for practitioners and administrators. The creation of the National Adult Literacy Database has revolutionized the organization of information and research on adult learning and literacy in Canada. Every reference in this chapter can be traced through NALD. What has not yet been achieved is a national electronic discussion list, such as the National Literacy Advocacy list in the United States, through which policy issues can be discussed and rapid response to political issues can be generated. To date, the western provinces and Ontario have preferred to use their own communication systems for policy discussions. A national vision has not yet prevailed.

More recently, the NLS has funded *Connect*, a national newsletter on technology for literacy practitioners. Available in print and on-line, every issue includes regular features such as Software Reviews, Navigating the Web, Lesson Plans, Reports from Learners or Reports from the Field, and Technical Tips. *Connect* assumes that most literacy workers in Canada are new to, apprehensive about, or perhaps resistant to technology and need to be guided through it gently in the familiar medium of print, but it also supports more experienced users. *Connect* was originally funded as a short-term publication, but the NLS seems to recognize that the effective integration of new technology in literacy teaching will require long-term support through the medium of print.

The challenges of integrating technology into adult literacy practice are similar to those in the United States. They include a need for
long-term professional development, a need to determine the most
appropriate uses of particular technologies, the recognition that practitioners and students do not have equal access to various technologies in all parts of Canada, and the recognition that a permanent
technical infrastructure and support system are required. With many
isolated models of excellence, Canada has a rich, if scattered, experience on which to build in integrating technology into adult basic education. The challenge is complicated by a Canadian tradition of
creating provincial models and resisting national ones.

## Redefining the Roles of Practitioners and Volunteers

The trends toward greater professionalization, the development of new
approaches to teaching, and the demand for program accountability
are calling into question the appropriate role for both volunteers and
practitioners in adult literacy education.

The contribution of volunteers to adult literacy across Canada must
be acknowledged. Volunteers were the backbone of Canadian adult
literacy provision before ABE was officially sponsored. In some parts
of the country, particularly in remote rural regions where practitioners are not available, volunteers have been the sole providers of service. Today two of the six national organizations, Frontier College and
Laubach Literacy Canada, are volunteer organizations, and hundreds
more exist across the country. Volunteers constitute one group—and
a large proportion—of those teaching adult literacy today.

While volunteers have been among the strongest lobbyists for the
cause of adult literacy education and fill many other roles in the field,
the traditional and well-loved image of the volunteer is that of the
individual tutor working closely with one adult student whose life may
be changed as a result of the process. Since the early days of the Frontier College, the media have been enamored of the image of the
volunteer, and Quigley (1997) points out that the literacy community
itself often inadvertently contributes to it because such heart-warming
stories can open donor purse strings. It is this role of the volunteer
that has become subject to change as the call for professionalization
and accountability and the development of new approaches to teaching come more and more into play.

As early as the 1950s, the Canadian Association for Adult Education (CAAE) began to advocate for more professionalization of the field. British Columbia and Ontario universities offered the first adult education degree and certificate programs in English. Eventually a few other institutions added this specialization, with a small number specifically naming ABE/literacy. In the 1970s, the University of Quebec in Montreal offered the first certificate in adult literacy in French. Thus, over the past fifty years, a community of practitioners with academic credentials for teaching ABE has developed. Another group of ABE practitioners are teachers who moved over to ABE from the regular elementary or secondary school system. Although their academic training was not in ABE, they were nonetheless trained as teachers. As in the United States, practitioners with other, varied degrees of training and experience exist.

The question of accreditation has been hotly debated for several years. Surveys in a number of provinces have found that many practitioners would welcome a formal accreditation as literacy/ABE educators. The question then becomes, What kind of accreditation? Even among provinces offering university certificates or degrees, there is no consistent requirement in practice from one province to another. And until there is a stable, systemic provision of services with equitable working conditions for teachers, there is unlikely to be a universal requirement for university accreditation. Under current conditions, few ABE/literacy instructors have job security or benefits. Many have only sessional contracts and take on as many classes as they can manage because they are never certain if they will work in the next session.

In an attempt to respond to the call for professionalization while also heeding the reality of the circumstances in which practitioners teach, some local equivalency types of accreditation have been developed that in fact apply to volunteers as well as practitioners. The Nova Scotia Tutor Training Certification Program is a thirty-hour program that introduces volunteers to theories of reading, writing, and numeracy, with an emphasis on practical applications. The Nova Scotia Department of Education, acknowledging that it cannot afford to pay many full-time teachers, wants volunteers to use a common approach to teaching. On the other hand, STAPLE 1 and 2 (Supplemental Training for Literacy Practitioners), a CD-ROM-based professional development program created by Literacy Coordinators of Alberta, is an elaborate yet highly accessible training program that assumes some formal education background on the part of enrollees. It was designed by university-based literacy specialists to be used at a distance. There are also some excellent models of volunteer programs that provide ongoing tutor training and monitor student progress. Prospects Literacy in Alberta has developed a computerized management system called Litnet that allows it to track data such as hours of training, hours of tutoring, lessons covered, competencies achieved, levels completed, and more. Numerous well-designed volunteer tutor program evaluation kits have also been developed across Canada (Thomas, 1989). Each province is promoting consistency of training and evaluation within its borders; there is no general agreement nationwide as to how teachers should be trained or evaluated.

As suggested by the example of the Nova Scotia program for volunteer training and evaluation, newer approaches to teaching are also having an effect on the roles that volunteers and practitioners play. Some community-based programs now use a participatory education model in which the curriculum is created collectively with the students. Two Alberta programs, the Learning Center Literacy Association (Edmonton) and the Write to Learn project, and the Adult Basic Education Writing Network in Newfoundland are outstanding models of community-based participatory education. Each of these programs has developed materials and guides for engaging adult learners in writing that builds on learners' strengths. Their publications have won recognition and respect beyond the literacy community (Norton & Campbell, 1998; Morgan, 1998; Woodrow, 1995). In Quebec, francophone educators have developed a model of "popular education," similar to participatory education (Wagner, 1990), carried out by paid educators adapting a Freirian empowerment philosophy. The model is not widely known in the rest of Canada, or even in the English community of Quebec, and is no longer as strong in Quebec as it was in the 1970s and 1980s, but it is worth examining as an effective alternative model for literacy education. (For a detailed description of Freire's philosophy, see Chapter Two in this book.) These models of participatory/popular education are quite different from the models of volunteer one-on-one tutoring and teacher-as-classroom-authority popular in most parts of the country.

Government demand for program accountability and measurable outcomes is also having an effect on the roles of volunteers and practitioners. Many formal programs in various provinces, caught between the conflicting demands of adult education funders and welfare reform funders, have begun to accept only higher-level learners who have a better chance of succeeding within a fixed time frame. Lower-level learners are being referred to the community and volunteer sectors (Ziegler, 1996; Smith, 1997, 1998). This trend highlights the question of who is best equipped to teach each of the different segments of ABE learners and what level of training can or should be required of providers. Learners at beginning levels of literacy will probably always need a person to guide and give them confidence. The need for volunteers to fill this role is likely to continue. Moreover, adult learners have different needs, some of which may require professional intervention and some of which may not. Even in urban areas, there are students who are not willing or able to attend a class because of embarrassment or disability or because they have a short-term goal and do not want or need certification. Volunteers have a role to play in these cases as well. They may also come to work as teachers' aides, a common role for volunteers in the K–12 system. The match between service and need in adult literacy is not easily made (ABC Canada, 1997). Despite the growing dialogue between practitioners and volunteers across the country, in most places, there are still differences in beliefs about the best way to approach learning and literacy (Hambly, 1998).

In the future, it is likely that apart from those cases where a volunteer is a better option or the only option, if provision is well funded and stable, the role of volunteers could become similar to that of hospital auxiliaries, indispensable but not the primary or sole service providers. Canada is not yet close to this possibility.

## Improving Family and Workplace Literacy

Family literacy and workplace literacy have been getting more attention over the past decade; increased funding for such programs is evidence of this trend. Policymakers and providers are optimistic that family literacy can achieve what more traditional models could not: a long-term commitment from adult learners motivated by wanting to help their children. Workplace literacy is tied to the rhetoric of employability and productivity in a global economy. Both models seem to offer more measurable outcomes than the more traditional models of ABE. The resulting challenge to the field is twofold. First, with disproportionate amounts of ABE funding being directed to these two sectors, there is a corresponding decrease in funding appropriated for other education options. Second, sufficient longitudinal research has not been conducted to justify the shift of so much of the available resource base to these two program options.

A research study tracing the development of Canadian family literacy programs showcased some best practices across the country. By the time the book was published (Thomas, 1998), however, several of the featured programs were no longer in existence. Many attempts to document the results of other family literacy programs and workplace literacy programs throughout the 1990s have been frustrated by the short-term nature of the programs (see Taylor, 1997a). As one researcher noted,

> Future policy decisions regarding family literacy will increasingly depend on research. Nevertheless, there is no coherent strategy in place for developing a Canadian research base in family literacy. At the present time, program design and practices are only loosely related to a research base, and community-based implementation decisions often appear fragmented. Because local program developers have little access to program evaluation results of similar programs . . . Canadian family literacy intervention has been characterized by relatively short-term, low-intensity programs. [Thomas, 1998, pp. 21-22]

Since that pronouncement, the commitment to family literacy has grown as several provinces, such as Alberta and British Columbia, have undertaken intensive initiatives under the heading of early intervention and prevention. This allows for shared federal funding, which would be seen as overstepping jurisdictional bounds if children, rather than the family as a whole, were the direct targets of the programs. The NLS research strategy is supporting some three-year studies. The challenges, in addition to those noted by Thomas, include a tendency to focus on children more than parents (unlike the highly structured model promoted by the U.S. National Center for Family Literacy). Some literacy advocates worry about the burden of responsibility being placed on mothers.

Workplace literacy has a longer history of support in Canada than does family literacy. It addresses workers' needs directly and has been justified through economic arguments, although it has generally been difficult to get employers to invest directly. The provincial record on such programs has also been checkered. Ontario created a well-funded ministry to support workplace literacy and set up programs across the province. But the more right-leaning Conservative government elected in the mid-1990s had dismantled the entire workplace component by the end of the decade, arguing that employers should not receive public funds for this purpose. A few enlightened employers and industry groups across Canada have identified their own self-interest in workplace literacy, but such initiatives have not been widespread. In the early 1990s, ABC Canada, with NLS support, created a Workplace Education Center (WEC) that developed an excellent model for literacy needs assessment and offered assessment and consulting services across Canada (Folinsbee & Jurmo, 1994; Belfiore, 1996). This program created resentment at local levels. Many provincial organizations that had their own workplace programs and assessment models complained that a Toronto-based organization was offering services to employers who could have bought the same or equivalent services from local providers. The WEC closed in 1998.

The expertise gained over the decade is nonetheless being tapped through more research. One of the first proposals funded under a research initiative called Valuing Literacy was a three-year ethnographic study of the impact and outcomes of a workplace literacy program. As more evaluation and research are conducted and more strategic funding provided, indicators should emerge as to whether the current shift in literacy investment has been justified.

## Encouraging Partnerships

Encouraging partnerships is an international trend that has worked well for the literacy field in Canada. The practice was formalized through NLS policy, which states explicitly that the NLS works through the model of partnerships with literacy organizations across the country. This policy has resulted in some dynamic projects and strong alliances, although the concept of partnership can also be problematic when there is an imbalance of power. A partnership implies equality or parity between partners; the question then arises: Can an organization be a partner with its primary or only funder? While the NLS has generally been perceived as fair, there is no doubt that its policies drive many of the ABE activities in progress across the country.

Literacy organizations across Canada also benefit from other kinds of partnerships. One example is the tripartite Workplace Education Manitoba Steering Committee of labor, business, and government, which has been highly effective in identifying ways of developing the skills of the province's workforce, with a heavy emphasis on basic skills

(Despins, Maruca, & Turner, 1997). The strength of the Manitoba model is its diversified funding. If one of the funders were to withdraw, the others could continue with modified programs while rebuilding the funding base.

Because of the jurisdictional and funding complexities in Canada, many in the literacy field have formed partnerships with business or made alliances with colleagues in other sectors when there is common cause. One of the outstanding examples is in the health sector, where the Canadian Public Health Association has forged a partnership of more than two dozen health-related professional associations, such as the Canadian Medical Association, to raise awareness of the connections between health and literacy and to advocate for changes in professional practice around the use of plain language communication.

Some leaders see this trend toward strategic alliances as one that will carry literacy into the future. The hope is that work with antipoverty groups, women's and children's rights groups, human rights and criminal justice groups, and health and environmental groups will embed the cause of adult literacy within all these issues and make it eligible for funding from sources other than the traditional ones.

## Improving ESL/FSL Literacy

The interface between ESL/FSL and literacy in Canada is charged with all the tensions accruing to the language conflicts between English and French speakers and between Quebec and the rest of Canada. The issue of English or French being a second language occurs mainly in urban areas of the country with large immigrant populations. The funding for such programs is difficult to trace, and the practice of placing second-language learners in regular literacy classes is not uncommon. Such placement sometimes occurs because there are not sufficient numbers to make up full classes of either group; sometimes it is because more funding is available for one than for the other. Whatever the reason, providers are generally reluctant to discuss the question, but the mixing of the groups creates challenges for providers in terms of the appropriate methodologies to use. It creates challenges for students who find themselves in the same class but whose needs are radically different; what is the common ground between a physician from a foreign country and a Native speaker with third-grade education? The programs best able to meet these challenges are in Toronto, which has large programs serving both client groups.

A more complicated aspect is the provision of French literacy to francophones outside Quebec. The LSUDA and IALS corroborated that francophones had more serious literacy problems than anglophones. The francophones' advocacy organization, the FCAF (see Exhibit 6.2), argues that they need to learn their mother tongue as a prerequisite for learning English. There are those within the English literacy community who argue that if "refrancization" is included within the boundaries of literacy, then the same option should exist for immigrants who are not literate in their mother tongue. Other than St. Christopher House in Toronto, no programs offer mother tongue literacy to immigrants. This is one challenge not likely to be addressed too soon because it is too politically fraught.

## Working Sustainability into the System

The greatest challenge facing the field is sustainability. Throughout the 1990s, report after report confirmed that students do not have equal access to adult basic and literacy education in every province and that in many provinces, provision is not part of a stable, funded education system (Darville, 1991; White & Hoddinott, 1991; Barker, 1992, 1999; Hoddinott, 1998). Both the dependency on the NLS for so much project funding and the model of project funding itself are problems. Some practitioners believe that provincial and territorial governments have not responded as strongly to the need for provision of adult literacy education as they should have because they too have become reliant on short-term federal grants that can be made to appear provincial. Until the provinces create a system of provision and support, making ABE a permanent part of the education system, as is K–12, access by students to programs will be temporary.

The Council of Ministers of Education is in an excellent position to initiate provincial cooperation by encouraging education ministers across Canada to expand systems to include statutory provision of adult education. Making space for adult literacy and learning on the continuum of lifelong learning would not address all the challenges facing the field, but it would go far in ensuring some degree of quality and equity of provision.

The concept of lifelong learning, which until now has been mainly a catch-phrase, could become the lever to propel change. A 1998 discussion document prepared for the Council of Ministers of Education on essential skills for the workplace, which included literacy and numeracy, analyzed the question of sustainability in relation to workplace basic skills. It called Canada's funding traditions "woefully inadequate for the future" and called sustainable funding "the life-support system of workplace learning initiatives [which] must be as well thought out and seamless as that of the K–12 and PSE [Post-Secondary Education]" (MacLeod, 1998, p. 11). The document recognized the diverse circumstances of each province in developing public policy but also suggested some broad principles that could be adapted to foster more sustained sources of funding. One such principle is that of the public-private partnership, exemplified by the tripartite committee in Manitoba.

## CONCLUSION

The achievements of the adult literacy field in Canada have been the establishment of an infrastructure for resources and communication, including a network of resource centers and use of the Internet; production of high-quality educational materials, print and electronic, for both students and providers that reflects regional and national perspectives on literacy; a more knowledgeable and well-trained cadre of practitioners and volunteers; support for more credible research; greater public awareness; and a move toward redefining the problem from one of illiteracy to degrees of literacy. All of these accomplishments can be seen as necessary but not sufficient. The groundwork for sustainable provision has been laid. To make it a reality, the federal government should become permanently responsible for sustaining infrastructure, a responsibility that legitimately falls within current jurisdictional divisions of power, as does the responsibility for the public broadcasting service. The federal government could thus be responsible for communication networks, resources, and support for credible research, both academic and community-action based. The provinces would have to take responsibility for making adult education a statutory part of the K–12 system, and partnership among the education, community, and business sectors, of which Canada has developed many workable models, could become the principle for sustainability. The question is whether there are sufficient commitment and will to work against all the historical, political, and philosophical barriers to ensure equitable provision of high-quality adult basic education services across Canada.

## Appendix A: Chronology of Events in the Development of Adult Basic Education and Literacy Nationwide

| | |
|---|---|
| 1899 | The Canadian Reading Camp Movement is founded. Becomes Frontier College in 1922. University students were sent to the Canadian wilderness to teach laborers, mostly lumberjacks and miners, how to read and write. (See Exhibit 6.2 for more information on Frontier College.) From this time until the 1930s, ABE was not significantly distinguished from other adult education initiatives, which were carried out through YMCAs and YWCAs, Mechanics' Institutes, churches, labor unions, farm organizations, traveling circuit lecturers and teachers, and other organizations. |
| 1935 | The Canadian Association for Adult Education (CAAE) is founded as a clearinghouse to serve professionals in the field. The CAAE was the first national organization dedicated solely to adult education and laid the groundwork for the adult literacy organizations that eventually became central to the field. The CAAE became a developer of educational programs with a focus on citizenship, dedicated to informing adults about political, social, and economic issues. It was the main source of adult education publications until the 1950s and nurtured some of the early researchers who separated out for study high-school-equivalent education (sometimes referred to as ABE in Canada) and pre-high-school-equivalent education (sometimes referred to as literacy education). The CAAE 1985 report, *Educationally Disadvantaged Adults: A Project*, contributed to the pressure for government action on literacy. Its leadership role diminished in the late 1980s, and it folded in the mid-1990s. |
| 1960s | The decade was characterized by idealistic social consciousness and nationalist feeling in Canada and Quebec, waves of immigration, and broad |

social reforms, such as the war on poverty. Means of waging the war on poverty included expanded federal funding for technical and vocational education, which led to the exposure of undereducation among adults.

1960      The Technical and Vocational Training Assistance Act authorizes Ottawa to join the provinces in funding capital costs for vocational training facilities. Within six years, projects valued at more than $1.5 billion served to create 662 new schools through which passed 439,952 students (Stamp, 1970). Because of federal-provincial conflict over roles and differences between Quebec and other provinces, this act was the last federal investment in capital and operating costs for technical and vocational education. Many institutes of technology created through this act were converted to community colleges.

1967      The Adult Occupational Training Act is passed, focusing on unemployed and underemployed workers and on short-term retraining. It led to the development of NewStart, creating six private nonprofit corporations to promote "experimentation in methods which would motivate and train adults who were educationally disadvantaged" (Selman & Dampier, 1991, p. 166). Without intending to do so, NewStart revealed that a number of Canadian adults were not educated enough to qualify for retraining; the need for adult basic education was out in the open for the first time (Thomas, 1983; Selman, 1995).

1969      The Official Languages Act is passed, leading to an explosion of second-language teaching across the country and further contributing to the awareness of the large numbers of undereducated adults.

Late 1960s/early 1970s      Federal Basic Training and Skills Development (BTSD) and early Basic Job Readiness Training

(BJRT) are developed to target adults who could be trained or retrained in short-term programs leading directly to jobs. BTSD was intended to provide the elementary and high school levels of education that were prerequisites for vocational training.

1970s    The decade was characterized by a retrenchment in spending on adult learning and literacy. After reviews of BTSD and BJRT showed these programs were not meeting the anticipated goals of skills training, funds were restricted, and by the end of the decade "provision for the most undereducated adults had almost ceased to exist" (Thomas, 1983, p. 65). Simultaneously a series of provincial reports and commissions highlighted the needs of illiterate and undereducated adults. A number of national reports from various government committees (such as the Senate Committee on Poverty in 1971 and the Senate Finance Committee in 1976) raised the same concern in the context of other social issues. The first major study of illiteracy in Canada was written, and the first organization dedicated exclusively to adult learning and literacy, Movement for Canadian Literacy, was founded. (See Exhibit 6.2 for more information.) A concern for literacy as a social justice issue was dominant among activists.

1970    The first Laubach tutor training workshop was offered in Canada. Laubach councils were set up across the country during the next decade. (See Exhibit 6.2 for more information.)

1976    *Adult Basic Education in Canada and Literacy Activities in Canada, 1975/76,* the first detailed analysis of illiteracy in the country, is published. Written by Audrey M. Thomas for World Literacy of Canada, it used census data on school grade completion to estimate the number of adults in need and collected all available data on provision

|       | across the country from federal and provincial sources and from numerous organizations of different types—government, research, and community based. |
|-------|---|
| 1977  | First national conference on literacy in Ottawa brings together key people in the field and leads to the creation of the Movement for Canadian Literacy to advocate for the cause. (See Exhibit 6.2 for more details.) |
| 1979  | *Report of the Commission of Enquiry on Educational Leave and Productivity* (for the federal labor minister) is released and includes recommendations on adult illiteracy, calling for incentives and establishment of an adult literacy education fund that would offer grants to employers, trade unions, educational organizations, and individual workers to upgrade basic skills (report cited in Adams, Draper, & Ducharme, 1979). Although this fund did not materialize, the recommendations contributed to setting the stage for a federal response to adult literacy. |
| 1980s | The decade was characterized by an increasing number of federal government department reports on adult illiteracy as a social and economic issue. Provinces studied the issue, developed policies, and expanded provision of innovative services (in the community-based and institutional sectors), although there was little coordination within different provincial departments funding different types of services. |
| 1981  | Laubach Literacy of Canada is established to coordinate and represent the Laubach Reading Councils across the country. (See Exhibit 6.2.) |
| 1983  | *Adult Illiteracy in Canada—A Challenge,* an occasional paper for the Canadian Commission for UNESCO, written by Audrey Thomas, is released. It was the most comprehensive national assessment yet produced in Canada, contextualizing the |

problem in relation to world literacy and characterizing the Canadian situation as one of undereducated adults. Thomas described provincial and federal activities as well as those in the volunteer sector and pointed out the fragmentation of services. The juxtaposition of data on labor force participation, educational attainment, and training activities was effective in making connections between the social justice and economic motives of literacy advocates. The paper also identified groups in need of specialized response—the incarcerated, indigenous people, the disabled, immigrants, women, the elderly, and school dropouts—thus emphasizing that adults with literacy problems were not a homogeneous group.

1986

On October 1, in the Speech from the Throne, the occasion on which the government announces its focus for the coming year, the federal government pledges to "work with the provinces, the private sector and the voluntary groups to develop resources to ensure that Canadians have access to the literacy skills that are the prerequisite for participation in our advanced economy" (Selman & Dampier, 1991, p. 168). The task of developing a national strategy within the jurisdiction of the federal government was given to the Department of the Secretary of State, which began a lengthy process of consultation with all possible stakeholders.

In a December meeting at a site called Cedar Glen, a coalition of national groups promoting literacy in the volunteer sector crafted a public policy statement. They called it the Cedar Glen Declaration and published it as an open letter to the prime minister and provincial and territorial premiers and leaders. This declaration marked the beginning of a public awareness campaign and a new point in the literacy movement when national organizations could speak with common cause.

1987

The Southam newspaper chain, one of the largest publishers in the country, undertook a survey (Creative Research Group, 1987) and published a series of articles on adult illiteracy in Canada. (The articles were reprinted in Calamai, 1987.) This was the first assessment in Canada to test literacy using "real tasks" rather than by extrapolating literacy levels from years of schooling. The Southam survey sent shock waves across the country and brought the issue to public attention.

The National Literacy Secretariat was founded to fund literacy initiatives.

1988

A study by the Canadian Business Task Force on Literacy estimates the annual cost to business of illiteracy in the workforce at $4 billion and the cost to society at $10 billion. The group did not use scientific methods to reach these estimates but hypothesized that many errors required work to be redone and that many accidents in the workplace resulting in loss of life or property could be attributable to illiteracy. Although the text contained a disclaimer about the accuracy of the estimates, very few people read the disclaimer; only the figures made headlines. Accurate or not, publicity about the costs of illiteracy, added to all the other discourse, contributed to government's decision to take action (Darville, 1988).

The Council of Ministers of Education, the association that brings together all provincial and territorial education ministers to share information, aware of some potential loss of provincial prerogative, responded to the 1986 Throne Speech by commissioning its own survey of literacy and ABE. The resulting report, *Adult Illiteracy in Canada*, published in February 1988, outlined provincial programs and policies where they existed (Cairns, 1988). These descriptions were taken directly from provincial government documents. The analysis updated and expanded the themes of the 1976 and 1983 Thomas reports. Lifelong learning was a theme.

The prime minister announces a federal national literacy strategy with funding of $110 million over five years.

1989    The National Adult Literacy Database, ABC Canada, and the Fédération canadienne pour l'alphabétisation en français are created. (See Exhibit 6.2.)

The National Literacy Secretariat funds the national *Survey of Literacy Skills Used in Daily Life*, a well-respected and widely read report on literacy in Canada and the first official document to focus on the concept of literacy as opposed to illiteracy, as reflected in its title.

1990s    The decade was characterized by the creation of an infrastructure to support literacy activities across the country, including resource centers, electronic networks and communication systems, and provincial and territorial coalitions, all funded partially or entirely by the NLS. Through the funding of more than forty-five hundred projects, the NLS also supported the creation of teaching materials and increased support for academic and community-based research. While most provinces and territories increased spending on adult literacy education, provision of services to students has remained inconsistent from one part of the country to another (Hoddinott, 1998). The decade ended with attempts to assess, consolidate, and share the best of what had been developed (Barker, 1999), with repeated references to a future model of lifelong learning.

1994    *The International Adult Literacy Survey*, conducted by Statistics Canada in partnership with the Organization for Economic Cooperation and Development in seven countries, including Canada, provides an updated profile of literacy in Canada.

1997              The federal government increases the annual
                 allocation of the NLS to $30 million and targets
                 the additional money to family literacy,
                 workplace literacy, and new technology. The
                 move was seen as a sign of continuing federal
                 commitment, which some in the literacy field had
                 feared might end at the close of the decade when
                 the UNESCO International Decade of Literacy
                 came to an end.

## Appendix B: Agencies, Organizations, and Programs

*National Literacy Organizations and Agencies*

ABC CANADA
333 King Street East
Toronto, Ontario
Canada M5A 4N2
Phone: (416) 350–6270 or 1–800–303–1004
Fax: (416) 350–6262
Web site: http://www.abc-canada.org/

Fédération canadienne pour l'alphabétisation en français
235, chemin Montreal, bureau 205
Vanier, Ontario
Canada K1L 6C7
Phone: (613) 749–5333 or 1–888–906–5666
Fax: (613) 749–2252
E-mail: alpha@facf.franco.ca
Web site: http://www.franco.ca/alpha

Frontier College
35 Jackes Street
Toronto, Ontario
Canada M4T 1E2
Phone: (416) 923–3591 or 1–800–555–6523
Fax: (416) 923–3522
Web site: http://www.frontiercollege.ca/

Laubach Literacy Canada
70 Crown Street, Suite 225
Saint John, New Brunswick

Canada E2L 2X6
Phone: (506) 634–1980 or 1–877–634–1980
Fax: (506) 634–0944
Web site: http://www.laubach.ca/

Movement for Canadian Literacy
180 Metcalfe Street, Suite 300
Ottawa, Ontario
Canada K2P 1P5
Phone: (613) 563–2464
Fax: (613) 563–2504
Web site: http://www.literacy.ca/

National Adult Literacy Database
Scovil House
703 Brunswick Street
Fredericton, New Brunswick
Canada E3B 1H
Phone: (506) 457–6900 or 1–800–720–6253
Fax: (506) 457–6910
Web site: http://www.nald.ca

National Literacy Secretariat
Learning and Literacy Directorate, HRDC
Jos. Montferrand Building
170 Hotel de Ville, Eighth Floor
Hull, Quebec
Canada, K1A 0J9
Phone: (819) 953–5280
Fax: (819) 953–8076
Web site: www.nald.ca/nls.htm

*Other National Organizations Supporting Literacy Projects or Programs*

Canadian Labour Congress
2841 Riverside Drive
Ottawa, Ontario
Canada K1V 8X7
Phone: (613) 521–3400
Fax: (613) 521–4655
Web site: http://www.clc-ctc.ca/

Canadian Public Health Association
400–1565 Carling Avenue
Ottawa, Ontario
Canada, K1Z 8R1
Phone: (613) 725–3769
Fax: (613) 725–9826
Web site: http://www.cpha.ca

CONNECT
c/o Diane McCargar
LBS/ESL/LINC Department
Ottawa-Carlton School Board
515 Cambridge Street South
Ottawa, Ontario
Canada K1S 4H9
Phone: (613) 239–2583
Fax: (613) 239–2324
Web site: http://www.nald.ca/connect.htm

Learning Disabilities Association of Canada
323 Chapel Street, Suite 200
Ottawa, Ontario
Canada K1N 7Z2
Phone: (613) 238–5721
Fax: (613) 235–5391
Web site: http://www.ldac-taac.ca/

*Selected Provincial Programs*

AlphaPlus
2040 Yonge Street, Third Floor
Toronto, Ontario
Canada, M4S 1Z9
Phone: (416) 322–1012
Fax: (416) 322–0780
Web site: http://alphaplus.ca/index1.htm

Centre for Literacy of Quebec
3040 Sherbrooke Street West
Montreal, QC
Canada H3Z 1A4

Phone: (514) 931–8731, ext. 1415
Fax: (514) 931–5181
Web site: http://www.nald.ca/litcent.htm

SkillPlan BC
4303 Canada Way
Burnaby, British Columbia
Canada V5G 1J3
Phone: (604) 436–1126
Fax: (604) 437–7539
Web site: http://www.nald.ca/skill.htm

## Notes

1. Figures for all dollar amounts throughout the chapter are in Canadian dollars; as of year-end 1999, $1.00 Canadian was the equivalent of about $0.68 in the United States.
2. The term *formal* as used in this chapter refers to programs offered and accredited through academic institutions, public and private. While some volunteer and other "informal" community-based programs are also recognized, many offer educational services needed by their clientele without official accreditation. Increasingly, the lines between these categories are blurring.
3. It is worth knowing that some provinces requested and paid for the over-sampling of subpopulations. For example, Ontario and New Brunswick oversampled minority-language French speakers; Quebec, however, did not oversample minority-language English speakers. Consequently figures for Quebec's English-speaking population are unreliable.
4. Joyce Fairbairn, a Liberal senator, was for several years the special minister responsible for literacy, until the position was dropped in 1997. She has been a personal champion and literacy advocate since the 1980s and is considered by many to have been instrumental in building much of the parliamentary support accorded to literacy in the past twelve years. She has worked tirelessly behind the political scenes and taken on a public profile, traveling from coast to coast to preside over literacy events, always dressed in a signature red suit. In any full history of literacy in Canada, her name will figure prominently. She remains an important voice on Parliament Hill.
5. I thank Mary Norton and Audrey Thomas for their comments that helped shape this segment of the chapter.

## References

ABC Canada. (1997). *Are we meeting Canadian literacy needs? A demographic comparison of IALS and LEARN research respondents.* Toronto: ABC Canada.

Adams, R. J., Draper, P. M., & Ducharme, C. (1979). *Education and working Canadians: Report of the Commission of Inquiry on Educational Leave and Productivity.* Ottawa: Labour Canada.

Barker, K. C. (1992). *Adult literacy in Canada in 1992: Initiatives, issues, and imperatives. A report for the Prosperity Secretariat.* Ottawa: Prosperity Secretariat.

Barker, K. C. (1999). *Adult literacy: "Lessons learned" project technical report.* Ottawa: Human Resources Development Canada.

Belfiore, M. E. (1996). *Understanding curriculum development in the workplace: A resource for educators.* Toronto: ABC Canada.

Cairns, J. C. (1988). *Adult illiteracy in Canada.* Toronto: Council of Ministers of Education of Canada.

Calamai, P. (1987). *Broken words: Why five million Canadians are illiterate. A special Southam survey.* Toronto: Southam Newspaper Group.

Canada Standing Committee on Aboriginal Affairs. (1990). *"You took my talk": Aboriginal literacy and empowerment.* Fourth Report. Ottawa: House of Commons of Canada.

Creative Research Group. (1987). *Literacy in Canada: A research report.* Toronto: Southam News.

Darling, S. (1993). *Literacy: Its role in the implementation of Yukon land claims.* Whitehorse, YT: Yukon Literacy Council.

Darville, R. (1988). Framing il/literacy in the media. *Learning, 5*(1), 9–11.

Darville, R. (1991). *Adult literacy in Canada: Results of a national study.* Ottawa: Statistics Canada.

Darville, R. (1992). *Adult literacy work in Canada.* Vancouver: Canadian Association for Adult Education and Centre for Policy Studies in Education, University of British Columbia.

Despins, R., Maruca, G., & Turner, S. (1997). What makes a successful workplace education partnership? In M. Taylor (Ed.), *Workplace education* (pp. 41–53). Toronto: Culture Concepts.

Folinsbee, S., & Jurmo, P. (1994). *Collaborative needs assessment: A handbook for workplace development planners.* Toronto: ABC Canada.

Francis, R. D., Jones, R., & Smith, D. B. (1992). *Destinies: Canadian history since confederation* (2nd ed.). Toronto: Holt, Rinehart and Winston of Canada.

George, P. (1997). *Vision guiding Native literacy.* Owen Sound, ON: Ningwakwe Clearinghouse.

Godin, J. (Ed.). (1996). *Working in concert: Federal, provincial, and territorial actions in support of literacy in Canada.* Ottawa: National Literacy Secretariat.

Hambly, C. (1998). *Behaviour and beliefs of volunteer literacy tutors* (Working Paper No. 3). Montreal: Centre for Literacy of Quebec.

Hautecoeur, J.-P. (1978). *Analphabetisme et alphabétisation au Québec.* Quebec, QC: Gouvernement du Québec, Ministère de l'education du Québec, DGEA.

Hautecoeur, J.-P. (1990). Literacy policy in Quebec: A historical overview. In J.-P. Hautecoeur (Ed.), *Alpha 90: Current research in literacy* (pp. 13–51). Hamburg: UNESCO Institute for Education.

Hawkins, F. (1988). *Canada and immigration: Public policy and public concern.* (Rev. ed.). Montreal: McGill-Queen's University Press.

Hoddinott, S. (1998). *Something to think about: Please think about this. Report on a National Study of Access to Adult Basic Education Programs and Services in Canada.* Ottawa: Ottawa Board of Education.

Horsman, J. (1999*). Too scared to learn.* Toronto: McGilligan Books.

Jones, S. (1993). *Reading, but not reading well: Reading skills at level 3.* Ottawa: National Literacy Secretariat.

Larimer, S. J. (1999). *A brief history of the Ontario literacy movement.* Unpublished paper.

Lower, A. (1977). *Colony to nation, a history of Canada.* Toronto: McLellan & Stewart.

MacLeod, C. (1998). *Updating essential skills for the workplace: A paper.* Toronto: Council of Ministers of Education.

McConnell, W. H. (1977). *Commentary on the British North America Act.* Toronto: Macmillan of Canada.

Miller, L. (1990). *Illiteracy and human rights.* Ottawa: National Literacy Secretariat.

Ministry of Education of Quebec. (1994). *Basic school regulation respecting educational services for adults in general education.* Quebec, QC: Ministry of Education.

Morgan, D. (1998). *Writing out loud.* Canmore, AB: Write to Learn Project.

Norton, M., & Campbell, P. (1998). *Learning for our health: A resource for participatory literacy and health education.* Edmonton: Learning Centre Literacy Association.

Organization for Economic Cooperation and Development. (1995). *Literacy, economy, and society: Results of the first international adult literacy survey.* Paris: OECD Minister of Industry.

Organization for Economic Cooperation and Development. (1997). *Literacy skills for the knowledge society*. Paris and Ottawa: OECD, Human Resources Development Canada, and Minister of Industry.

Palmer, H. (Ed.). (1975). *Immigration and the rise of multiculturalism*. Vancouver: Copp Clark.

Parkland Regional College. (1998). *Reaching the rainbow: Aboriginal literacy in Canada*. Melville, SK: Parkland Regional College.

Quigley, B. A. (1997). *Rethinking literacy education*. San Francisco: Jossey-Bass.

Rodriguez, C., & Sawyer, D. (1990). *Native literacy research report*. Salmon Arm, BC: Okanagan College.

Selman, G. (1995). *Adult education in Canada, historical essays*. Toronto: Thompson Educational Publishing.

Selman, G., & Dampier, P. (1991). *The foundations of adult education in Canada*. Toronto: Thompson Educational Publishing.

Smith, J. (1997). *Literacy, welfare, and work: Preliminary study*. Brandon, MN: Coalition for Brandon Literacy Services.

Smith, J. (1998). *Literacy, welfare, and work: Year II*. Brandon, MN: Coalition for Brandon Literacy Services.

Stamp, R. M. (1970). Government and education in post-war Canada. In J. D. Wilson, R. M. Stamp, & L.-P. Audet (Eds.), *Canadian education: A history* (pp. 444–470). Scarborough, ON: Prentice-Hall of Canada.

Statistics Canada. (1991). *Adult literacy in Canada: Results of a national study* (Statistics Canada Catalogue No. 89–525-XPE). Ottawa: Minister of Industry, Science, and Technology.

Statistics Canada. (1996). *Reading the future: A portrait of literacy in Canada* (Statistics Canada Catalogue No. 89–551-XPE). Ottawa: Statistics Canada and Human Resources Development Canada, National Literacy Secretariat.

Sticht, T. G. (1999). How many low literate adults are there in Canada, the U.S. and U.K.? Should the IALS estimates be revised? *Literacy Across the CurriculuMedia Focus, 14*(3–4), 21–22.

Taylor, M. (1997a). *Workplace basic skills: A study of ten Canadian programs*. Ottawa: University of Ottawa.

Taylor, M. (1997b). *Workplace education: The changing landscape*. Toronto: Culture Concepts.

Thomas, A. (Ed.). (1998). *Family literacy in Canada: Profiles of effective practice*. Welland, ON: Editions Soleil.

Thomas, A. M. (1976). *Adult basic education and literacy activities in Canada 1975–76*. Toronto: World Literacy of Canada.

Thomas, A. M. (1983). *Adult illiteracy in Canada: A challenge* (Occasional Paper No. 42). Ottawa: Canadian Commission for UNESCO.

Thomas, A. M. (1989). *Adult literacy volunteer tutor program evaluation kit.* Victoria, BC: Ministry of Advanced Education and Job Training.

Wagner, S. (1990). Literacy and the assimilation of minorities: The case of francophones in Canada. In J.-P. Hautecoeur (Ed.), *Alpha 90— Current research in literacy* (pp. 55–80). Hamburg: UNESCO Institute for Education.

White, J., & Hoddinott, S. (1991). *Organizing adult literacy and basic education in Canada: A policy and practice discussion document.* Ottawa: Movement for Canadian Literacy.

Woodrow, H. (1995). *A Newfoundland spell.* St. John's NF: Harrish Press.

Ziegler, S. (1996). *The effectiveness of adult literacy education: A review of issues and outcomes-based evaluation of literacy programs.* Toronto: Ontario Literacy Coalition.

# CHAPTER SEVEN

# Organizational Development and Its Implications for Adult Basic Education Programs

*Marcia Drew Hohn*

—*∿*—

An organization is an entity where groups of people, connected through common purpose, come together to achieve particular ends (Morgan, 1997a). In the case of adult basic education (ABE), a typical organization would be a local program where teachers, counselors, directors, coordinators, and administrative and other staff come together to provide learning services for particular groups of adult students. Or it might consist of the people who work in a state or federal agency that oversees policy, funding, and support for local programs. Organizations do not exist independently of the people who populate them. In fact, all aspects of organizations ultimately flow from the individual thoughts and actions of members of the organization and their interaction with one another (Morgan, 1997b; Pfeiffer & Ballew, 1991). Understanding organizations therefore is about understanding the behavior of the groups and individuals within them. Organizational development and change are about seeing, understanding, and structuring processes; facilitating relationships; and leading groups and individuals within the organization to learn, grow, and work creatively together in achieving a common purpose and goals.

Organizational development is not an area that has received much attention in ABE. Historically, ABE has been a marginalized field with fragmented and inadequate resources. However, resources and recognition for the field are rising. Funding is rising at the federal level and in many states, and with these funding increases come different requirements and expectations. The Workforce Investment Act (WIA) of 1998 places ABE squarely within the context of workforce development. This may be an opportunity to play a more meaningful role in the workforce development system, or it might be a barrier. The National Reporting System (NRS) has narrowed measures of assessment to three core indicators of performance accountability. As Bingman, Ebert, and Bell (2000) point out, the purpose of ABE as defined in WIA and the NRS is much narrower than the goals of many adult learners. This poses a serious dilemma for programs that serve adult learners.

Organizational development is a tool that can be used to help those in the field of ABE deal with the calls for change inherent to these challenges and others. It can be used to develop a clearer articulation of the values and principles that guide this work, a better understanding of the nature of interactions within and between organizations, more effective communications, both internal and external, and a more informed commitment to learning and growth as individual organizations and as a larger field of work. The goal of this chapter is to help to facilitate that commitment.

## THE EVOLUTION OF ORGANIZATIONAL DEVELOPMENT

In the first half of the twentieth century, organization theory was dominated by classicists who viewed organizations as rational systems and valued efficient operations above all. They promoted the idea that management is a process of planning, organization, command, coordination, and control and that the design of an organization should be like that of a machine. This concept spawned the modern bureaucracy (Morgan, 1997a).

Morgan points out that bureaucracies are an ideal form when we think of organizations as machines: "We arrive at the kind of organization represented in the familiar organization chart: a pattern of precisely defined jobs organized in a hierarchical manner through precisely defined lines of command or communication" (1997a, p. 18). Although they are frequently vilified as mindless, rigid, and dehumanizing and sometimes appear to be instruments of oppression, bureaucracies remain a highly prevalent organizational form. Many of the organizations we interact with every day are bureaucracies: the school our children attend, the Department of Education where we attend a meeting, the bank where we cash a check, the insurance company where we take out a new policy. Bureaucracies have remained a popular organizational form because they are an efficient approach to routine tasks. They have also persisted because they "offer managers the promise of tight control over people and their activities" (Morgan, 1997a, p. 31; Morgan 1997b). Moreover, they are representative of the Western analytical worldview deeply ingrained in people by means of societal institutions and educational systems (Capra, 1982; Morgan, 1997a; Wheatley, 1992; Wheatley & Kellner-Rogers, 1996).

The mechanistic perspective that characterizes the bureaucracy also underlies the theory of scientific management developed by Frederick Taylor in the early 1900s. Taylor was an engineer who worked in a time in which industrial mass production was posing enormous problems in the workplace. The huge disparity between rewards for owners and workers generated conflict and hostility. Waste, injuries, and costly mistakes were commonplace. Taylor championed the idea that the work of human beings could be measured in the same way that the output of a machine can be measured, the objective being to design that work in the most efficient configuration possible. His principles include a belief that managers should do all the thinking about the planning and design of the work and, guided by scientific methods, should determine the most efficient work methods. They should also select and train the best person for the work design and then monitor performance. Taylor's work was associated with time and motion studies, which even then were seen as cold, calculating, and unconcerned with workers' needs and humanness; it has earned him scorn in much contemporary writing on management theory (Weisbord, 1987).

In spite of being maligned and criticized, Taylor has had an enormous impact on organization theory. His principles of scientific management provided the framework for work design throughout the century. Fast food restaurants, in which the work is broken down into carefully controlled parts networked to function like a machine, are the epitome of Taylorism. Similar methods have found their way into innumerable organizations trying to streamline their operations, including hospitals, retail outlets, and factories (Morgan, 1997a; Senge, 1990; Senge, Kleiner, Robers, Ross, & Smith, 1994).

Once in place, the limits of the mechanistic perspective, scientific management, and bureaucracies rapidly became apparent. Bureaucracies, in particular, were criticized for their dehumanizing effects on the people who worked in them, for stifling creativity, inhibiting personal growth, and causing people to be fearful and untrusting of management. Critics contended that by assuming people need to be watched, controlled, and held accountable for every minute of their time at work or would otherwise "screw up or screw off," bureaucracies miss out on a large part of the ability, talent, and potential brainpower of their workers.

Promoting a different perspective, Douglas McGregor articulated a powerfully positive view of human nature in his 1960 book, *The Human Side of Enterprise.* In presenting his "theory Y," McGregor (1960/1985) put forth a set of assumptions that Malcolm Knowles (1989) himself attributed as part of the underpinnings of his principles of adult learning. Theory Y assumes that (1) physical and mental effort is as natural as play, (2) the individual will exercise self-direction and self-control in the service of objectives, (3) the individual, under the right conditions, will learn not only to accept responsibility but to seek it, and (4) the capacity for imagination, ingenuity, and creativity in problem solving is widely distributed in the population (Hohn, 1998a).

McGregor was strongly influenced by psychologist Abraham Maslow's theory of a hierarchy of needs, which is based on the idea that after safety and security needs are met, individuals require more intangible rewards—status, recognition, and responsibility (Maslow, 1954). Another important influence on McGregor was Kurt Lewin (1951), who promoted the idea of "learning by doing" as key to helping people find meaning in work—the original "action research" that is frequently employed in ABE. Lewin's work also joined scientific thinking with democratic values and, as Weisbord (1987) points out, gave birth to the concept of participatory management, in which those directly involved in a work issue or problem participate in its analysis and resolution. McGregor wove ideas from Maslow, Lewin, and others into his own to produce a new concept of management, one that embraced the capacity of the human spirit to transform and the idea that each of us has individual perceptions about how the world works.

Weisbord (1987) believes that McGregor's greatest contribution to organization theory is the idea that because social change starts from deep within the individual, individuals need to be freed to make choices and work together to develop solutions to problems. In the work setting, these ideas and concepts translate into such activities as self-directed work teams, managers as coaches and mentors, and shared leadership. These ideas and concepts were also in sync with those emerging in education in the late 1960s and the 1970s: Freire's participatory education, Highlander's participatory research, and Knowles's principles of adult learning. The work of all three promotes the view that (1) the people most affected by a problem or work issue need to be involved in solving that problem in a manner that respects their needs, intelligence, and dignity; (2) the problem must be approached from the perspective of "we and us," not "I and them"; and (3) change evolves in the context of the local environment and its values (Hohn, 1998a). These are ideas that underlie the contemporary Total Quality Management (TQM) movement and much of current thinking about learning organizations as places where all the members of an organization are encouraged to learn together to solve problems and think creatively about achieving the organization's purpose and goals.

During the 1970s and into the 1980s, the practice of organizational development shifted away from a focus on the individual and a process-oriented philosophy to a focus on the organization itself (Bolman & Deal, 1997). This new focus, developed through the work of Trist and Emery (from the 1950s into the 1970s), led to the view of organizations as systems of integrated processes framed within particular paradigms and initiated the intensive engagement with what is now called systems thinking (Morgan, 1997a).

## SYSTEMS THINKING

Systems theory is a way of thinking about how the world operates—about the assumptions, beliefs, values, and symbols that characterize it. It is about the paradigm, the worldview, the vision of reality that helps a society maintain order. Deeply ingrained assumptions about how the world works shape the habits of our hearts and minds and our organizations in a continuous process of reinforcement. When worldviews are stable and held uniformly, they tend to be unseen and unquestioned. But when worldviews are in flux or challenged by different ways of thinking, controversy and turmoil ensue. At this time in history we seem to be caught between two ways of thinking: analytical thinking and synthetical, or systems, thinking (Capra, 1982; Hohn, 1998b; Morgan, 1997a, 1997b).

In analytical thinking, the world is seen as a machine in which the underlying assumption is that phenomena can best be understood by being reduced to their individual parts, with each part then being examined. As Ackoff (1981) explains, this approach involves taking things apart and studying the behavior of each part separately, then aggregating the explanation of the parts into an explanation of the whole. The assumption is that if each part functions as efficiently as possible, the system will operate optimally. The scientific method and objectivity are promoted, and the values of participants and the context of immediate environments are seen as irrelevant. Thinking focuses on straight-line cause and effect and on dichotomies of either-or. Analytical thinking underlies the classical management theory of rational planning, command, and control processes; it informs Taylor's work in scientific management, which breaks down work into smaller and smaller parts to be studied for optimal efficiency; and it leads to bureaucratic organizations with a top-down hierarchical structure and distinct departments, functions, and roles.

Synthetical thinking, now better known as systems thinking, emphasizes cohesion. According to Capra, contemporary systems thinking "looks at the world in terms of interrelatedness and interdependence of all phenomena, and in this framework an integrated whole whose properties cannot be reduced to those of its parts is called a system" (1982, p. 43). In this view, the system as a whole is greater than the sum of its parts, and the behavior of the system can be understood only in terms of its role and function within its containing whole (Ackoff, 1981). Localness, harmony, cooperation, and a sense of mutual dependence among system parts are promoted. Each individual part is considered in relation to all of the other parts, and respect for the values and thinking of individuals and groups involved is inherent in the system. Systems thinking underlies most contemporary approaches to management and leadership, one of which promotes the idea of "the learning organization," popularized by Peter Senge in *The Fifth Discipline* (1990).

## THE LEARNING ORGANIZATION:
## SYSTEMS THINKING IN ACTION

Senge's concept of the learning organization encompasses a broad range of approaches to developing the capacity of organizations to learn for continuous improvement. But the heart and soul of the learning organization is systems thinking. Senge believes that organizations need to stop focusing on pieces of the system and to understand the organization as a whole, with a deep appreciation of the interrelatedness of the various parts. A system is seen as a perceived whole whose elements hang together, affect one another, and operate toward a common purpose. Examples of systems are the human body, families, factories, chemical reactions, communities, teams, and all workplaces. In the workplace, the pattern of the relationships shared by key components of a system—work flow, the cultural system (composed of the attitudes, beliefs, and values of the employees), the quality of products or services, decision-making processes, and so on—need to be examined to discover how changes in any one of the components might affect the others and how small changes in components might leverage big changes in the system. Because teams and collaborative thinking are vital to the examination of these interrelationships, systems thinking by necessity assumes that everyone in the organization is engaged in this process (Senge, 1990; Senge et al., 1994).

As an example, consider the perennial problem of retention in ABE programs from a systems perspective. The common wisdom about why so many ABE students leave programs prematurely is that they have too many problems in their lives to stick with learning. But what if the starting point were different? What if the assumption was that the cause of the retention problem lay not with the student but with the system, with the way that program processes do or do not interrelate? A systems approach to solving the problem would engage in putting together teams made up of people from throughout the organization to look at the way program processes interrelate: intake and assessment, attendance policies, support services, opportunities for student leadership, curriculum and instruction, and so on. Data about how these various components work together and affect one another would then be generated and analyzed. This would likely lead to changes in the various components, linking and aligning them so that the optimum environment for students' successful completion of educational programs is established.

An ABE program in Tennessee initiated a process of systems thinking in 1997. The Knox County Adult Literacy Program used the Malcolm Baldrige educational criteria for performance excellence as its change process framework (these criteria apply TQM concepts that are based in systems thinking). The staff considered their program to be a strong one, but they wanted to establish a process through which they could continuously improve it. Teams of staff, students, board members, and volunteers were put together, and these teams identified vital areas for improvement. Data on these areas were generated through examination of records, interviews, and other information-gathering tools and then analyzed through the lenses of interrelatedness (how each worked or did not work with one another) and customer satisfaction (students' opinions).

Among several surprising and disturbing revelations, the systems analysis revealed that enrollment and assessment policies, teacher training, curriculum and instruction, and student leadership opportunities were not well linked and aligned; rather, they were riddled with gaps that created confusion, misunderstandings, inconsistency in program practices, and uncertainty among students and staff. For example, the analysis revealed that teachers were not incorporating training ideas and materials from in-service programs into their classrooms. To address this problem, the focus of training shifted from putting on a workshop to involving teachers in curriculum development and bringing together teachers who worked in different parts of the program. The increased exchange of ideas and information among teachers led to the development of significantly more positive attitudes toward the program and the incorporation of new ideas and methods into classrooms (Cody, Ford, & Hayward, 1998).

The program began an attempt to link and align internal operations, organization leadership, systems (such as data management), and processes (such as intake and assessment), as well as sound literacy practices in a long process that has been a reeducation for everyone. Program staff find their world to be more complex because they understand how the parts of the program are interrelated. They have discovered the need to be open to change and to solicit and receive feedback in a way that honors and values the perspectives of all those involved. And they have come to realize that there are no quick fixes; the best way to bring about program improvement is by means of an ongoing commitment to do so on the part of students, staff, board members, and volunteers (Cody, Ford, & Hayward, 1998; Mincey & Bingman, 2000).

The members of Knox County Adult Literacy Program were able to engage effectively with systems thinking, although not without a struggle. Systems thinking represents a dramatically different way of thinking about organizational issues. It requires a reexamination of assumptions about how things work and a kind of skill and patience in executing change that some organizations do not have.

## PARADIGMS, MIND-SETS, AND ORGANIZATIONAL CHANGE: THE EXPERIENCE WITH TQM

An example of how difficult it can be to implement organizational change when it challenges traditional ways of thinking and operating is the experience of educational institutions in their attempt to adopt TQM concepts in the late 1980s and early 1990s. The theory of TQM was articulated primarily by W. Edwards Deming (Hohn, 1996), who worked with the Japanese on corporate approaches to management in the post–World War II era. Deming promoted the idea of training everyone in an organization to become engaged in process improvement and quality management up-front rather than relying on post-production inspection. These methods produced spectacular improvements in the quality of Japanese products, the Toyota line of cars being a notable example.

Most American businesses became engaged with the idea of TQM because they saw the competitive environment as a wolf at the door. The options were to change or cease to exist. Educational institutions were more likely inspired to engage with TQM because of its transformational potential and the idea of continuous improvement; often a particular individual or group within the institution was excited about TQM and rallied to its cause (Seymour & Collett, 1991). Here was a management approach that seemed relevant and workable for educational institutions. It made sense to many educators to form teams to examine the organizational processes, develop and analyze concrete data generated by TQM methods and tools, and then empower employees to make decisions based on the analysis that would foster continuous improvement of the institution. The emphasis on customer satisfaction was seen as a way to recast conversations on improvement of the system so that the focus would be customer (student) needs and interests rather than a quagmire of personal (faculty) opinions. Many educators were probably drawn to TQM because it embraced democratic principles, recognizing the dignity and worth of all individuals and seeking to include voices across traditional boundaries.

TQM promoted employee participation and power sharing throughout an organization, and it introduced new ways of thinking about relationships within organizations. Therein lay the problem. A critical assessment of the TQM experience at some twenty-two institutions of higher education indicated that the shift in mind-set that implementation of TQM required significantly stymied its adoption by many institutions (Hohn, 1996; Seymour, 1993; Seymour & Collett 1991). The assessment showed how difficult it is to break free of deeply ingrained analytical ways of thinking that constitute the operating paradigm of educational organizations.

In the institutions studied, the experience with TQM yielded some significantly positive results. Chief among the benefits was the fact that employees acquired a voice in the decision-making process. Teamwork brought employees together, often for the first time; they engaged in networking and developed a greater appreciation for the complexity of the organization. This led to changes in the organization's psychological climate: improved morale, reduced grievances, and less use of sick time. Processes and procedures were streamlined, and problem prevention strategies reduced the need to correct errors. One college claimed to have reduced its overall purchasing, warehousing, and delivery of equipment errors by 78 percent. Another college worked to improve its graduation rate, reaching nearly 80 percent matriculation rate over three years (Seymour & Collett, 1991).

Frustration and lack of progress was enormous, however. Overt problems, such as the time needed to train staff and for teams to meet, surfaced immediately. Then more subtle problems emerged. Many revolved around issues of power. Middle managers, in particular, had a hard time letting go of decision-making authority and were fearful of losing control, thereby undermining or ignoring recommendations from employee teams. Employees were also highly sensitive to what they perceived as mixed signals from the top, indicating a lack of commitment to or understanding of TQM. There was a sense that top management did not support the work of employee teams. This led to mistrust, cynicism, and a sense of betrayal that eroded morale and lessened productivity. Issues of power and control are bound up in what one believes about the nature of power. When managers believe that power is finite, they are reluctant to give up any portion of it. This belief is inherent in analytical ways of thinking. The belief that power grows through sharing is inherent in systems thinking, with its emphasis on interrelationships and interactions.

Other challenges included the lack of underlying skills to work in teams and lead teams. Skills in listening, giving feedback, generating ideas, equalizing everyone's voice within teams, reaching consensus, and dealing with conflict all demanded team participation and facilitation skills that employees and managers simply did not have and that were often not highly valued in the organization. Facilitation skills were often seen as too "soft" or too "feminine" to get the "real work" done. The need for additional training to develop team skills was sometimes resisted and certainly exacerbated the problem of time management.

What proved extremely difficult for the people in these educational institutions was thinking in terms of processes and their interrelationships and interactions. Not only was it an unfamiliar and therefore difficult way of thinking, but it did not produce enough tangible results to warrant the time and effort it required. The staff members were anxious about the challenge of working through that ambiguous time during which old ways of doing things are given up but there is no clarity about what will replace them. People were concerned about the ramification of change for both the organization and themselves as individuals. All of this made people resistant to change. Ultimately some institutions abandoned TQM because the overall benefits did not seem substantial or immediate enough to warrant the time, expense, and effort required to integrate it fully into the institution. Others, however, cited TQM as transforming their organizations and preparing them to meet the challenges of the twenty-first century.

One experience of ABE with TQM yielded similar results. In 1994, Massachusetts introduced a program and staff development process involving the application of TQM concepts. This process supports a participatory approach to organizational planning intended to link staff learning to the agenda for the program's growth and to address weaknesses in program systems. All staff are to be involved in decision making and work individually and in teams to learn about the issues identified and to carry out the work needed to address them. For some programs, the experience led to a new world of thinking, growing, and doing—although not without some difficulties—that transformed their program management and operations. For others, the process never became integrated into the organization and rapidly disappeared, usually because the process challenged the same mindset that undermined TQM in higher education (Hohn, 1996, 1998b).

## CONCLUSION

Insights into people's motivation to do good work, their need to be recognized as capable and self-directed, and the necessity of honoring the perspective of those closest to the work are becoming more common in contemporary organizations. In fact, teamwork and employee empowerment now operate in many organizations, flattening the organization into a less hierarchical arrangement that allows for swifter problem solving and directs the collective creativity and energy of employees toward achieving the organization's vision, purpose, and goals. Managers function less as controllers or dictators than as mentors, coaches, and facilitators of relationships. These concepts and ideas find congruence with many of the principles and practices found within ABE, especially in Knowles's principles of adult learning, Freirean participatory education, and Highlander's participatory research. They promote inclusion of those closest to the work in solving problems, an approach that honors local knowledge and perspectives and urges a melding of different perspectives to reach new levels of potential. In some places, ABE already thinks in a systems way.

The continuously evolving and increasingly complex problems that ABE organizations face require a change from traditional, top-down management hierarchies. But no one should be naive about what it takes to bring about a genuine shift in thinking about how the organizations operate. The experience with TQM, the enormous difficulties organizations have had in applying the concepts of the learning organization, and the pervasive and persistent presence of bureaucracies in our everyday lives collectively show how difficult it is to shift paradigms. Embarking on such a program of change means starting down a long and difficult road. New ways of thinking and working together need to be supported through time and training at all levels, and there needs to be strong, continuous, and consistent leadership that values input from many perspectives. People need to see the benefits of changing in relationship to personally meaningful issues so the stress of uncertainty does not dominate their thinking. As the Knoxville, Tennessee, program shows, the perspective needed for a paradigm shift requires a willingness for "constant reflection, evaluation, and experimentation" to move beyond the comfort of current, "good enough" work to the risk and uncertainty in realizing their potential through continuous improvement (Bingman, Ebert, & Bell, 2000).

## References

Ackoff, R. (1981). *Creating the corporate future*. New York: Wiley.

Bingman, M. B., Ebert, O., & Bell, B. (2000). *Outcomes of participation in adult basic education: The importance of learners' perspectives*.

Cambridge, MA: National Center for the Study of Adult Learning and Literacy.

Bolman, L. G., & Deal, T. E. (1997). *Reframing organizations: Artistry, choice, and leadership.* San Francisco: Jossey-Bass.

Capra, F. (1982). *The turning point: Science, society and the rising culture.* New York: Bantam Books.

Cody, J., Ford, J., & Hayward, K. (1998). The story of improvement. *Focus on Basics, 2*(C).

Hohn, M. D. (1996). *Total quality management.* Unpublished manuscript.

Hohn, M. D. (1998a). *Partnering for empowerment.* Dissertation study.

Hohn, M. D. (1998b). Why is change so hard? *Focus on Basics, 2*(C).

Knowles, M. (1989). *The making of an adult educator.* San Francisco: Jossey-Bass.

Lewin, K. (1951). *Field theory in social science.* New York: HarperCollins.

Maslow, A. H. (1954). *Motivation and personality.* New York: HarperCollins.

McGregor, D. (1985). *The human side of enterprise: 25th anniversary edition.* New York: McGraw-Hill. (Original work published 1960)

Mincey, R., & Bingman, M. B. (2000). *Challenges of Change: The Program Improvement Process of the Knox County Adult Literacy Program.* Knoxville: Center for Literacy Studies, University of Tennessee.

Morgan, G. (1997a). *Images of organization.* Thousand Oaks, CA: Sage.

Morgan, G. (1997b). *Imaginization: New mindsets for seeing, organizing, and managing.* Thousand Oaks, CA: Sage.

Pfeiffer, J. W., & Ballew, A. C. (Eds.). (1991). *Theories and models in applied behavioral science, 4.* San Diego: Pfeiffer & Co.

Senge, P. (1990). *The fifth discipline: The art and practice of the learning organization.* New York: Doubleday.

Senge, P., Kleiner, A., Robers, C., Ross, R. B., & Smith, B. J. (1994). *The fifth discipline fieldbook: Strategies and tools for building a learning organization.* New York: Doubleday.

Seymour, D. (1993). *Total quality management in higher education: Clearing the hurdles.* Methuen, MA: GOAL/QPC.

Seymour, D., & Collett, C. (1991). *Total quality management in higher education: A critical assessment.* Methuen, MA: GOAL/QPC.

Weisbord, M. R. (1987). *Productive workplaces: Organizing and managing for dignity, meaning, and community.* San Francisco: Jossey-Bass.

Wheatley, M. (1992). *Leadership and the new science. Learning about organization from an orderly universe.* San Francisco: Berrett-Koehler.

Wheatley, M., & Kellner-Rogers, M. (1996). *A simpler way.* San Francisco: Berrett-Koehler.

# Resources on Organizational Development

*Marcia Drew Hohn*

T he following selections provide sources for readers interested in pursuing the topic of organizations and their development. The annotations note the recommended audience for each title, its focus, and what that audience can expect to find when turning to it. Some titles, for example, focus on the kind of leadership believed to be necessary to carrying an organization through systemic change (examples are Stephen Covey's "Three Roles of the Leader in the New Paradigm," Edgar Schein's "Leadership and Organizational Culture," and Sally Helgesen's *The Web of Inclusion*). Others focus on the special demands of initiating change in nonprofit organizations (John M. Bryson's *Strategic Planning for Public and Nonprofit Organizations*), resources on applying systems thinking in organizations (Margaret Wheatley's *Leadership and the New Science*), and practical strategies to support organizational change (Roger Fisher's *Getting to Yes*).

Most of the following resources are readily available through public libraries, libraries in higher education institutions, or publishers or booksellers. A few, such as articles and collections of articles published by Harvard Business School Press, are available only by direct order from that publisher. I have included on-line ordering information for each publisher.

## BOOKS

Alvarez, R., & Luterman, K. G. (1979). *Discrimination in organizations.* San Francisco: Jossey-Bass. 396 pages. Out of print but available at libraries.

*Focus:* Racism, sexism, and other forms of discrimination that thwart organizational development.

*Recommended audience:* Anyone interested in discrimination in organizations.

*Discrimination in Organizations* is a series of essays by twenty-five authors who examine five aspects of discrimination in organizations: access to opportunity and power, the extent of sexism and racism, the effects of outside influence (such as dominant ethnic groups) on organizational staffing, the representation of women and minorities by organization level, and institutions of social control, such as courts, public schools, and government agencies. The essays are a call for action.

Bennis, W. (1993). *Beyond bureaucracy: Essays on the development and evolution of human organization.* San Francisco: Jossey-Bass. 254 pages. Can be ordered on-line at www.josseybass.com.

*Focus:* The organization as embedded in external environments.

*Recommended audience:* Those both new to and somewhat familiar with the field of organizational development.

Bennis argues that the bureaucracy is in a state of decline as an organizational form, being too big and too slow to respond to the rapid pace of change in technology, the labor market, and the global economy. He also believes that the democratization of the workplace will speed the demise of the bureaucracy—that is, the emerging participatory nature of workplaces is incongruent with the command-and-control approach inherent in bureaucracies. Bennis supports his case by citing trends in the evolution of organizational development, such as employee empowerment and teamwork, and by examining the assumptions, such as the human need for recognition, that underlie his theory. He discusses changing patterns of leadership in the past few decades from authority and control to facilitation of relationships for developing a vision to achieve the organization's potential and suggests several possible approaches through which to direct organizational change.

Bolman, L. G., & Deal, T. E. (1997). *Reframing organizations: Artistry, choice, and leadership.* San Francisco: Jossey-Bass. 450 pages. Can be ordered on-line at www.josseybass.com.

*Focus:* Organization spirit and transformation.

*Recommended audience:* Those interested in a broad perspective on organizational development; useful as both a primer and for those familiar with the field.

This book is about understanding and changing organizations. It explores the development of thinking about organizations through a series of frameworks: structural, human resource, political, and symbolic. It also reviews the historical development of the field of organization development and cites the work of its significant theorists and thinkers. The author offers an extensive discussion on how leadership practices can be improved by drawing on the knowledge gained through the integration of organizational theories.

Bryson, J. M. (1995). *Strategic planning for public and nonprofit organizations.* (Revised edition.) San Francisco: Jossey-Bass. 348 pages. Can be ordered on-line at www.josseybass.com.

*Focus:* Nonprofit organizations.

*Recommended audience:* Directors, managers, and staff of nonprofit organizations.

This is a guide to the strategic planning process written by a highly experienced consultant in organizational planning to assist nonprofits in strengthening and sustaining organizational achievement. The recommended cycle for strategic change has ten steps, and all the processes within each step are explained in detail. Steps range from identifying and clarifying organizational mandates and mission to developing, implementing, and integrating a strategic vision. Special attention is paid to the role of leadership in making strategic planning work. This guide is best read in conjunction with resources that emphasize a systems approach to planning, such as Peter Senge's *The Fifth Discipline* (reviewed later in this bibliography), so that the reader develops an appreciation of how the complexities of interrelationships and interactions in organizations can affect planning initiatives.

Bryson, J. M., & Alston, F. K. (1995). *Creating and implementing your strategic plan: A workbook for public and nonprofit organizations.* (2nd edition.) San Francisco: Jossey-Bass. 140 pages. Can be ordered on-line at www.josseybass.com.

*Focus:* Nonprofit organizations.

*Recommended audience:* Directors, managers, and staff of non-profits interested in implementing strategic planning.

This publication takes readers through a step-by-step process in which they create and implement a strategic plan (described above in Bryon, *Strategic Planning for Public and Nonprofit Organizations*). It also explains strategic planning and its value to nonprofit organizations as an alternative to other internal planning options, such as customer-focused processes. To be implemented effectively, this process requires a facilitator skilled in assisting organizations with planning.

Capra, F. (1983). *The turning point: Science, society, and the rising culture.* New York: Bantam Books. 419 pages. Available at www.amazon.com.

*Focus:* Organizations as systems.

*Recommended audience:* Useful as a primer on systems thinking.

Capra, a physicist, explores how the mechanistic worldview developed from the time of Descartes and Newton and how this perspective pervades society and institutions today. Capra goes on to discuss the reason that mechanistic ways of organizing inhibit creative problem solving. He then explains his interpretation of a systems view of life and the ways in which that view can help in solving critical social problems. Capra does a good job explaining complicated concepts and theories. The book is a fine introduction to systems thinking and the influence the mechanistic worldview has on contemporary work and social and family life.

Clegg, S. R., & Hardy, C. (Eds.). (1999). *Studying organization: Theory and method.* Thousand Oaks, CA: Sage. 480 pages. Can be ordered on-line at order@sagepub.com.

*Focus:* Analysis of organizations.

*Recommended audience:* Researchers.

The contributors to this collection are academics and researchers who are writing for other academics and researchers in the field of organization theory. The chapters in Part One provide frameworks such as ecology and economics for the analysis of organizations. Those in Part Two are essentially reflections on research, theory, and practice. The chapters are on such topics as structural contingency theory, organizational ecology, feminist approaches in the workplace, the role of emotion in the workplace, and organizational culture. This book has an extensive bibliography that makes it a good reference.

Edwards, P., Edwards, S., & Benzel, R. (1997). *Teaming up.* New York: Putnam. 385 pages. Can be ordered on-line at www.putnam.com/putnam.

*Focus:* Practical strategies for organizational change.

*Recommended audience:* Anyone whose organization may be entering into an alliance or merger with another organization.

*Teaming Up* was written with small businesses in mind, but it has many ideas and strategies that will be useful to adult basic education programs that are contemplating a collaboration, alliance, or merger. Of particular interest are the chapters on legal and financial issues, the psychology of making relationships work, a troubleshooting guide, and the process for determining whether breaking up is the best thing to do. This book is written in a trendy style that educators may find irritating, but there are nonetheless a lot of useful ideas in it.

Fisher, R., Ury, W., & Patton, B. (1981). *Getting to Yes*. New York: Penguin Books. 200 pages. Can be ordered on-line at www.amazon.com.

*Focus:* Practical strategies for organizational change.

*Recommended audience:* Anyone whose organization may be entering into an alliance, collaboration, or merger with another organization.

*Getting to Yes* is a classic text on negotiation that has been used by businesses, churches, and other organizations. It is an excellent resource for adult basic education programs entering into collaborations, alliances, or mergers. Chapter topics include how to avoid bargaining over two different positions, how to focus on method (separate the people involved from the problem, focus on mutual interests and gains, invent options for mutual gain, and insist on using objective criteria), and how to address some of the more difficult areas of negotiation, such as dealing with more powerful organizations. This book has also been used increasingly for problem solving in families, especially those with teenagers.

Fletcher, J. K. (1999). *Disappearing acts: Gender, power and relational practice at work*. Boston: MIT Press. 175 pages. Can be ordered on-line at www.mitpress.mit.edu.

*Focus:* Workplace environments with a focus on gender issues.

*Recommended audience:* Anyone interested in the psychological environment of the workplace.

Relational practice is a term coined at the Center for Research on Women and the Stone Center at Wellesley College, a by-product of the research of Jean Baker Miller and others who have developed theories of how women learn and grow in the context of relationships. *Disappearing Acts* is based on Fletcher's study of female design engineers and details how the need for relational skills and emotional intelligence that is associated with teamwork and employee empowerment in the modern organization is often undervalued or undermined when it bumps up against male-oriented images of what it takes to be successful. The very behavior that organizations say is needed disappears. Fletcher suggests some ways that individuals and organizations can make the hard work of collaboration and teamwork visible and underscores its importance for organizational competence.

*Harvard Business Review on change.* (1998). Boston: Harvard Business School Press. 240 pages. Can be ordered on-line at custserv@hbsp .harvard.edu.

*Focus:* Organizational change and transformation.

*Recommended audience:* Those interested in reading about the experience and results of a variety of organizational change initiatives.

This is a collection of eight articles first published in the *Harvard Business Review* and written by organizational consultants and practitioners. Each article represents a particular perspective or case study on organizational change. Among the articles are "Why Transformation Efforts Fail" (Kotter), "Building Your Company's Vision" (Colline & Porras), "Managing Change" (Duck), "The Reinvention Roller Coaster" (Goss, Pascale, & Athos), and "Reshaping an Industry" (Augustine). The articles are of varying quality and relevance to adult basic education, but they provide a good overview of current strategies for initiating organizational change.

Helgesen, S. (1995). *The web of inclusion.* New York: Doubleday. 288 pages. Can be ordered on-line at www.amazon.com.

*Focus:* Organizational change.

*Recommended audience:* Those who want to know about models for inclusion and how they are developed for empowerment of voices within and between organizations.

Helgesen's thesis is that the modern organization relies on the ideas and talents and energy of its employees and that top-down bureaucratic organizations smother this creativity and energy. To support her thesis, she examines five organizations (three businesses, a newspaper, and a hospital) that have developed structures and processes that allow individuals and groups to create flexible and ever-changing webs of relationships, both internal and external, in order to respond rapidly to the demands of the workplace. The emphasis is on facilitation of relationships, employee empowerment, and inclusion of voices from across an organization.

Kanter, R. (1997). *On the frontiers of management.* Boston: Harvard Business School Press. 320 pages. Can be ordered on-line at www.hbsp.harvard.edu.

*Focus:* Organizational change and transformation.

*Recommended audience:* A good resource for readers with some grounding in organizational theory and behavior.

The writing in this book tends to be sweeping, with little underlying theory explored or explained. However, the author does paint a vivid picture of contemporary thinking about management and leadership and provides useful guiding principles for organizational development. Of particular interest is the chapter on change, in which Kanter emphasizes that change-friendly organizations are future oriented. Such organizations seek to close the gap between their current performance and their potential by means of a "learning together" approach that is characterized by the participation of employees at all levels and from all areas of the organization. Change-friendly organizations form internal and external networks around common interests and needs through which they can exchange knowledge and view differences in opinion as opportunities to grow. Their leaders create cultures in which people are encouraged to take risks. The emphasis of this book is on viewing employees as assets to the organization and defining management's role in creating an environment where employees can flourish.

Kotter, J. P. (1996). *Leading change.* Boston: Harvard Business School Press. 186 pages. Can be ordered on-line at www.hbsp.harvard.edu.

*Focus:* Organizational change and transformation.

*Recommended audience:* Anyone involved in or leading an effort to initiate organizational change.

The eight-stage process for leading change that Kotter describes includes establishing a sense of urgency to change, creating a coalition to guide the change, developing a vision of the outcome of the change, communicating that vision through the organization, empowering employees to contribute to the change effort, generating short-term "wins" to encourage people to keep moving toward the larger goals, consolidating gains (interrelating key changes to leverage still more change), and anchoring new approaches in the culture of the organization (integrating changes into norms of behavior and shared values). What is most compelling about this book is its description of the needs of the organization and its people at each stage of the change process; it rings true. The writing is practical and personal. No attempt is made to provide a theoretical base or to explain underlying assumptions or beliefs. This is Kotter telling the reader what he thinks it takes to make change happen.

Martin, J. (1992). *Cultures in organizations: Three perspectives.* New York: Oxford University Press. 240 pages. Can be ordered on-line at www4.oup.co.uk.

*Focus:* Organizational culture.

*Recommended audience:* Anyone interested in a synthesis of the research and writing on organizational culture.

Studying organizational culture—the shared mental models or meanings that influence people's behavior in organizations—was a fad in the 1980s, and much of the writing on this subject is fragmented and centered on case studies. Martin tries to make sense of this confusing array of research and writing by organizing it into three categories: integration, differentiation, and fragmentation. She uses case study materials from a Fortune 500 company to illustrate her points.

Morgan, G. (1997). *Images of organization.* Thousand Oaks, CA: Sage. 498 pages. Can be ordered on-line at order@sagepub.com.

*Focus:* A broad perspective on the nature of organizations and organizational development.

*Recommended audience:* Anyone interested in developing an understanding of organizations. An especially good introductory resource.

This 1997 edition of *Images of Organization* is the updated version
of the original 1986 edition, which electrified the organization world
with its innovative approach to understanding organizations. As
Morgan writes, the "book is based on a very simple premise: that all
theories of organization and management are based on implicit images
or metaphors that lead us to see, understand, and manage organizations in distinctive yet partial ways" (p. 4). This premise leads Morgan
to explore organizations as modeled on machines, organisms, the brain,
cultures, political systems, and psychic prisons. He discusses the way
each image plays out in organizational design and management, traces
its theoretical roots, and cites theorists and thinkers who have contributed ideas and concepts. The chapter on organizations as instruments of domination is excellent. Morgan writes in a clear and
compelling style and has fresh perspectives, ideas, and insights.

Morgan, G. (1997). *Imaginization: New mindsets for seeing, organizing, and managing.* Thousand Oaks, CA: Sage. Now also available in
paperback from Berrett-Koehler. 388 pages. Can be ordered on-line
at www.bkpub.com.

*Focus:* Organizational change and transformation.

*Recommended audience:* Those new to and experienced in organizational change.

Morgan introduced the term *imaginization* to give a name to the
process through which people can free themselves of an organization's
dysfunctional mind-sets. He sees metaphor as the primary means
through which people forge their relationship to their work; the individual's image of self and the world, he believes, can either constrain
or expand the potential for transformation. By developing an image
of an organizational structure, a problem area, or some aspect of the
future, Morgan says, it is possible to gain insight into how an organization operates and what it will take to change it. Nature is seen as a
good source of images to use in this process. For example, a person
might "image" an organization as an ant colony, a spider plant, a
river, or a spider's web to develop and communicate his or her

understanding of how the organization operates. *Imaginization* can be read as a companion piece to Morgan's *Images of Organizations* or on its own.

Scholtes, P. R., with Joiner, B. L., Braswell, B., Finn, L., Hacquebord, H., Little, K., Reynard, S., Streibel, B., & Weiss, L. (1988). *The team handbook.* Madison, WI: Joiner Associates. 219 pages.

*Focus:* Practical strategies for organizational change.

*Recommended audience:* For anyone undertaking leadership of or involvement with teams.

*The Team Handbook* was written to help companies implement Total Quality Management (TQM) and other quality initiatives (it contains introductions by W. Edwards Deming, a major force in the TQM movement, and Malcolm Knowles, a well-known adult educator and consultant to business). Despite its focus on quality initiatives, it is an excellent resource on teams and teamwork, which are here to stay in modern organizations. Included are discussions on holding productive meetings, maintaining record-keeping systems, and determining the best way to meet goals. The most valuable chapters have to do with the dynamics of team formation and growth, the highs and lows all teams face, and problem-solving and team-building guidelines and activities.

Senge, P. (1990). *The fifth discipline: The art and practice of the learning organization.* New York: Doubleday. 360 pages.

*Focus:* Organizations as systems.

*Recommended audience:* Those interested in understanding the learning organization as it was introduced to the business community.

*The Fifth Discipline,* which popularized the concept of the learning organization, electrified the business community when it was published in 1990. A decade later, it still impresses for its ability to capture the essence of leadership. Senge believes that five important components, or "cornerstones," as he calls them, characterize the learning organization: (1) a shift in focus from the individual parts of a system to its functioning as a whole, with a deep appreciation of the interrelatedness of the various parts; (2) personal mastery, in which the individual clarifies and deepens his or her personal vision of what to accomplish; (3) an understanding of mental models (the paradigm or mind-set through which the organization operates); (4) the building of a shared vision of the organization; and (5) an effort to break old habits through disciplined dialogue. The writing is somewhat dense and convoluted. See *The Fifth Discipline Fieldbook* (Senge et al.) for a simpler presentation of the learning organization and for guidelines on how to create one.

Senge, P. M., Kleiner, A., Roberts, C., Ross, R. B., & Smith, B. J. (1994). *The fifth discipline fieldbook: Strategies and tools for building a learning organization.* New York: Doubleday. 560 pages.

*Focus:* Organizations as systems.

*Recommended audience:* Those interested in learning more about the way a learning organization works.

While many were inspired by the concept of the learning organization that Senge described in his path-breaking book *The Fifth Discipline* (1990), many also found it difficult to implement. Consequently Senge and his coauthors developed *The Fifth Discipline Fieldbook,* which outlines strategies and tools for building a learning organization and includes case studies as well as references to other theorists. The five cornerstones of the learning organization (see the annotation of Senge's *Fifth Discipline*) are explained simply and clearly. This is an implementation guide, but it can also be used as a companion to the original book, which is somewhat dense and can be difficult to follow.

Stern, G., for the Drucker Foundation. (1998). *The Drucker Foundation self-assessment tool: Process guide and participant workbook.* San Francisco: Jossey-Bass. Process guide: 176 pages; participant workbook: 80 pages. Can be ordered on-line at www.josseybass.com.

*Focus:* Planning for organizational change.

*Recommended audience:* Organizations interested in implementing a program for change.

This package, which consists of a facilitator's guide and participant workbooks, is meant to be used in training sessions to help nonprofits implement a planning process. It is the replacement for a previous publication of the Drucker Foundation (Peter Drucker is a writer, teacher, and consultant in management and leadership), *The Ten Most Important Questions You Will Ever Ask About Your Nonprofit Organization,* a guide to customer-focused planning for nonprofits. This revised version retains a customer focus and takes an organization through an entire self-assessment process for internal planning purposes. It is a useful tool for nonprofits, including adult basic education programs, but a facilitator experienced in a variety of forms of planning (for example, customer focused, strategic, and participatory) is needed to guide the process.

Stivers, C. (1992). *Gender images in public administration: Legitimacy and the administrative state.* Thousand Oaks, CA: Sage. 176 pages. Can be ordered on-line at order@sagepub.com.

*Focus:* Racism, sexism, and other forms of discrimination in organizations.

*Recommended audience:* Anyone interested in discrimination issues in organizations, particularly those of gender.

Stivers's book is likely to strike a note of recognition with many women who are "on tap but not on top" in public administrative agencies. She defines herself as a woman who had been ambivalent about feminism but could no longer ignore the impact of organizational concepts and theories being framed by an exclusively masculine perspective. She could also no longer ignore the fact that women have not often been in positions at high levels of organizations that would allow them to reshape the dialogue and the action. She organizes the book in terms of basic dilemmas in which professional women are likely to find themselves—for example, the "dilemma of expertise," which confines a woman to a particular niche where she is unable to influence the overall organization, and the "dilemma of leadership," in which women are expected to seem "ladylike" but act "tough" and in other ways associated with masculine behavior. One chapter explores feminist theory and suggests that many of its underlying values and concepts (such as the power of relational intelligence) need to be brought into the workplace.

Weisbord, M. R. (1987). *Productive workplaces: Organizing and managing for dignity, meaning, and community.* San Francisco: Jossey-Bass. 433 pages. Can be ordered on-line at www.josseybass.com.

*Focus:* Organizational change and transformation.

*Recommended audience:* Readers new to the arena of organizational change.

In this memoir-like book, Weisbord tells how he learned about organization, management, and leadership as he helped to transform his own workplace and later used this experience when working as a consultant for other organizations. Writing in an engaging and personal manner, Weisbord explains how the work of five innovators (Taylor, Lewin, McGregor, Emery, and Trist) informed his understanding of the productive workplace. He makes connections to their work but does not pretend to give the reader a broad, balanced introduction to the field of organizational development. Weisbord also discusses case studies that exemplify methods of diagnosis and action in solving organizational problems, the importance of improving whole systems (as opposed to focusing on pieces of the organization), and the application of contemporary theories such as Total Quality Management to the design and practice of work processes.

Wheatley, M. J. (1992). *Leadership and the new science: Learning about organization from an orderly universe.* San Francisco: Berrett-Koehler. 151 pages. Can be ordered on-line at bkpub@bkpub.com.

*Focus:* Organizations as systems from a chaos perspective.

*Recommended audience:* Anyone interested in how organizational development can be informed by natural systems.

*Leadership and the New Science* excited the business world on its publication and has since stirred new thinking about leadership across many types of organizations, including religious, social, and educational institutions. Working from a "chaos" mind-set, in which there is disorganization but underlying order, Wheatley invites the reader to look at natural systems such as rivers and forests for clues about organizing human endeavor. In this new paradigm, the central metaphors are organisms (such as plants) and ecological systems (the relationship between organisms and their environment), the strategic objectives are adaptation and continuous improvement, and the primary sources of value are information and knowledge. In the workplace, it is desirable to develop self-organizing teams that can form quickly to respond creatively to changes in the external environment.

Contributions from physics and evolutionary biology are explored. The writing is clear, but some of the biology and physics may be difficult for lay readers, who may want to refer to *A Simpler Way* by Wheatley and Kellner-Rogers.

Wheatley, M. J., & Kellner-Rogers, M. (1996). *A simpler way.* San Francisco: Berrett-Koehler. 168 pages. Can be ordered on-line at bkpub@bkpub.com.

*Focus:* Organizations as systems from a perspective of chaos.

*Recommended audience:* Readers new to systems thinking and chaos theory.

*A Simpler Way* is a simpler version of the main ideas put forth in Wheatley's *Leadership and the New Science* (see the previous entry). Like its predecessor, this book illuminates a whole new way of thinking about organizations. Wheatley proposes that we can learn from natural systems—systems as large as rain forests and as small as the circulation system of the tiniest of organisms—by looking at patterns within patterns within patterns for clues about how to build human organizations and organizational life. The emphasis is on the essential simplicity of natural systems and their participatory and open nature. The book can be read as a companion piece to *Leadership and the New Science* or on its own.

## ARTICLES AND ESSAYS

Covey, S. R. (1996). "Three roles of the leader in the new paradigm." In F. Hesselbein, M. Goldsmith, & R. Beckhard (Eds.), *Leader of the future.* Drucker Foundation for Non-Profit Management. 10 pages. Available on-line through Jossey-Bass at www.josseybass.com.

*Focus:* Organizational culture.

*Recommended audience:* Anyone interested in ethical issues in management and leadership and the role of the leader in creating organizational culture.

Covey, author of *The Seven Habits of Highly Effective People, Principle-Centered Leadership,* and *First Things First,* discusses the leader who creates a culture or value system centered on principles of humility, courage, and integrity. He defines leadership in terms of three roles: pathfinding (developing a compelling vision and mission), aligning (forming continuity between the vision and the mission), and empowering (viewing employees as assets through which the vision and mission can be achieved). He thereby presents a paradigm that is different from traditional thinking about the nature of management, which does not emphasize the value of such personal qualities as humility. He stresses the importance of leaders in establishing organizational culture and broadens the scope of leadership to include people's work in community organizations, churches, and other life arenas. Covey's books and essays have been widely sold, and he presents regularly at conferences and seminars and in video broadcasts on management and leadership. His work has inspired many to look more deeply at their role as leaders.

Harvard Business School Publishing. *Control versus empowerment: Achieving a balance.* Reprint Collection of the *Harvard Business Review* (1999). Harvard Business School Publishing product no. 39104. Can be ordered on-line at custserv@hbsp.harvard.edu.

*Focus:* Organizational culture.

*Recommended audience:* Anyone interested in issues of power and control in organizations.

Empowerment is a natural outgrowth of new organizational designs and is integral to the spirit of learning organizations. It is also a term that has been so overused as to become almost meaningless. People who populate organizations are beginning to discern that there are limits to empowerment in the organizational culture and that with empowerment come new responsibilities and challenges. One of the greatest challenges is that of power sharing. *Control Versus Empowerment* contains seven articles by change consultants, practitioners, and theorists. Of particular interest is an article by Chris Argyris, who has studied and written about organizations since the 1950s. In "Empowerment: The Emperor's New Clothes," he explores how empowerment has remained mostly an illusion, despite all the hype, and how it too often enters the realm of political correctness in which no one can say what he or she is thinking. He posits that true power sharing requires sincere commitment, such that what is being asked for (more involvement and autonomy) is not undermined by information systems, processes, and tools designed to control.

McCambridge, R., & Weis, M. F. (1997). *The rush to merge: Considerations about nonprofit strategic alliances.* Boston: Boston Foundation. Can be ordered from the Boston Foundation, One Boston Place, 24th Floor, Boston, MA 02108.

*Focus:* Points to consider when developing alliances and collaborations with nonprofit organizations.

*Recommended audience:* Anyone whose organization may be entering into an alliance, collaboration, or merger with another organization.

This slim volume provides sound guidelines on how the nonprofit organization should approach alliances, collaborations, and mergers. Nonprofit organizations increasingly are being asked to enter into community planning, collaborate with other providers, and develop alliances with organizations concerned with a common population. Behind this trend are some unexplored assumptions about the benefits of this activity. What questions should be raised before an organization enters into such negotiations? What concerns must be addressed so that the alliance will have the best chance for success? What are the structural options of strategic alliances? These are the kinds of questions that McCambridge and Weis explore.

Schein, E. H. (1996). "Leadership and organizational culture." In F. Hesselbein, M. Goldsmith, & R. Beckhard (Eds.), *Leader of the future.* The Drucker Foundation for Non-Profit Management. 11 pages. Can be ordered on-line at www.pfdf.org or www.josseybass.com.

*Focus:* Organizational culture.

*Recommended audience:* Anyone interested in organizational culture and the ways in which it relates to the type of leadership needed.

In this short essay, Schein looks at leadership as it relates to an organization's particular stage of development: beginning, building, maintaining, or changing. He examines the ways in which an organizational culture is built and in which it may need to be gently changed so as to deal with new challenges. He cautions leaders about the human costs—such as job loss and a sense of betrayal—that change may create. Leadership is not, he concludes, a one-size-fits-all proposition for organizations.

# ⟶ Name Index

**P**

Padak, G., 90
Padak, N., 90
Padmore, S., 71
Pagano, J., 153
Palmer, H., 193
Palmer, T., 131
Parkland Regional College, 195
Pastore, A., 112, 123
Patton, B., 260
Penrod, D., 88
Perl, S., 65
Peyton, J. K., 87, 88, 89
Pfeiffer, J. W., 242
Pottmeyer, D., 180, 186n.3
Pugsley, R., 15
Purcell-Gates, V., 58n.2, 77–78, 81

**Q**

Quigley, B. A., 17, 26, 37, 155, 218

**R**

Raimes, A., 74–75
Ramirez, J. D., 74
Rance-Roney, J., 98
Raspberry, W., 23
Read, C., 64
Reder, S., 71, 73, 85, 86, 92, 98
Reed, E., 75–76
Reid, J. M., 75
Reno, J., 138
Rethemeyer, R. K., 91
Reumann, R., 152
Reynard, S., 265
Rhoder, C. A., 88
Rhum, M., 88
RMC Research Corporation, 152, 155
Robers, C., 244, 248
Roberts, C., 266
Roberts, J., 122
Robinson, J., 101
Rodriguez, C., 194
Roemer, T., 23
Rogan, L., 75–76, 76
Rogers, W., 122
Rose, A. D., 153, 154
Rose, M., 65, 68, 69

Rosen, D., 96
Rosen, H., 64
Ross, R., 131, 244, 248, 266
Rubin, H., 76
Russell, M., 77, 91
Ryan, T. A., 146n.3

**S**

Sawyer, D., 194
Sawyer, T., 23
Scardamalia, M., 67–68
Scheffer, L., 88
Schein, E., 255, 271–272
Schneider, P., 90
Scholtes, P. R., 265
Scribner, S., 70
Selman, G., 228, 231
Senge, P., 244, 247–248, 248, 258, 265–266
Sentencing Project, 118
Seymour, D., 250, 251
Shannon, P., 31
Shaughnessy, M. P., 64
Sherman, R., 181
Shohet, L., 189
Shor, I., 26, 30–31, 34, 35, 37, 38, 40–41, 41, 42, 43, 44, 45, 46, 47, 48
Silva, T., 73–74
Simon, P., 20, 21, 22, 23, 25n.1
Smith, B. J., 244, 248, 266
Smith, C., 15, 151
Smith, D. B., 190
Smith, J., 200, 221
Snyder, T., 118
Sommers, N., 65
Spack, R., 75
Specter, A., 138, 144n.3
Speights, D., 1
Spence, A. M., 125
Spencer, S., 176–177
Stamp, R. M., 228
Statistics Canada, 199–200, 201, 202
Staton, J., 87
Stein, S., 60n.9, 95
Stephan, J., 145n.3
Stern, G., 266–267
Steurer, S., 129–130, 132, 136, 144n.3

# ～ Subject Index

Minority language speakers, 38; and appropriation of dominant language, 40; assessment of, 93; in Canada, 191–192, 194–195; current research on writing of, 74–75; and dominant language, 39; Internet resources for, 96; reading experiences of, 74; and standardized tests, 74; storytelling styles of, 39; and teachers, 39; and transitional programs, 98; and writing process, 73–75, 88. *See also* Bilingual education; ESOL programs

Models: Hayes-Flower, 65–67, 66f; knowledge-telling, 67; knowledge-transforming, 68; TIE, 134

Movement for Canadian Literacy, 211, 212e; contact information for, 235

Multicultural education, 34

**N**

NAACP. *See* National Association for the Advancement of Colored People (NAACP)

NAAL. *See* National Assessment of Adult Literacy (NAAL)

NAEP. *See* National Assessment of Educational Progress (NAEP)

NALD. *See* National Adult Literacy Database (NALD)

NALS. *See* National Adult Literacy Survey (NALS)

National Adult Literacy Database (NALD) (Canada), 211, 212e, 217, 233; contact information for, 235; Web site, 212e

National Adult Literacy Survey (NALS), 16, 19, 142, 143n.2; of inmates, 119–120, 120t, 121

National Affiliation for Literacy Advance, 212e

National Alliance of Urban Literacy Coalitions, 5

National Assessment of Adult Literacy (NAAL), 19, 142

National Assessment of Educational Progress (NAEP), 83–84, 88, 89

National Association for the Advancement of Colored People (NAACP), 23

National Association of State Directors of Adult Education, 14

National Center for Adult Literacy, 23

National Center for Education Statistics (NCES), 20

National Center for Family Literacy, 23

National Center for the Study of Adult Learning and Literacy (NCSALL), 23, 25n.1

National Center for the Study of Writing, 82

National Coalition for Literacy (NCFL), 4, 5, 12, 13, 23, 24

National Council of La Raza, 23

National Council of State Directors of Adult Education, 23–24

National Education Goals Panel, 60n.9, 94

National Even Start Association, 13

National Institute for Literacy (NIFL), 4, 12, 21, 23, 25n.1, 60n.9; and correctional education, 127, 135, 141; and trends in writing instruction, 94–95

National Institute of Corrections, 143

National Institute of Justice, 143

National Literacy Act (NLA), 1, 5, 13, 23, 144n.3, 151, 155

National literacy agenda, 23

National Literacy Report Card, 22

National Literacy Secretariat (NLS) (Canada), 200, 217, 222, 223, 232, 233; contact information for, 235; and funding, 234; and support for adult basic education, 205–211; Web site, 207

National Literacy Summit, 1, 2, 20, 23–24, 24, 25n.1

National Opinion Survey on Crime and Justice (1995), 126

National Reporting System (NRS), 7, 14–15; and accountability, 14–15; and evaluation, 14, 15; and organizational development, 243